THE ACADEMY OF
ST MARTIN
IN THE FIELDS

The Academy of
St Martin
in the Fields

Meirion and Susie Harries

MICHAEL JOSEPH

First published in Great Britain by Michael Joseph Ltd
44 Bedford Square, London WC1
1981

To M.M. and N.M.

ISBN 0 7181 2049 3

Typeset, printed and bound in Great Britain
by Fakenham Press Limited

Contents

Preface and Acknowledgements

This book, prompted by the Academy's coming-of-age in November 1980, tells the story of the orchestra's first twenty-one years. It was not commissioned by the Academy – self-publicity has never been their forte; the initiative was ours, and the book presents our own view of the orchestra's career. We are, however, particularly grateful for the help and encouragement given to us by the directors, Neville Marriner, Malcolm Latchem and Stephen Shingles; by Molly Marriner; and by Sylvia Holford, the Academy's General Manager.

Throughout the book, we have relied heavily on interviews with members of the Academy, past and present, and with the orchestra's friends and critics. We have used a large number of photographs and illustrations supplied by the Academy themselves: otherwise we have had generous assistance from the publicity departments of Phonogram, Decca and EMI, and from the organisers of the many festivals at which the Academy have appeared. We should like to thank the following, all of whom have helped to make the writing of this book both possible and a pleasure:

John Amis, David Attenborough, Dame Janet Baker, Judith Barber, William Bennett, Sir Lennox Berkeley, Christopher Bishop, Elisabeth-Anne Black, Cynthia Bonham-Carter, Victor Bonham-Carter, Eleanor Boulter, Michael Bowie, Michael Bremner, Joanna Brendon, Iona Brown, James Burnett, Humphrey Burton, Marion Butler, Patricia Byrne, Quita Chavez, John Churchill, Richard Cisek, Trevor Connah, Barbara Cooper, Tony Cooper, Geoffrey Crankshaw, Gordon Crosse, Martin Dalby, Andrew Dalton, Jim Davidson, Charles Davis, Sir Colin Davis, Albrecht Deininger, Keith Dugdale, Eve Edwards, Stuart Eltham,

Mike Evans, Carolyn Fearnside, Carol Felton, John Fraser, Jenny French, Tristan Fry, Peter Gammond, Roger Garland, Philippa Garner, Stan Goodall, John Gray, Edward Greenfield, George Guest, Nadia Haggar, Margarita M. Hanson, Lynn Harrell, Kitty Harries, Eleanor Hayes, Chris Hazell, Frank Healey, Maud Heath, Laszlo Heltay, Elisabeth Hermann, Christopher Hogwood, Antony Hopkins, Anthony Howard, Pen Ibberson, Gerald Jarvis, Anthony Jenkins, Carmel Kaine, Kambara Music Office, Brian Kay, Raymond Keenlyside, Don Kennedy, Robert Key, Nicholas Kraemer, David Laing, Steve Lawrence, Margaret Leask, Philip Ledger, Arthur Leggatt, Alan Loveday, Philippa MacLeish, Hugh Maguire, George Malcolm, John Manduell, Andrew Marriner, Ethel Marriner, Nicholas Maw, Andrew McGee, Louise A. McKellip, Jane Miles, Nicholas Morrell, Bea Musson, Georgina Natzio, Norman Nelson, Celia Nicklin, Manoug Parikian, J. A. Parkinson, György Pauk, Gerald Peacocke, Simon Preston, Andrew Raeburn, Jan Rubinstein, Malcolm Russell, Stanley Sadie, Hans Ulrich Schmid, Christopher Senior, Mary Shillabeer, Marjorie Sims, Erik Smith, Roger Smith, the Society of Authors, Simon Streatfeild, Professor S. W. Sykes, David Takeno, Marilyn Taylor, Robert Tear, Hans Tecker, Charles Tindall-Lister, Graham Turnbull, Harley Usill, Frans Vanagt, Denis Vigay, the Reverend Christopher Walker, Sir William Walton, Raymond Ware, Johannes Wasmuth, Elizabeth Watson, Harry M. Weinrebe, Doreen Wells, Alan Wilkinson, Kenneth Wilkinson, Sir David Willcocks, the Reverend Prebendary Austen Williams, Elizabeth Williams, Dolly Williamson, Clive Wilson, Roger Witts, Katy Woolf, Jagna Wright, Stephen Wright and Peter Younie.

The Academy's association with Alfred Brendel started in 1971, when together they embarked on the first of their recordings of Mozart piano concertos. This special relationship is an important aspect of the orchestra's career, and we are particularly grateful to him for writing the introduction to this book.

We are also very grateful to Hilary Bacon and Joe Stern for their help in preparing the text, and in particular to our editor, Jennie Davies.

Meirion and Susie Harries
London, 18 May 1981

Introduction by Alfred Brendel

It took me years to remember the Academy's full name correctly. A group with such an impossible name had either to be dreary, or become a legend. It became the latter, and this book shows the reality behind it.

The name is not the only thing about the Academy that is strange, unlikely, and entirely unorthodox. It was formed as a democratic ensemble of part-time, and pastime players, and yet developed its own unmistakable style, *senza maestro*. It gained a reputation first through recordings and only later embarked on an international concert career. It started off as a baroque group, and has ended up in matters of repertoire as probably the most adventurous chamber orchestra under the sun. It may be the most improvisatory among orchestras of repute in the use of its players, and the most flexible in size according to the works performed; yet such fluidity, instead of being demoralising, in fact works as a safeguard against routine.

Neville Marriner's career is hardly less unusual. To emerge as the conductor of a group that gathered with the aim of avoiding conductors is rare enough, even for its principal violinist. Still harder for any director of a chamber orchestra to achieve is the transition to an international conducting career. Neville has calmly and brilliantly succeeded, and yet has not lost touch with the group which formed him and which he has formed.

I have spent many happy musical hours with the Academy and Neville, relishing their unique blend of freshness and refinement. A warm welcome, then, to this book; in dealing with the reality of the musical profession, it should make us all the more aware of the mystery of music.

Alfred Brendel
London, May 1981

1

An Appeal to all Music-Lovers

It has been three hundred years since the church of St Martin last stood 'in the fields'. The present building stands at the heart of London's West End – facing Trafalgar Square and backing towards Charing Cross Station and the Strand – a position which has helped to make it a famous and effective centre for social service. The church's eponymous saint was a Roman centurion who shared his cloak with a beggar by the roadside, and subsequently saw in a vision that the beggar was Christ. Martin, later to become Bishop of Tours, is revered as 'the lover of the poor', and since the days of the Reverend Dick Sheppard, Vicar from 1914 to 1927, his church has been a refuge for the lonely and derelict, and a source of help, moral and material, to anyone in need in one of the world's most crowded and expensive cities.

Perversely, when the church *did* stand in fields, its name did not at first reflect the fact. The chapel built in the thirteenth century to the glory of St Martin, midway between the City of London and the Abbey church of Westminster, was referred to as the church of 'St Martin nigh the Cross' or 'St Martin by Charing', and it was not until the end of the fifteenth century that the designation 'St Martin in the fylde besid Charing Cross' came into common use. The description remained accurate for approximately two hundred and fifty years: the Agas Map of 1570 shows the church still looking over open arable fields, but by the end of the following century houses surrounded it on all sides.

As buildings gradually closed in around it, the old church (whose design has been preserved in drawings by George Vertue) was becoming something of a focal point in London life. Francis Bacon is said to have been baptised there, and Shakespeare to have been a

*Opposite,
St Martin-in-the-Fields,
Trafalgar Square*

George Vertue's 'West Prospect of St Martin's Church', c. 1720

Below, 'A Conversation of Virtuosis ... At the King's Armes, 1735', James Gibbs fifth from left (painting by G. Hamilton)

2

Left, *Gibbs's circular design for St Martin's; right, Gibbs's design (dedicated to George I) for the present church*

regular worshipper; Oliver Cromwell's daughter Frances was married at St Martin's in November 1657, and Charles II's mistress Nell Gwyn would have been buried in its public graveyard but for the virtuous outcry against the proposal. The Vicar at that time, Dr Thomas Tenison (later Archbishop of Canterbury), was a friend to Nell in her old age, and had promised her burial at his church: in order to keep his word, he was obliged to place her remains with those of past clergy in the Vicars' private vault. (She was later to be joined in the crypt by a curious assortment of London's notables, from Nicholas Hilliard and Thomas Chippendale to the eighteenth-century cat-burglar Jack Sheppard.)

By the start of the eighteenth century the old church was in a precarious state of disrepair: in 1710 the Vestry had it surveyed by several master-craftsmen, who reported, 'We are . . . of opinion that the said Church cannot be supported by repairing but must be rebuilt' – on the not unreasonable grounds that the walls, originally constructed of rubble, were slowly subsiding under the weight of the roof. Accordingly, the clergy approached James Gibbs, a friend of Sir Christopher Wren and one of the most successful architects of the day, who was also the designer of the Radcliffe Library in Oxford and the Senate House in Cambridge. Gibbs produced several plans – one an elegant circular design, another rectangular with a columned front in the style of a Greek temple, surmounted by a tapering steeple of contemporary design. The circular design he considered 'more capacious and convenient'; it was also more expensive, and the clergy settled for a rectangular church which itself cost a total, including Gibbs's fee, of £33,661 16s 7¾d.

The building of the present church started in 1722 under the aegis of King George I; it was at this stage that St Martin's links with the throne – it is the Royal Parish Church, with Buckingham Palace just down the Mall – were firmly established. Henry VIII could be said to have taken an interest in the old church inasmuch as in 1542 he constituted round it an independent parish, to avoid 'the danger of infection which might happen to our Court by the carrying of dead bodies past our royal palace to be interred at St Margaret's [Westminster]'; henceforth St Martin's dead were to be buried in St Martin's ground (a decree which became all too relevant in 1665, when the church was in one of the areas of London worst affected by the Plague). But George I's interest in the new church of St Martin was more positive. He followed its construction attentively; his Royal Arms are carved on the pediment, and his private box can still be seen above and to the left of the altar. Furthermore, on its completion and consecration in 1726 he requested, and not unnaturally received, the post of Churchwarden.

George was an ardent patron of music – he presented the church with a magnificent organ, at a cost of £1500 – and St Martin's was built with music in mind. Its elliptical ceiling ('much better for the voice than the semi-circular', according to Gibbs) gave it a fine acoustic, and it attracted London's leading musicians. Among them was Handel, whom George, as Elector of Hanover, had previously employed as Kapellmeister. Relations had become strained when Handel, twice granted leave of absence from his post in Hanover to come to England, succumbed on his second visit to the adulation he was receiving and failed to return. His thoughts on hearing that the Elector was to follow him to England as King may be imagined, but by the time St Martin's was completed the rift had been healed – with the aid of the 'Water Music' which Handel composed as a peace offering (so the story has it, though Handel scholars have their doubts). It was natural, therefore, that Handel should play the organ at his sovereign's church; his presence was recorded by the contemporary commentator Dr Charles Burney – 'It was the fashion for

Interior of St Martin's

the first musicians in London to frequent that church; I have often seen Mr Handel there' – and it is pleasing to picture Mr Handel looking across from the organ loft at the royal churchwarden.

The tradition of music at St Martin's continued after Handel's death, but by the twentieth century the church's reputation was more for its far-reaching social work than for its involvement in the arts. When, however, in 1949 John Churchill was appointed Organist and Master of Music at St Martin's, he made no secret of his ambition to renew the church's musical links with the past and make it again a centre where 'the first musicians in London' could be seen. One of his first acts was to initiate the twice-weekly lunchtime concerts of solo and duo recitals given in the church by young professional musicians; three decades later these are still a regular feature of music in the West End. He also trained and conducted the church choir and arranged for it to be accompanied by a scratch orchestra of volunteers. But from the start he wanted to form a permanent orchestra based on the church, to give concerts and to accompany the choir. For this

5

*The Reverend
Austen Williams
in 1958*

purpose, in the early 1950s he put the scratch orchestra on to a more regular footing as the 'St Martin's Chamber Orchestra'. However, it slowly became obvious that busy professional players could not afford to give such an orchestra any priority in their lives; it was one thing to give their services for occasional concerts, quite another to give up unpaid the time for the rehearsals and performances involved in belonging to a regular orchestra, and the St Martin's Chamber Orchestra gradually ceased to operate.

One of its viola players, Michael Bowie, was an ex-pupil of John Churchill's and a member of the St Martin's Music Committee. A strong supporter of the idea of a permanent orchestra for the church, he thought it worth an attempt to raise money to *pay* for one – a small group of top professional players (possibly from his own orchestra, the London Symphony Orchestra) which would start by playing a series of concerts in the church. With two interested colleagues from the LSO, Simon Streatfeild and Norman Nelson, who had also played at concerts in St Martin's, he took the idea to John Churchill. The project, and the possible ways of raising the money for it, were put to the Vicar, the Reverend Austen Williams, who since his appointment in 1956 has always been a loyal and enthusiastic supporter of music in his church. Reverend

6

Williams took the initiative by publishing in the September 1958 issue of the *St Martin's Review* 'An Appeal to All Music-Lovers':

> This autumn John Churchill completes ten years at St Martin's, ten years in which he has patiently built our music and taught us how it can find a place in our church. We have never been able to help the music financially as much as we would like because of our heavy commitments in other fields (social service, overseas work and so on) and since it is clear that the concerts and recitals are going to need a sound backing if we are to go forwards as we would wish, we are launching a special appeal to those who are interested in music and would like it to grow here at St Martin's. John Churchill has the plans – a small professional orchestra is one of them – and we must try to help him.

The response from the many friends of St Martin's was generous and the Music Committee, convinced of a future for the venture, began in earnest the task of bringing the orchestra into being.

From the outset it was to be a string ensemble concentrating on the period of the late baroque, the 'golden age' of string music in which both John Churchill and Michael Bowie had a particular interest, and aiming at authenticity of style; much of the music of Vivaldi, Bach and Handel needed only small forces, and it suited the interior of the church, also baroque, to perfection. This decision to specialise in the music of the late seventeenth and early eighteenth centuries does not seem especially adventurous now. But in the 1950s, interest in baroque music, previously considered specialist and 'highbrow', was only just beginning to spread to a wider audience with the advent of the BBC's Third Programme and the development of the long-playing record, and the Music Committee's project was in the vanguard of popular taste.

With the general aims of the orchestra outlined, and the problem of finance solved (at least in the short term), the Music Committee turned to the question of whom they should ask to found and lead it. They chose Neville Marriner, a colleague from the London Symphony Orchestra who met the two essential requirements of experience in chamber music and a detailed knowledge of the baroque repertoire.

Neville Marriner's involvement in chamber music had started at the Royal College of Music, where in 1949 he had formed a trio

7

*John Churchill
and Neville
Marriner*

with violinist Alan Loveday and pianist Antony Hopkins. It has to
be admitted that the purpose of this trio was as much social as
musical; they toured the country playing golf in the afternoons,
giving recitals to unsuspecting music clubs in the evenings, and
finishing the nights playing poker, in the course of which Antony
(who had never played poker before the trio's formation) invariably
lost his newly-earned fee. Their repertoire was drawn largely from
the baroque period but extended as far as Martinu and Bartok, and
included pieces specially composed by Antony. The usual format
for recitals was a trio, followed by a piano solo, a violin duo, and
another trio to conclude the first half; in the second half, the pattern
would be repeated – trio, solo (often the kind of illustrated talk for
which Antony is famous), duo and a final trio. The sequence took
on a new and entertaining dimension when the trio was booked to
play to a music club in Newport. It was winter and freezing; with no
prospect of golf, they decided to travel up from London by train,
arriving at 6.30 for the concert at 8 pm, but on arrival at the station
were horrified by the general prevalence of Welsh accents, signify-
ing Newport, Monmouthshire, while 120 miles away an eager
audience was awaiting them in Shropshire. Leaping on to the

express to Hereford, and into a taxi for the remaining 80 miles to Newport, Shropshire, stopping every ten miles to report their progress, they arrived half an hour late to find the members listening to recordings of Jascha Heifetz, which did little to calm violin-playing nerves. They launched into the opening trio dressed as they were in snow-covered duffel-coats, and while Antony played his solo, Neville and Alan donned regulation tails for their duo – during which Antony went off to change: by the concluding trio, they were all in white tie and tails, and spent the interval in heated discussion about how good a joke it would be to reverse the procedure in the second half and finish the concert in duffel-coats.

After leaving the Royal College, while freelancing with most of London's symphony orchestras, Neville formed a second and more serious-minded trio – the Virtuoso String Trio – with Alexander Kok and Stephen Shingles, a future Academy member. He also joined the Martin String Quartet as second violin to David Martin, and the years spent with the quartet were vital to his musical development, teaching him to identify and deal with problems of ensemble, intonation and internal balance. His appointment in 1956 as principal second violin in the LSO gave him the added experience

The Hopkins–Loveday–Marriner Trio in characteristic pose

9

*The Virtuoso
String Trio*

of controlling a section of strings; it was here that he learnt the art of inducing musicians to make their entries precisely together (conductors having a tendency to concentrate on the more prominent first violins and leave the second violins largely to their own devices).

Throughout this period, Neville was also playing a good deal of baroque music, an interest aroused through his friendship with Robert Thurston Dart which had begun at the end of the Second World War. Thurston Dart was both an eminent mathematician and a brilliant musician who, with his ex-service gratuity, had gone to Belgium to study the early keyboard repertoire with the distinguished musicologist Charles van den Borren. On his return to England in 1947, he joined forces with Neville (then in the Martin String Quartet), first in a duo and later in the Jacobean Ensemble, putting his ideas on authentic performance to the test. He was a formidable scholar – later to become Professor of Music at Cambridge University – and one of the first musicologists to insist on taking early music and styles of performance seriously; his book *The Interpretation of Music*, published in 1954, acted as a catalyst to a whole generation of scholars and performers of the baroque. In

10

Neville Marriner and Thurston Dart

preparing performing editions, he tried scrupulously to identify the composer's precise intentions, but applied theory to practice in an exuberant and inventive way, approaching baroque music with confidence and a completely unacademic vitality. In the process, he transformed the hitherto rather dowdy image of the harpsichord – Simon Preston, now Organist and Master of the Choristers at Westminster Abbey, remembers the 'tremendous flamboyance of this enormous man playing these tiny little pieces'. Thurston Dart was in the forefront of the post-war baroque revival; his practical and resolutely un-precious attitude appealed enormously to Neville, and the Academy's performances were always to reflect his approach.

The other major influence on Neville's playing came, surprisingly perhaps, from a singer. According to Leopold Mozart, writing in the eighteenth century, 'instruments should imitate the voice', and in the singing of Alfred Deller, with whom he had worked in the early days of the Third Programme, Neville found the naturalness of phrasing which for him epitomised good baroque style. The influence of Deller and Dart, combined with his own innate musicality, made Neville one of the leading baroque violinists of his day – as the British

11

magazine *Gramophone* observed in 1962: 'Tonally and technically he evokes the early eighteenth century in a way that few other violinists can, and artistry of this kind is worth any number of chromium-plated fiddlers, as alike as so many balls in a bearing.'

It was this background that decided the St Martin's Music Committee and, one evening during the autumn of 1958, in a pub near Trafalgar Square, Michael Bowie, Simon Streatfeild and Norman Nelson asked Neville to take on the task of forming and leading the orchestra. He accepted immediately and in an enthusiastic discussion fuelled by many pints of bitter, the principles which were to govern the orchestra were thrashed out. The basic ensemble was to be eleven string players with harpsichord continuo played by John Churchill. Wind instruments could be added from time to time as the repertoire demanded, but these were always to be regarded as extras. In true baroque style the group would be led from the first desk of the violins, and no conductor would be permitted to hold sway over it: this was an unusual approach at that time as, in England at least, ensembles larger than an octet were almost always conducted. In addition, although the players would be obliged to give some degree of priority to the orchestra, their commitment would only be part-time and they would be at liberty to work with other ensembles – a feature which has continued to the present day.

Various possible titles for the new orchestra were discussed. It was decided that the name should naturally reflect the connection with St Martin's, but that it should also underline the members' personal interest in the repertoire and their willingness to meet and play it through for their own pleasure. The name 'Academy' which they ultimately chose expressed this enthusiasm. Academies, which had flourished throughout Europe in the baroque era, were for the most part societies dedicated to cultivating learning and the arts, with the emphasis on practice rather than theory. Hence musical academies were dedicated to extending knowledge of music not through teaching, but through performance and discussion; at their meetings (the forerunners of the modern concert), groups of musicians both amateur and professional would play under the direction of a leader to a small knowledgeable audience of members and invited guests.

Through their ardour and skill, academies set high standards of musicianship and taste in European life in the seventeenth and eighteenth centuries, and one English academy provided a particularly good model for the new orchestra. The eighteenth-century Academy of Ancient Music met weekly at the Crown & Anchor Tavern in the Strand. 'It is our design,' wrote the society's secretary in 1731, 'to search for what is beautiful in the works of the ancients, and to seek out those things that have been either neglected or forgot.' The Academy of St Martin in the Fields shared this enthusiasm and philosophy, and they were to cling to their unwieldy name through repeated efforts over a decade and a half to change it.

2

Refugees from the Conductor

With the framework for the orchestra agreed and a name chosen, Neville began the search for players to fill the seven places remaining. He had been greatly impressed by the way in which Walter Legge had made the Philharmonia one of the finest orchestras in Europe by handpicking each player for his skill and style, and he adopted a similar approach. The players had to be first-rank – but they also had to have the style and sound best suited to baroque music. This Neville saw as being a 'white' sound, not neutral but not highly-coloured either, with clean intonation and precise articulation with the bow. The group needed players who would be willing, without losing all personality, to subordinate their own carefully nurtured individual styles to an overall sound; there would be no place for the 'star' instrumentalist. In an 'academy' which was going to be playing more for pleasure than for money, there would be no room for self-indulgent temperament either – it was vital that the atmosphere should be relaxed and uncompetitive.

The result was an ensemble of friends and known quantities – colleagues from the Royal College of Music or the LSO and Philharmonia, all of whom shared an interest in baroque music and the desire for a change. In practical terms, playing in a symphony orchestra in the late 1950s could be tiring, repetitive and limited. It could mean a great deal of touring, giving concerts on one rehearsal, performing in uncomfortable conditions and, worse, playing the same part in the same pieces time and time again. The musician, because of his place in the layout of the orchestra, would often be unable to hear the piece as a whole, or evaluate his own contribution to it – this contribution being in any case strictly controlled by somebody else. Academy players were described in the early days as

The early Academy: clockwise – Neville Marriner, Norman Nelson, Raymond Keenlyside (first violins); Simon Streatfeild, Michael Bowie (violas); Wilfred Simenauer, Kenneth Heath (cellos); John Gray (double bass); Malcolm Latchem, Anthony Howard, Tessa Robbins (second violins); John Churchill (harpsichord)

'refugees from the conductor'; tired of playing to order, they wanted more influence over the final performance, and saw in chamber music the way to keep themselves musically alive and creative. The Academy, small and conductorless, was an attractive proposition, offering fresh repertoire, more say in interpretation, and the opportunity to establish and maintain a distinctive corporate style and identity, safe from the idiosyncracies of conductors.

Rehearsals began at once. The Academy's early days were characterised by a prodigious number of rehearsals, often as many as ten per programme, possible only because the players rehearsed for nothing (a phenomenon on which early members look back with some pride). Times were erratic because they had to be fitted in with the players' regular bread-winning jobs; a 5.15–7.15 pm rehearsal was not uncommon, squeezed between rehearsal and performance of a symphony concert. The places where the group met to rehearse were equally varied at first. The church proved unsatisfactory: although its acoustics were excellent, it was always too busy, crowded with tourists or with the tramps and homeless to whom St Martin's has always offered refuge. John Churchill remembers rehearsals disturbed by 'people wandering about in the church, tapping players on the shoulder and whispering "Are you the

Rehearsal in the church

Vicar?" ' – ripostes became increasingly un-Christian. The crypt was impossibly hot in summer, cold in winter and much too resonant, and eventually the players gravitated to the Marriners' flat in Cornwall Gardens where they rehearsed (to the qualified rapture of the neighbours) in the drawing-room, fortified at suitable intervals by tea and digestive biscuits. The only disturbance here was the occasional high note from Joan Sutherland rehearsing in her flat on the other side of the Gardens.

Procedure at these rehearsals was elaborate. A performing edition of every piece would be prepared in advance by Michael Bowie from the most reliable sources available (which invariably involved a visit to the British Museum), taking into account all known conventions for performing baroque music. Authentic performance of early music is complicated by the fact that what is written rarely corresponds exactly with what the composer would have expected to hear in performance; composers of the seventeenth and eighteenth centuries were far readier than their modern counterparts to trust to the performer's training, musicianship and sense of tradition in interpreting their music, and they inserted few indications of phrasing, tempo or dynamics. Michael's job was to mark

*First run-through
– Neville
Marriner and
Kenneth Heath*

these details into the music as a guide to the players, and as a
starting-point for detailed discussion.

The section leaders would then meet to run through the music,
identify potential problems and suggest bowings; finally at full
rehearsals the others would have their say. Every aspect of the
interpretation of a piece was ultimately decided collectively: the
early Academy was one of the few musical institutions in England
where *everybody* had a voice. Players joined, stayed and rehearsed
endlessly without being paid because they knew their individual
contributions were welcomed and valued. There was no conductor
to impose an interpretation from outside, and every player could be
confident that his own feelings about the piece would be somehow
reflected in the final performance. The Academy prided themselves
on working like a string quartet, each player listening to every
other, striving to blend his sound and style into a balanced whole,
and to achieve this the orchestra practised its corporate technique
much as a soloist would his own.

The consequence was rehearsals which regularly went on until
midnight, or for as long as it took to get it right. Discussion
frequently became heated – Michael, as custodian of the text and

17

watchdog over the authentic baroque style, recalls being shot down often – but the end product was an interpretation which carried conviction. This made Neville's task as leader much simpler; his direction was informal and unobtrusive, consisting of indicating tempo and nuance by his playing. It was his job to look after ensemble problems as they arose – and in the early days of the Academy, with the first and second violins sitting on opposite sides of the orchestra in authentic eighteenth-century style, the smallest flip of the bow or nod of the head was enough to control tempo or co-ordinate an entry.

During these first rehearsals the Academy evolved the distinctive style which characterised their early years as a baroque orchestra. The insistence on authenticity was carried over into the playing style, the main feature of which was vigorous and exact articulation. In line with Corelli's insistence (reported by his pupil Geminiani) that 'bows should move exactly together, all up or all down', the Academy's bowings were conscientiously standardised (the synchronised but diverging actions of the left-handed Simon and the right-handed Michael landing the viola section with the title 'Boeing 707'), and its articulation was kept crisp and détaché, imitating the action typical of the bow used in the baroque period – the so-called 'Corelli bow'. Similarly, the texture of the music itself was clarified to bring out the bones of the piece, its rhythmic and harmonic structure. The brilliance of the upper violin line was emphasised by carefully standardised phrasing and attack, and by the endless pains taken to ensure uniform intonation. The bass line was accentuated by unusually short and precise articulation which underpinned the music with strong rhythmic patterns. Perhaps most important, the middle line carried by the second violins and violas, often neglected, was brought out firmly to play its full part in the structure of the music.

The first demonstration of the Academy style came in five trial concerts at St Martin's in the winter of 1958/9, the first of them on 26 October 1958. Unfortunately, the clarity for which the orchestra had striven was not reflected in the weather, and the first two concerts took place with thick fog blanketing Trafalgar Square. Few people attended the first, and even fewer the second – the absentees included the double bass player booked to play that

*The Academy's lynch-pin
– John Gray*

evening, who lived outside London and could not get in to Trafalgar Square through the fog and traffic jams in time. At very short
notice and with no rehearsal, a deputy was brought in – and stayed
for more than fifteen years. John Gray became the Academy's
regular double bass and remained their lynch-pin until his emigra-
tion to Australia in 1977.

Nor did the fog help to attract attention to the concerts from the
Press and music critics. The main problem in publicising the new St
Martin's orchestra was one of image; as John Churchill has
observed, 'Anything which goes on in a church outside its normal
functions is looked upon as "village hall" by both general public
and critic.' To some extent the atmosphere at those first concerts
may well have seemed 'village hall', as the sparse audience was
heavily weighted with friends and relations of the players. Nobody
had paid to get in: a silver collection was taken to cover expenses,
and the musicians received fees which even at that time were low –
thirty shillings a head, rehearsals free. The harpsichord was also
free, lent by the eminent instrument-maker Thomas Goff, who
generously continued to support the Academy in this way
throughout their early years.

19

Thomas Goff (standing) and Thurston Dart, with a Goff clavichord

There was, however, nothing amateur about the programmes, careful compilations of concertos by Vivaldi, Bach, Handel and lesser-known composers such as Manfredini and Albicastro. In these early concerts the Academy initiated the policy, which has continued to the present day, of using their own members as soloists. Both Alexander Murray, the flute soloist in the fourth concert, and Roger Lord, the oboe soloist in the fifth, were in the LSO, and both were to play regularly with the Academy whenever wind instruments were needed. (On one occasion in the early 1960s when Alexander Murray could not manage an Academy rehearsal, the deputy he sent was James Galway – later to appear with the

20

orchestra in rather more of a stellar role).

By the time of the last concert in the series, the Academy had attracted enough attention to merit their first review in *The Times* – 'The performances were at once more inward and more lively than some we have heard just across the river at the South Bank. The highly-praised Italian groups such as I Musici or the Virtuosi di Roma are perhaps more rigidly disciplined, but they tend to exaggerate both fast and slow rhythms, and particularly slow ones. This is a trap into which John Churchill and his very experienced players never fell.' This was enough to earn the Academy their first date with the BBC – a modest half-hour of Handel, Albicastro and Corelli, recorded on 5 August 1959 – and to justify another series of concerts in the church.

This second series was a far more highly organised affair, and the players now see it, and the first concert on Friday, 13 November

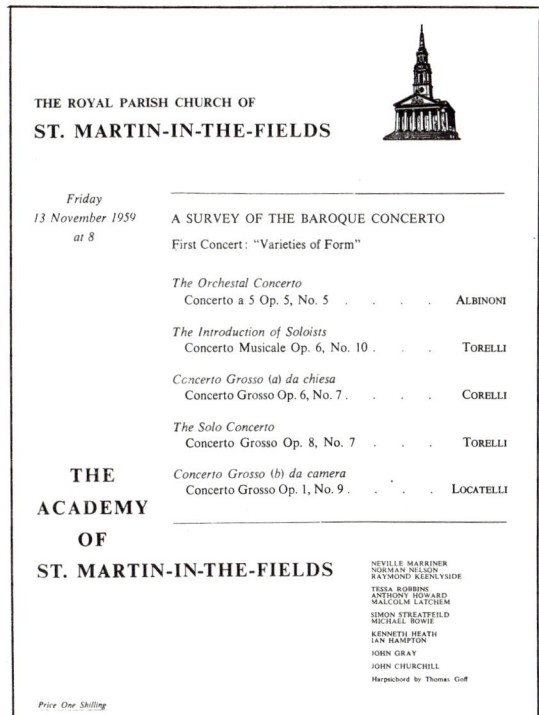

The first professional concert

21

1959, as marking the start of the Academy's professional career. The orchestra's style had crystallised, and they were playing with more confidence and panache. They had acquired management – in the person of Neville's wife Molly, who did such paperwork as was necessary on the kitchen table at home – and a small publicity leaflet had been issued. As for their repertoire, although this remained almost exclusively baroque, the second series of concerts was more ambitious in its approach. Taking as its overall title 'A Survey of the Baroque Concerto', it set out to trace the development of the concerto in the seventeenth and early eighteenth centuries, contrasting the forms it took in the different countries of Europe.

The next venture was similarly scholarly, with the Academy and the St Martin's Cantata Choir giving the first performance of the Watkins Shaw edition of *Messiah*. Queues for the performance, on 8 December 1959, stretched right round the church into Adelaide Street, and Norman Nelson remembers, 'When we arrived at the church to rehearse, there were people all around it. There are a lot of bus stops in the area, and I remember thinking that the bus system must have gone mad, before I realised that they were queuing for our concert.' Despite the fact that the orchestral parts for the new edition were not ready and John Churchill had to conduct from a vocal score while the orchestra played from old parts covered with pencil alterations, the performance was received with gratifying enthusiasm by the Academy's first full house.

However, this proved little more than that the Academy were developing a following among the people who had always supported music at St Martin's; outside the church, they had had little exposure and a correspondingly limited impact. It became apparent that they were going to have to branch out in order to survive at all; the church could only afford to offer from the money already raised very low pay for what was in effect all overtime work – and now even that money was beginning to run out. In the attempt to keep the orchestra together, the players started to accept outside dates. Five of them – Neville, Norman, Simon, John, and the new principal cellist, Kenneth Heath – were involved, in the guise of the Ambrosian Players, in a BBC radio series of music from stately homes. Each programme, devised by the musicologist Denis Stevens and introduced by Richard Dimbleby, was built around

the musical establishment of the house in question. Simon has particular reason to remember the programme from Hampton
Court. Responsible for booking the players, he had forgotten that
continuo would be needed, with the result that the group found
itself at the last minute in Hampton Court with a recording crew
waiting and no harpsichord player. Fate took a hand: 'The most
extraordinary thing happened – there was a chap looking round the
pictures, a visitor, who took pity on us. He wasn't a member of the
Union or anything, but he could play the harpsichord quite well
enough – and he saved the broadcast.'

Another attempt to preserve and promote the Academy met with
no such good fortune. In April 1960 the group gave, at its own
expense, its first recital at the Wigmore Hall. The experiment did
not pay off; the reviews with which the group was going to sell
itself never materialised, and it proved an expensive gesture. But the
concert did mark the first appearance with the Academy of one of
their most long-standing friends – George Malcolm, whom they
accompanied in a Bach harpsichord concerto.

It was rather in this spirit – of chasing up work wherever it was to
be found – that the Academy made their first tour abroad. Neville
and Molly had spent some time writing to potential 'customers' –
music clubs, concert societies, and local arts associations – including, at John Churchill's suggestion, the Royal Dublin Society. The
Society's offer of two concerts was consolidated by an invitation
from the Waterford Music Society to give another, and the
Academy decided to accept.

The tour, though well-received, probably did more to develop
team spirit in the Academy than it did to promote the love of
baroque music in Eire. It took place in a particularly inclement week
in December 1960, and a series of mishaps did much to diminish
artistic fervour. The two concerts in Dublin took place on the same
day, one in the afternoon and one in the evening. The hall proved
bitterly cold, and for the evening performance a paraffin heater was
put on the platform, strategically placed behind the second cello's
chair. It was in the middle of the first half of the concert that the
unfortunate cellist was observed to be green and sweating; he
retired shortly afterwards, overcome by the fumes, leaving Ken
Heath to play as loudly as he could for the rest of the evening.

THEY GAVE R.D.S. RECITAL

Members of The Academy of St. Martin-in-the-Field who gave a recital at the Royal Dublin Society. They will visit Waterford to-day. Front (from left): Violins, Messrs. Neville Marriner, Norman Nelson, Raymond Keenlyside, Anthony Howard, Malcolm Latchem, Gerald Jarvis. Second row: Violas, Simon Streatfield, Michael Bowle; Violoncellos, Kenneth Heath, Stanley Mant. Behind: John Churchill (Piano) and John Gray (Double Bass).

Impeccable Style

B.Y MARY MacGORIS
"Irish Independent" Music Critic

IMPECCABLE ensemble and musical style marked the playing of a chamber orchestra, The Academy of St.-Martin-in-the-Field, whose wholly enjoyable performance was heard at the latest of the R.D.S. series of Monday recitals.

Devoted to music of the 18th century, the programme deployed all the charm of the period and, in the afternoon, avoided monotony by ranging from Handel's theatrical Berenice Overture to Mozart's most gallant style, deliciously exemplified in the Divertimento K. 136.

A particularly nice choice of tempo at all times was emphasised by the rhythmic verve of the group and the welcome vitality which distinguished the entire performance

ANOTHER ASPECT

The fine playing from the four soloists in a Vivaldi Concerto, excellent in itself, was merely another aspect in the excellence of the group, whose clear tone, mellow or vivid as required, and musicianly phrasing served all the music well.

John Churchill, w h o m one assumes to be responsible for this ensemble of 11 strings and piano, was the pianist. His discreet accompaniment, combined with the lower strings, contrived to suggest at times an organ continuo, occasionally even seeming to add touches of wind colour especially in the G minor Overture attributed legitimately one felt in this performance, to Bach.

The Academy travelled down to Waterford on the following day. The hotel's heating was discovered on arrival to be inadequate to such a degree that to get their circulation going in time to play, the performers found it necessary to spend the half hour before the performance in bed in full concert dress and their overcoats. The concert passed relatively uneventfully, but the bus taking the orchestra back to Dublin afterwards for their flight home that night had no heating at all and several windows were jammed open. After one bow arm had frozen to the window as its owner dozed, the band wrapped themselves in the *Irish Independent* to stay alive.

The weather had not finished with the Academy. Half the players had been given leave of absence from the LSO to do the Irish tour on strict condition that they were back in time to go with the orchestra to Israel. The LSO was due to leave for Tel Aviv from Gatwick four hours after the Academy arrived back from Dublin at Heathrow, and Molly had arranged a mini-bus to transfer the players from one airport to the other with an hour to spare. This was reckoning without the fuel-loaders' strike which greeted the Academy at Dublin airport and appeared likely to delay their flight by four hours. The stranded players included more than one LSO principal, and they knew that if they failed to turn up, even if they kept their jobs, it was unlikely that further leave of absence would be granted in the future – which could mean the end of the Academy. Panic threatened to set in and was averted only by an early morning telephone call made with extreme difficulty from a noisy phone box at the airport to the manager of the LSO, which revealed that dense fog – for once on the Academy's side – had grounded all planes at Gatwick.

Opposite, *The Academy in Dublin*

25

3

Sell Another Sheep

The months immediately after the Irish tour were crucial for the survival of the Academy. There were a few changes in the group's membership (including the loss of Michael Bowie, who emigrated to Canada in 1961), but then it settled in a form that was to remain largely unchanged for several years – Neville Marriner, Norman Nelson, and Raymond Keenlyside as first violins; Trevor Connah, Anthony Howard and Malcolm Latchem as second violins; Simon Streatfeild and Stephen Shingles as violas; Kenneth Heath and Denis Vigay as cellos; and John Gray as double bass, with John Churchill as harpsichord continuo.

The early 1960s were difficult for the music profession as a whole. Music clubs and societies, plentiful in the 1930s, had declined dramatically in number after the war with the advent of television and the long-playing record, and with the clubs went the means for many freelance musicians of making a secure living. The Academy were fortunate in having the opportunity to give concerts in St Martin's, and they also established an early connection with the BBC; their work for the Third Programme was frequent and varied, ranging from a programme of Handel arias with Alfred Deller to the twentieth century and Britten's 'Simple Symphony'. The players quickly mastered the techniques of recording for radio, including that of meeting deadlines: during one long-drawn-out session, where they were being obliged to justify every phrase and nuance of their performance to the producer, Neville was forced to the expedient of taking an extended coffee break during which he telephoned an urgent message through to the Academy's adversary, summoning him to a vital (and non-existent) meeting with the BBC's Head of Music. In the producer's absence, the recital was recorded with time to spare, but as John Gray recalls, 'We didn't get many broadcasts for a while'.

Even with these two important links, it became obvious to the players that there was simply not enough work to keep the Academy in business. In the year of the orchestra's conception, the first stereo records had made their appearance in Britain, and it was in the rapidly-evolving recording industry that the Academy saw their best chance of survival as a professional group. They decided, in their search for a recording contract, to make an audition tape and hawk it round the record companies. For technical assistance they approached Jimmy Burnett, a producer with whom they had worked at the BBC and one who, having worked closely with Thurston Dart and Arnold Goldsbrough, had a considerable knowledge of baroque music and the chamber orchestral repertoire. For their first (and last) recording made in St Martin's, they chose a Handel concerto grosso, but had to wait to record it until 2 am, when the traffic noise from Trafalgar Square eventually died down. Jimmy Burnett edited the tape the next day, handed it over to Neville, and thought no more about it.

By one of those happy coincidences which have punctuated the Academy's life, the proprietor of the first company to which Neville sent the tape was a close friend of Jimmy Burnett's; and six weeks after Jimmy had finished the tape, it was back on his desk with a note asking for an opinion. Fortunately, from his earlier work with the orchestra he was able truthfully to reply (irrespective of his own contribution to the tape) that he thought the Academy were marvellous, and he recommended that they be asked to make a series of six records. This prescient advice was not immediately taken, but a single record was offered, which the players recognised as a make-or-break opportunity.

The company was L'Oiseau-Lyre and the Academy had been lucky, for this company was conspicuous for its willingness to record unusual repertoire and unknown artists, undeterred by the lack of commercial appeal. This adventurous and altruistic outlook it owed entirely to its founder, Mrs Louise Hanson Dyer, remembered with gratitude by the Academy as the eccentric Australian millionairess to whom much of their early success was due. Born into a prominent Melbourne family, Louise Dyer had trained as a singer (for a time as a pupil of Dame Nellie Melba), but in 1927 she came to Europe, fell in love with France, and decided to make it her home.

Dame Janet Baker, who made some of her first solo records for Mrs Dyer, remembers her with awe as epitomising all that the public expects an 'artist' and impresario to be. Extraordinary and glamorous in the flowing dresses, long white gloves and large picture hats that she customarily wore, she had the 'star quality' of a past era, when people were afraid neither of being, nor of being thought to be eccentric. She lived a life of great elegance, dividing her time between a house close to the Palace in Monaco and a flat on the right bank of the Seine overlooking the Trocadero and the Eiffel Tower. Her art collection included a Blue Period Picasso bought from the artist himself after a six-month war of attrition; he had finally agreed to part with it only on condition that she offered an interpretation of the painting with which he was satisfied. As this story suggests, Mrs Dyer was a woman of intelligence, charm and an iron will: Jimmy Burnett remembers her as 'someone who could have succeeded in *anything* she chose to do'. What she did choose was the preservation and promotion of the music which she loved

Mrs Dyer in her Paris flat

28

*Les Éditions of
1934, bound in
Australian
blackwood –
'Polyphonic
Music of the XIII
Century'*

and felt to have been unjustly neglected. Moving to Paris, she founded the Lyre-Bird Press in 1932 and gathered around her some of the leading musicologists of the day, to produce scholarly and moderately-priced editions of previously unexplored repertoire – which at that time included Couperin, Lully and Rameau. 'Les Editions de L'Oiseau-Lyre' were welcomed by universities and libraries throughout the world, and it was not long before Mrs Dyer and her second husband, Dr Jeffrey Hanson, took the next logical step and started to illustrate the editions with performances, recorded on 78 rpm discs, which paid close attention to authenticity. She was subsequently among the first to introduce long-playing records to France, and L'Oiseau-Lyre's recordings of repertoire that would otherwise have gone unheard rapidly built up a reputation for enterprise and high standards of performance.

With the growing demand for the records came the need for wider distribution, and Mrs Dyer decided that this could best be

provided by the Decca Record Company, whose producers, engineers and equipment she already used for most of the recordings she made in England. On a flying visit to Decca House she convinced the Chairman, Sir Edward Lewis, of the desirability of this arrangement – which would have surprised nobody familiar with her force of character. At times this dynamism made life difficult for Raymond Ware, who was responsible for the liaison between Decca and L'Oiseau-Lyre until Decca finally took over the recording catalogue in 1970. Now manager of the L'Oiseau-Lyre label for Decca, he recalls meetings with Mrs Dyer during which, if it looked as though she was not going to get her own way, she would rise to her feet, reach for her parasol and hammer the desk with it crying, 'But you *will* do it for me, won't you?!' His most vivid memory of her persistence is an occasion in Paris when, suffering from a severe case of influenza, he was induced to try her patent (and wholly successful) remedy – large quantities of champagne drunk from her shoe.

Mrs Dyer liked challenges and underdogs, and when she saw that she had succeeded in encouraging interest in her chosen repertoire, which other companies were now eager to record, she changed the emphasis of the recording side of L'Oiseau-Lyre. The Lyre-Bird Press continued to produce editions of rare music and is still a thriving specialist music publishing house, but Mrs Dyer's new 'cause' on records was to help young and little-known artists to become established. She had an extraordinary talent for spotting potential: over the years she was to record Joan Sutherland, Dame Janet Baker, Sir Colin Davis, Thurston Dart and the Melos Ensemble very early on in their careers. The lyre-bird motif she had chosen for her enterprises was a symbol both of her Antipodean origins and of the art of music itself, and it became a tradition for her to present her female artists with a lyre-bird brooch, an Australian opal set in silver. Dame Janet Baker fondly remembers hers, bestowed rather in the style of the *Good Housekeeping* 'Seal of Approval' to denote a promising career.

It was into this category of new talent that the Academy fell. Their first record for L'Oiseau-Lyre – 'A Recital by the Academy of St Martin in the Fields' – was made in Conway Hall, Red Lion Square, and released in 1961. Mrs Dyer did not view her recordings as profit-making ventures – it became a standing joke among the members of the Academy that every time she wanted to make a new record, she had to sell another sheep to pay for it. Her dedication to music as an end in itself was genuine – and she expected the same altruism from her artists. She would never fly first-class on the grounds that with the money she saved by going second-class she could make another record. In the same spirit, no royalties were paid, fees were low (dispensed by her in person in crumpled pound notes from a large white handbag) and session time was limited. The Academy received £5 a head for their first record, and were given only two sessions in which to record a 40-minute programme of rarely heard works by Corelli, Torelli, and Locatelli (irreverently referred to by the players as 'the ice-cream makers'), Albicastro and Handel, in editions prepared by Michael Bowie. (Record companies today, faced with this kind of 'bitty' programme, would rarely expect to be able to use more than eight or ten minutes of music per session.) Jimmy Burnett was the producer for the recording, and he remembers Mrs Dyer sitting in the control box with him, looking at her watch every few minutes to reassure herself that she was getting her money's worth. He also remembers the effect this had on the players: 'It was hair-raising, frenetic – Neville was sweating on the top line; there was no let-up whatsoever, and not one fraction of a second was wasted.' Despite the pressure, and the Academy's relative inexperience in the recording studio (John Gray remembers Neville making a last-minute dash to buy gut E-strings for the fiddle sections, the wire ones having proved unexpectedly shrill in the particular acoustic of Conway Hall), the record was a considerable success: *Gramophone* described it as 'played with precision,

*Claude Monteux,
Jimmy Burnett
and Neville
Marriner*

care, consummate musicianship, and with more sense of style than all the other chamber orchestras in Europe put together'.

The Academy have always been grateful for the reception the critics gave that first record, which encouraged Mrs Dyer to persevere – although she never ceased to wage war on overtime and extra sessions, and the Academy's recordings for L'Oiseau-Lyre invariably became a race against the clock. The 'Second Recital', released in the following year, should have been a more leisurely affair: because the repertoire was difficult (including Vivaldi's Opus 3, No. 10, a concerto for four violins, with Neville Marriner, Norman Nelson, Anthony Howard and Gerald Jarvis as the soloists), Mrs Dyer had budgeted for three sessions. But the easier pace promised never materialised because Jimmy Burnett, again the producer, was called to the telephone halfway through the second session to learn that his son had just been born, and the ensuing celebrations rather delayed matters. For their third record (entitled, a trifle unimaginatively, 'Recital for Strings'), the whole of the first session was allocated to recording the Telemann Viola Concerto in G with Simon Streatfeild as soloist. Ready to start at 10 am sharp,

A second recital by the ACADEMY OF ST. MARTIN in the FIELDS

Directed by NEVILLE MARRINER

The 'Second Recital' (cover photograph by Norman Parkinson)

the Academy were still waiting at 11 o'clock for the harpsichord to arrive; by the time it had been retrieved from Norwood, where the van bringing it had broken down, only an hour remained in which to record the concerto. Twenty years later, there are two passages which Simon still itches to re-record.

Mrs Dyer, who was ultimately to be awarded the Légion d'honneur for her services to music, died in 1962, and the management of L'Oiseau-Lyre passed to Dr Hanson. Over the next three years, the Academy were to make four more records for him – two of Bach cantatas with Dame Janet Baker, Robert Tear and John Shirley-Quirk; one of baroque solo concertos with Kenneth Heath, Roger Lord and Barry Tuckwell as soloists; and a recital of eighteenth-century flute concertos with Claude Monteux (whose father, the conductor Pierre Monteux, was to have a profound effect on the direction of the Academy's career). But it was Mrs Dyer's first make-or-break record which set the Academy on their way and prompted the critic Edward Greenfield, writing in the *Guardian*, to welcome 'what could well become the premier chamber group in this country'.

4

Cottage Industries

The Academy's potential as England's premier chamber group would not have been instantly apparent from their organisation in the early 1960s. Unlike most orchestras, with their administrators, librarians, accountants and secretaries, they were managed single-handed by Molly Marriner, who once remarked, 'A shoe-string would be an exaggeration for what the Academy's run on.'

Molly claims to have known little about music when she married Neville, at least from the professional performer's viewpoint, although she came from a family interested in music and remembers her father taking her to see Bruno Walter conduct in a cinema in Wigan. ('Nothing funny about that', she points out. 'After all, my father had seen Pavlova dance in a cinema in St Helen's.') Though she had little experience of the backstage workings of the music profession, she was to learn these rapidly and at first hand.

The Dutch magazine *Luister* once described Molly as the Academy's *organisietalent*, though at first she had no official title, becoming 'The Secretary' only when the Academy got their own headed writing-paper (also the moment at which the hyphens dropped out of their name). Her job, which was never paid, was never clearly defined either, covering everything from making the coffee and paying the players to turning the pages for the harp-sichordist and writing the programme notes. She was always amused by other people's expectations of a slick management machine, and remembers being convulsed when, for the Academy's first live concert for the BBC, the Corporation sent her four pairs of tickets – one each for the concerts manager, the librarian, the bookings manager, the secretary and their respective spouses. 'I took a lot of friends,' she recalls.

*Molly and
Neville Marriner*

In the earliest days, her job was to book (and remind) the players for each date – concert, broadcast or recording – and check that each piece had the instruments it required. For the baroque repertoire, the instrumentation remained reasonably constant – three or four first violins, three or four seconds, two violas, two cellos, double bass and harpsichord – and it was simply a question of ringing the regular players to ask if they were free. However, wind players were sometimes necessary – two oboes and bassoon for a Handel concerto grosso, for example, or oboes (*d'amore* or otherwise) and bassoon for a Bach cantata. On occasion the regular players would be unable to take the date, and Molly would then have to look further afield: a longer list would be drawn up, 'definites' down the left-hand side of the page, 'impossibles' across the bottom, and 'possibles' pencilled in as stand-bys in case of a change of plan. (A postcard cancelling two horns and ordering two trumpets records one such change: Molly had discovered at the last minute from the Haydn scholar H. C. Robbins Landon that the particular Haydn concerto for which she was booking players had, unusually, no horns.) Booking players in a busy freelance market is time-consuming and often frustrating, but she soon had it down to a fine art. One of the earliest members recalls, 'It was difficult to say "no" when Molly was trying to book you – she asked so nicely, and she was never disagreeable if you really couldn't do it; I think her charm persuaded a lot of people to play dates they hadn't really intended to do at all.'

The Academy's accounting system was no more than the booking-list. Against each 'definite' was marked the number of rehearsals he or she would attend, and the fee to be paid. Molly then kept track of the money coming into the Academy in a blue school exercise book, and handled the accounts for the money going out from the stubs of the Academy's cheque book: the players paid were ticked off on the booking sheet and that was it – no VAT, no accountant, and no electronic calculator. The Academy had a policy of paying players well to be sure of keeping happy the ones they wanted: the fee for each rehearsal or concert was, in the early days, standard Union rate plus a pound (as often as not a sizeable increase). For out-of-town dates each player would get, on top of his fee, his travel expenses (the double bass would also get porterage for his instrument), and subsistence money – one receipt solemnly

The cerebral part of the job

records 'afternoon tea for N. Marriner, K. Heath, and S. Shingles' at
2s 6d a head in a Cambridge hotel.

Molly's most complicated single task was organising the music.
In the first years of the Academy, the music was edited and assembled by Michael Bowie and Simon Streatfeild, with many of the
separate instrumental parts copied out by hand. As the orchestra got
busier and its repertoire began to grow, this became impracticable,
and Neville insisted that rather than hiring the parts for each date,
the Academy should buy their music and build up their own library
of parts: he designed a box file to suit the awkward shape of most
music, and Molly found a book-binder willing to make up a set.
The walls of their flat in Cornwall Gardens were slowly covered
with shelves full of concerto grosso parts, and Neville marshalled an
armoury of scissors, glue and 4B pencils for putting the Academy's
markings into their music. The library flourished – though miscal-
culations could occur: Molly recalls occasions when she would find
'Neville standing there in the hall shouting "Handel Opus 6, No. 11
– I need two more second violin parts by this afternoon" – and I
wouldn't have done the shopping for lunch yet, and would probably still be in my dressing-gown.'

Organising the music was the cerebral part of the job: the rest
Molly remembers as manual labour – 'peeling an onion with one
hand' (for the impromptu suppers she provided when rehearsals
spread themselves) 'and answering the telephone with the other'.
With twelve or more players to be fitted into the drawing-room for
rehearsals, furniture had to be moved and the kitchen denuded of
chairs so that meals in the flat became an impossibility and, after a
year of being rehearsed upon, every kitchen chair had developed a
permanent squeak. Hall and drawing-room were cluttered with
fiddle cases (as often as not cradling cats who found them the ideal
place for a sleep), and the double bass case was wedged under the
stairs. The Academy rehearsed to their own timetable – the players
took breaks not on the hour but when they were ready – and while
the music may have benefited from the absence of statutory inter-
ruptions, it meant Molly was tied to the kitchen, waiting for the
sounds of laughter and non-musical conversation that were the
signal for her to bring in the coffee, and a glass of milk and slice of
dry bread for the one with the ulcer. Occasionally she would bake

An early rehearsal in the recording studio for them – 'chocolate cake went well'. She would also be called upon to remove the cats if they became troublesome; Denis Vigay, then second cello, remembers rehearsals brought to a standstill by cats fighting noisily on top of the curtains.

In addition to stage-managing rehearsals, Molly was responsible for settling the players into the concert hall or recording studio. Stands had to be set up, music put out, and light and heat suitably adjusted. Cellos had to be provided with chairs of the right height for the instruments: too high a chair and the player gets backache, too low and the position of his bow arm is wrong, and Molly ransacked many a hall in search of the perfect chair. In recording sessions, time had to be allowed for John Gray to find the most resonant floor-board on which to rest the end-pin of the double bass. In Kingsway Hall he discovered that he could enhance the sound of the instrument by resting the spike over a particular joist; he used to carry an implement resembling a railway worker's wheel-tapper, armed with which he would crawl round the studio tapping assiduously until he located the joist – and Molly learnt in time to budget for this in preparing her setting-up schedules. At concerts, getting the orchestra on and off the stage in a seemly manner became a major preoccupation: her repeated attempts to coach them in platform deportment met with little success, however, and to this day, to quote one of the offenders, 'We remember to walk on smartly and in the correct order, but always forget at the end, and just shamble off.'

Molly's informal and unpaid management did much to foster in the Academy a corporate, almost family feeling which had its effect on the group's playing, full of an infectious pleasure in making music together. In the circumstances, the group could not have found a company better suited to develop their recording career after the death of Mrs Dyer (and that of her husband a few years later) than Argo Records, itself a 'cottage industry' in its early years. Harley Usill, the company's managing director, had founded Argo with a friend in 1950, almost as a hobby: they had been writing a musical comedy together, with Harley as librettist – but when it failed to reach the stage, they acquired a disc-cutting machine (this was still the age of 78s) and set up a record company instead.

Argo rapidly made a name for itself as a 'specialist' label, producing a few records of carefully chosen repertoire every year. The

Harley Usill

39

original intention was to specialise in English music performed by British artists – among them Thurston Dart, Alfred Deller, Malcolm Latchem and Stephen Shingles, two of the Academy's earliest members. However, the introduction of LPs, with their relatively silent surfaces and twenty-five minutes of uninterrupted playing time per side, encouraged Harley to pursue one of his own enthusiasms – the spoken word on record – and Argo is now recognised as a pioneer in this field. The company's first spoken-word recording was a reading by Robert Speaight of T. S. Eliot's *The Waste Land*. This was followed by a highly-acclaimed series of Shakespeare plays, performed by the Cambridge Marlowe Society, and by a poetry series made in conjunction with the British Council; and the Argo recording of the BBC production of *Under Milk Wood*, with Richard Burton as principal speaker, has been selling consistently for twenty years.

As Argo became securely established through the success of the spoken-word recordings, it began to expand its musical side: from purely British music it branched out into a variety of choral and chamber music, starting with 'A Festival of Lessons and Carols' from King's College, Cambridge in 1954, and moving into the *a capella* church music of rarely heard composers such as Taverner and Tye. It was at this stage that Harley first met Neville – as a member of the Jacobean Ensemble. He remembers a record of trio sonatas performed by Neville, Peter Gibbs and Desmond Dupré, which he produced, balanced and edited himself, and for which he cut the master discs, in the true spirit of the cottage industry. His friendship with Neville continued in the LSO, but on the cricket field rather than on the platform. Harley, invited to make a film about the LSO, became one of the stalwarts of the orchestra's cricket team; he remembers with some disgust his team's performance on the occasion when he was awarded his colours in a match against the London Philharmonic Orchestra. His main strength as a bowler was his ability to move the ball away from the bat – which presented many fine opportunities for catches behind the wicket; unfortunately, musicians are notoriously unwilling to risk their fingers catching fast-moving objects, and Neville, as the LSO's wicket-keeper, came in for his fair share of Harley's wrath.

Nevertheless, when Harley decided to move beyond small-scale

Recording session for Handel's Opus 3 concertos: left to right – Harley Usill, Neville Marriner, Kenneth Wilkinson, Michael Dobson, Andrew Raeburn

chamber and choral music, it was to the Academy that he turned. When in 1957 Argo had become part of the Decca Group, it had acquired both the capital necessary for further growth and the sales force of a major company; in 1964, confident of its ability to expand into the wider chamber orchestral repertoire, Harley offered the Academy a record with Argo. The producer was Andrew Raeburn, whom Neville already knew as the assistant manager of Thurston Dart's Philomusica, and the repertoire chosen was Handel's Opus 3, Six Concerti Grossi for Wind and Strings. It was an important project for the Academy, involving their first use of wind players on record; the set, edited by Simon Streatfeild with Thurston Dart in attendance at the sessions for advice and support, displays the quality in depth of the Academy's players, nearly all of whom played solo lines in one concerto or another.

The recording was made at Kingsway Hall, and the orchestra was fortunate in having on the sessions Kenneth Wilkinson, Decca's chief recording engineer; this was to be the first of the thirty or so recordings which 'Wilkie' has balanced for the Academy. Andrew Raeburn (now the Artistic Administrator of the Detroit Symphony Orchestra) made sure that the pressure on the orchestra was less than they had been used to with Mrs Dyer, and the recording was

41

allowed to spill over into an extra session.

The pains taken paid off – the British magazine *Records & Recordings* commented: 'They display an outstanding feeling for eighteenth-century performing style and, perhaps even more important, a uniformity in phrasing and attack that results in playing of exceptional energy and resilience.'

When Andrew Raeburn emigrated to America later in 1964, he was succeeded by Michael Bremner, who was to produce all the Academy's recordings for Argo until 1975. His first with the orchestra, early in 1965, was a collection of Handel's oboe concertos with Roger Lord as the soloist. It also included the 'lollipop' that virtually became the Academy's signature tune in the 1960s – 'The Arrival of the Queen of Sheba', from Handel's *Solomon* – and again the reviews were outstanding: 'If Handel had always been played like this, he would never have got the reputation, still held in some circles, of being a sanctimonious old stooge,' wrote *Gramophone*.

Mike had realised the potential of the Academy, and he suggested to Harley that they should be offered an exclusive contract. Although the orchestra had not been under contract to L'Oiseau-Lyre, the players felt a personal debt to the company. Accordingly, in the ensuing negotiations (which included the first of many attempts to change the Academy's name) they insisted that, although the Argo contract was otherwise to be exclusive, they should be at liberty to make a certain number of records with L'Oiseau-Lyre. With this single proviso, a contract was signed on 1 October 1965, under the terms of which the Academy became Argo artists for the next five years.

5

Make Sure Cambridge Is Warm

In the early 1960s, one of Argo's major assets was its association with the college choirs of Cambridge. It was recording a wide range of choral works, many of which required orchestral accompaniment, and the Academy's style was particularly well-suited to the repertoire in which Harley was interested. Their first recording in Cambridge came in 1964 – a recital of Purcell's 'Music for the Chapel Royal' with the Choir of St John's College, under the direction of Dr George Guest. Dr Guest was twenty-seven when he was appointed Organist and Choirmaster at St John's in 1951; he found the choir at a low ebb after the war years, and has spent the past thirty years successfully building up a new choir and restoring its public credibility through services in the chapel, BBC broadcasts, recordings, and concert tours throughout the world.

The Purcell recording was the first of many that the Academy were to make with Robert Tear, then at the start of his career. Among the other soloists was the Maori bass-baritone Inia te Wiata, who that year had started the carving of his massive 'Pouihi', a kind of totem pole representing Maori works of art, commissioned to decorate the foyer of New Zealand House in London, where it still stands.

The next project undertaken with St John's was an ambitious one – a set of Haydn's last six masses, written roughly one a year between 1796 and 1802 for the name-day of Princess Maria Hermenegild, wife of Haydn's patron Prince Nicolaus II Esterhazy. Only one of the six, the 'Nelson' Mass, had previously been recorded by Argo (with King's College Choir and the LSO under Sir David Willcocks), and before the sessions for the first in the set, Harley, naturally anxious to see how the relationship between the

Dr George Guest outside the Chapel of St John's College, Cambridge

Below, Inia te Wiata at work on the Pouihi

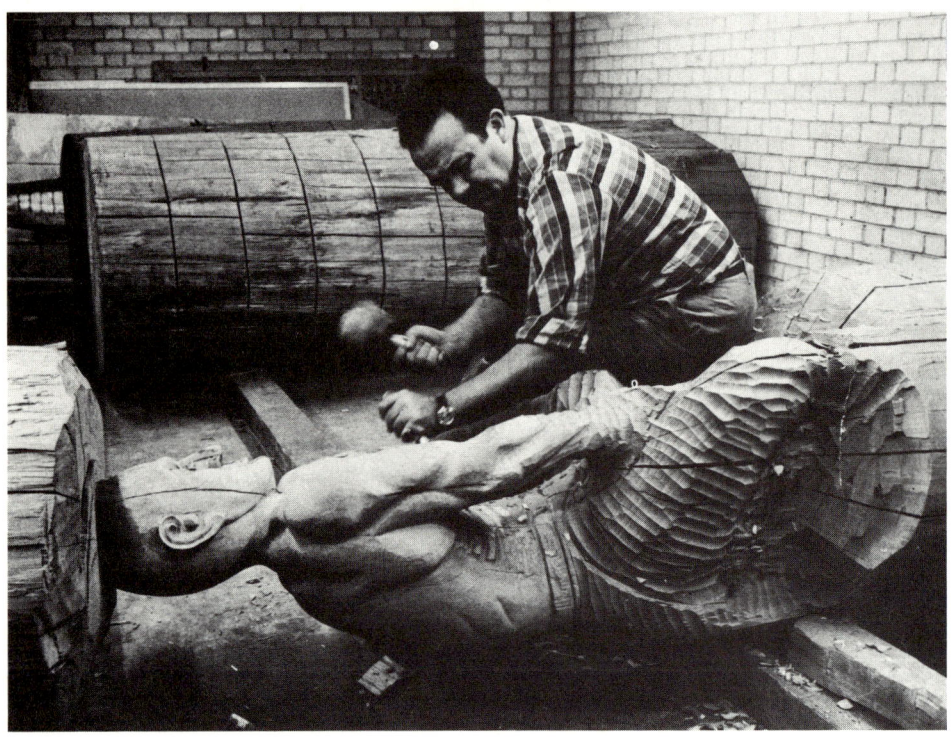

10, Downing Street.
Whitehall.

12 October, 1972

Dear Mr Dean,

The Prime Minister has asked me to thank you for your letter of 11 October.

The recordings of Haydn Masses which he gave to the Pope were the six recordings published by Argo; and of course, as you know, the St. John's College Choir are included in five of the six.

The Prime Minister is glad to think that it may please the Choir to know that the sounds of their voices may well be echoing round the Vatican.

Yours sincerely

Robert Armstrong

Academy and St John's was developing, arranged a live perform-ance in St John's College Chapel. In the event the trial run, the recording which followed, and the set as a whole were extremely well-received – a noteworthy tribute coming in 1972, when the Right Honourable Edward Heath, then Prime Minister, took the records with him to the Vatican as a present for Pope Paul VI.

In twelve records made since 1964, the Academy and St John's have covered a wide repertoire ranging from Monteverdi to Fauré. The relationship was from the start an especially happy one. The style of the orchestra blended well with that of the choir: George Guest shares the Academy's desire for clarity and he took pains to ensure that each strand of the polyphony was sharply distinguish-able amid the overall texture. Denis Vigay remembers him getting a bright Italian sound from the choristers which particularly suited the Academy's tone and attack. Orchestra and choir never met for rehearsal in advance, so the music had to be carefully prepared to save time at the sessions. Performing editions were marked up by Dr Guest, but were completed jointly, with the players entering bowings and discussing phrasing and dynamics in their usual style. Dr Guest remembers, 'Everyone put something into the perform-ance: every opinion, even that of a small boy, was taken seriously

George Guest conducting the Academy in St John's College Chapel

and usually proved to be of value.' The choir's work with the Academy was a team effort in every way: 'One happened to be playing the violin, one happened to be waving his hands about, others happened to be singing – but we were all working towards the same end.'

This friendship spilled over into off-duty hours; because of the boys, sessions rarely went on after 6 pm, and the evenings were free – a rarity for professional musicians, and much appreciated by the Academy. This unwonted free time was spent in various ways – George Guest remembers striking off into the country with Ken Heath and Steve Shingles in search of pubs serving real ale, while Denis Vigay recalls an unfortunate landlady spending sleepless nights listening to two of the fiddle-players teaching each other the Walton violin concerto and the first violin part from 'Scheherazade'. The orchestra also enjoyed working in the beautiful surroundings of Cambridge, and St John's Chapel itself has a handsome nineteenth-century interior and a fine warm acoustic. There was, however, one recurrent grumble: every session would start with complaints from players thwarted by the porters in their attempts to park in the Fellows' Car Park.

Vocal beauty: King's College Choir c. 1965 (Andrew Marriner third from left in the front row)

As Sir David Willcocks has pointed out, choral singing is one of the few spheres in which boys aged nine and ten can work on equal terms with the most experienced adults, and the professionalism and discipline of the boys at St John's meant that few allowances had to be made for them. However, choir schools necessarily put the education of the boys first, and record companies can generally work with them only in the school holidays; with St John's, the Academy could record only in the week before Christmas and the week or fortnight in June/July before the boys went on their summer holidays. The same restrictions applied to the boys of King's College Choir, and it became a habit for the Academy to spend their twice-yearly visits to Cambridge trooping up and down King's Parade and Trinity Street between recording sessions at the two chapels.

The 1954 recording of Choral Evensong at King's, under the direction of Boris Ord, was one of Argo's first musical ventures. Sir David Willcocks followed Boris Ord, and directed the choir from 1958 until 1974, when he left to take up his appointment as the Director of the Royal College of Music; he was succeeded at King's by Philip Ledger. Sir David made twelve records with the Academy

47

between 1965 and 1974, and remembers it as a close partnership, cemented by the presence in the choir of Neville's son Andrew (who earned his place less through vocal beauty than through his response to the polite enquiry designed by Sir David to put him at his ease before the audition: 'And how old are you, Andrew?' – 'Eight, sir. How old are you?').

The acoustic of King's College Chapel is one of its greatest beauties, but, with its long reverberation, it demands a sharper articulation than usual from the performers if the sound is not to be woolly and the phrases shapeless. The clipped consonants of the King's choristers are famous, and the Academy's instrumental style, with its crisp rhythms and exact bowing, matched this precision well. The boys sing with their 'head' rather than their 'chest' voice because of the resonant acoustic, and this produces a softly-grained sound; the care taken by the Academy to achieve a smooth, warm sound through uniformity of intonation and phrasing ensured a good blend.

To the Academy, used to being led from the front desk, being conducted by the Choirs' directors was a novel experience, but the collaboration worked smoothly. As at St John's, performing editions for King's/Academy recordings were prepared by the conductor – though it became clear at an early stage that the ideas of choir and orchestra on interpretation and technique were similar enough for little compromise to be necessary. The only discord arose from the fact that, whereas for professional players the first take is often in the nature of a run-through, for little boys, well-rehearsed and keyed-up, the first take is the big moment. The choristers tended to give their all first time through, and then grow tired or bored when asked to repeat themselves for the fourth or fifth time – by which stage the orchestra would be getting into its stride. Sir David used on occasion deliberately to leave details unrehearsed in order to have something to correct after the first take and to give the boys the stimulus and excitement of getting it right at the last moment. In more recent years, Philip Ledger has noticed the King's boys becoming cannier: they now save their best for the *second* take, giving the professionals time to get themselves sorted out.

With King's, the Academy have made records of varied reper-

toire, from Purcell's 'Funeral Music for Queen Mary' to Britten's 'St Nicholas Cantata'. For Argo they have recorded the smaller chamber works, including Handel's Chandos Anthems (which Sir David remembers with particular pleasure), the Vivaldi Gloria, and the Bach Magnificat. In addition, since 1970 they have taken on for EMI larger works requiring an expanded orchestra – *Messiah*, Haydn's *The Creation*, and Bach's *Christmas Oratorio* among them. (The *Messiah* sessions were particularly memorable for a bird noisily trapped in the roof of the chapel. Suggestions that it should be brought down with an air-rifle were not kindly received by those with an eye to the stained glass, and expensive session hours were lost while players, producer, choir and engineers flapped and shouted to dislodge it.)

Sir David Willcocks conducting the Academy in King's College Chapel

Both Argo and EMI have had to come to terms with the problems the chapel creates, in particular the acoustical ones. As Philip Ledger says, with some feeling, 'Everyone thinks we've got it made, that if you *sneeze* in the chapel it's going to sound lovely – well, it's simply not true. The chapel highlights everything: if you make an ugly sound, whether it be a harsh vocal sound or an ungainly string sound, the ugliness is exaggerated.' Chords linger for seven seconds, and the echo tends to come back flat in pitch. Soloists find it particularly difficult to secure good intonation, as the chapel has a tendency to depress the voice, and a miscalculation lasts not only for the duration of the note but the duration of the echo as

Philip Ledger conducting Elly Ameling, Dietrich Fischer-Dieskau and members of the Academy in King's College Chapel

well; it is here that singers trained in King's – Robert Tear among them – have the distinct advantage of knowing how to work with, and not against the acoustic. Balancing sound for recordings in the chapel is also exceptionally difficult; as one producer puts it, 'Once you get brass and timpani in there, you're in trouble; it all goes sailing off into the roof, and if you try and mike close enough to stop your trumpet disappearing into oblivion, it's right in your ear and everybody else could be in the next county.'

Another feature of the building is the sub-zero temperature it sometimes reaches, which affects both the players and the pitch of their instruments, and turns the heat-sensitive fire-opal worn by Marilyn Taylor, one of the second violins, a dark icy blue. Even at the height of summer the chapel is pleasantly fresh, and in winter the orchestra had regularly to be swathed in scarves and blankets. (Ken Heath had a fetching pair of fingerless mittens and a hip-flask reserved particularly for sessions in King's.) Christopher Bishop (now Managing Director of the Philharmonia Orchestra) who produced the majority of the King's/Academy records for EMI, remembers receiving a telegram from Dietrich Fischer-Dieskau, one of the soloists in the *Christmas Oratorio*, reading simply 'MAKE SURE CAMBRIDGE IS WARM'. Christopher did his best: the Academy's first oboe, Celia Nicklin, was deputed to fill hot water-bottles for

50

the soloists (who also included Elly Ameling, Dame Janet Baker, and Robert Tear) – but it was to little avail. Dame Janet recalls Fischer-Dieskau, muffled in his sturdiest overcoat with his breath coming in blue clouds, looking 'absolutely nithered'.

Nevertheless, for most people, the beauty of the surroundings more than compensates for the echo, the cold, and the added hazard of tourists loudly demanding admittance during sessions. Denis Vigay also remembers an Argo session disturbed by an excessively noisy lawnmower in the quad: it cost the producer £5 to ensure both its immediate retreat and the promise of a return the following week when EMI had some sessions. The technical problems of making music in King's College Chapel are easily outweighed by the inspiration that comes from the magnificence of structure and proportion in the building. Dame Janet Baker recalls 'a feeling of absolute enjoyment in making those records – a fantastic feeling of joyousness as a group. The Academy had an enthusiasm one didn't often find among professional orchestras, the choir was full of young singers eager to enter the profession; you'd hear this marvellous *obbligato* playing starting up behind you in this superb building – and it would all take off like a jet aeroplane.'

The Academy players greatly enjoyed working with the choristers, who seemed to regard sessions less as an imposition on their

MAKE SURE CAMBRIDGE IS WARM – Dietrich Fischer-Dieskau in King's College Chapel

Racing ants outside St John's College Chapel

holiday time than as an enjoyable opportunity to make extra pocket money. Dr Guest prizes a photograph of his choristers, gowns temporarily discarded, racing ants in the courtyard between sessions, and Sir David Willcocks recalls frequently having had to disperse cassocked and surpliced card schools which flourished in the breaks between takes. Trevor Connah remembers being particularly amused during the first sessions he did at King's by the sight of the little boys putting up their hands whenever they sang a wrong note. This practice, long used by choir masters as a means of saving time in rehearsal, identifies the culprit without its being necessary to stop the music, and makes him realise that each and every note is important. The system works well – but to Trevor it gave the impression of an exceptionally incontinent treble section. The corollary for the undergraduate choral scholars is to go up to the organ loft after the service or concert and apologise to the organist/director for any mistakes made. Philip Ledger, who studied under both Boris Ord and Sir David Willcocks, is still plagued by a feeling of guilt for mistakes, and has to repress the urge to apologise to the conductor if errors creep into his own solo performances.

The Academy made some of their firmest friendships in Cambridge. Besides George Guest (with whom they have now worked for over fifteen years), Sir David Willcocks and Philip Ledger (the pianist in the Academy's 1978 recording of Frank Martin's 'Petite Symphonie Concertante'), the orchestra worked regularly with several soloists – Helen Watts, Dame Janet Baker, April Cantelo, Felicity Palmer, Robert Tear and Ian Partridge among them. They rarely took continuo players with them to King's as the part was usually taken by the College organ scholars, two of whom – Andrew Davis and Simon Preston – were later to work closely with the Academy after coming down from Cambridge. They also spent a good deal of their spare time in the early days drinking, playing squash (and on one memorable occasion, cricket), and climbing in and out of College over the back gate with six of the King's choral scholars who had formed themselves into a close-harmony group under the name (the Academy have always had a fondness for long and complex titles) 'Schola Cantorum Pro Musica Profana in Cantabridgiense' – a group subsequently to become quite considerably better known as the King's Singers.

As Brian Kay, a founder member, has written, the King's Singers

Robert Tear

Cricket with the King's Singers (left to right – Mike Bremner, Tom Wheare, Simon Carrington, Roger Pullen, Alistair Thompson, Martin Lane, Roger Lord, Norman Nelson, Anthony Howard, Neville Marriner; kneeling – Alistair Hume, Brian Kay)

and the Academy 'have always had the feeling that we were in at the start together. . . One thing sticks in the mind from those early days, which I think formed the basis of the success of the Academy . . . a feeling of being young, vital and alert, closely aligned to a deep sense of fun, and a wealth of expertise and experience, which combined with devastating force, and produced the sort of unit for which the musical world was entirely ready. That desire to get away from the conductor's baton, and to form an ensemble which thrived on internal combustion, was very similar to our own ideals, and I imagine that the fact that the original players were friends before they started developing a musical relationship together accounted for the instant feeling of unity – a situation entirely reminiscent of our own.'

6

Love or Money

One of Norman Nelson's most searing memories of performing with the Academy is of a festival concert in Cambridge, arranged to coincide with sessions at King's. He and Neville were playing the Bach Double Violin Concerto (BWV 1043), and in one particularly piquant passage during which the two soloists are supposed to be playing a sixth apart, Norman was horrified to find that they were playing in unison. With lightning speed he dropped down a sixth to fill in the missing line – only to find that Neville had had the same idea, and they were back in unison again, albeit on the bottom line. History does not relate how, or if, they ever finished the piece, but for the rest of the concert the Academy's violin contingent was noticeably subdued.

Festivals like the one in Cambridge provided (and continue to provide) the Academy with the majority of their concert appearances in England. The orchestra could not afford at that stage to promote its own concerts – its Wigmore Hall enterprise had been an object lesson – and few but the best-supported music clubs could meet the expenses of an ensemble of twelve or more players. Festivals, aided by the Arts Council, were therefore a life-line. The Arts Council of Great Britain, set up in 1946, has over the past four decades provided money and ideas, both artistic and commercial, for an increasing number of festivals, which supplied the Academy, among many other artists, with the setting for their early appearances. The first to invite the Academy was the York Festival of 1963, at which the Academy played the whole of Bach's 'Musical Offering' in the candle-lit Minster, and over the next ten years they were to appear in places as diverse as Harrogate, Bath, King's Lynn, Edinburgh, Chichester and Norwich.

These appearances were not always characteristic. In Chichester, the Academy were directed from the piano (for the only time in their career) by Fou Ts'ong in three Mozart piano concertos; and on other occasions they found themselves back under the conductor's baton. In Bath, for example, they were conducted by Sir Michael Tippett in his anthem for double choir 'Plebs Angelica', in which they accompanied the Schola Cantorum of Oxford. In Norwich, the Festival's director, Antony Hopkins, took the baton for a performance of Stravinsky's 'Apollo' – and experienced at first hand the Academy's early aversion to conductors. He remembers with painful clarity the point at which, during a tricky passage with the sections entering one after the other in strict canon, one section anticipated its entry by a bar, throwing the pattern of the movement into confusion. With some neat stick-work he restored equilibrium by bringing in the remaining sections also one bar early, and hissing at the only section which had actually made a correct entry, 'Skip a bar, skip a bar.' But it had been an uncomfortable and potentially ruinous moment, and after the concert he went backstage to make his feelings known to the culprits; he remembers being halted in mid-diatribe with the inaccurate but heartfelt words: 'In the Academy we *never* take leads from conductors.'

Music festivals are special occasions, generally held in the summer, when more is packed into a few days than the host town or city might normally see or hear in a year. The organisers are eager to present 'big names' whose appearances might otherwise be confined to the capital, and the Academy in their early days were invited to accompany such internationally-known artists as Dietrich Fischer-Dieskau, Heinz Holliger, Jean-Pierre Rampal and Josef Suk. In one spectacular year at successive festivals they appeared with Ileana Cotrubas, Helen Watts, John Shirley-Quirk, George Malcolm, Heather Harper and Barry Tuckwell.

The organisers of a subsidised festival are generally readier to experiment than the commercial concert promoter, and audiences, in keeping with the festival spirit, are likewise more receptive towards new artists and specialist ensembles. An early prospectus for the Battle Festival – one of the earliest the Academy visited – describes its main characteristic as 'a feeling of friendliness and lack of restraint between artist and onlooker.' It was this atmosphere

*Bits of Bach –
John Gray and
Neville Marriner
in the Harrogate
Festival Club*

which the Academy enjoyed, and the players looked forward to their scattered public appearances as much in terms of the welcome they were given as the repertoire they were able to prepare and present to a well-informed festival audience.

There was the occasional administrative hiccup. Members of the orchestra spent an anxious day in Harrogate, feverishly snipping up full scores of the Bach Triple Violin Concerto (BWV 1064) to extract the three solo lines in time for the evening performance because the solo parts had inadvertently been left in London. The Academy have a long-standing and amicable relationship with the Harrogate Festival and its organiser Clive Wilson, and Molly recalls, 'We were particularly grateful for the facilities of the Festival Club that day; I'm afraid we littered it horribly, though, with sandwich wrappers and bits of Bach.'

Festivals apart, the Academy's exposure to the English public in their first decade was limited, though their connection with the BBC extended to television in 1965 for the first time, with a performance of Vivaldi's 'The Four Seasons' from Kenwood House, with Alan Loveday as soloist. The setting in the Orangery was exquisite; outside, conditions were less than ideal. Perversely

for March, it was a brilliantly sunny day, and Alan remembers being distracted during his performance of 'Winter' by technicians whom, out of the corner of his eye, he could see running round outside with watering cans, trying to create a suitably rain-swept effect. The mirth this provoked was not appreciated by the technicians, with whom some players had already crossed swords: the crew had wanted a shot of 'The Artists' arriving at the house, and were seriously displeased to find Peter Gibbs carrying his violin under his arm wrapped in old newspaper, *à la* fish and chips.

The orchestra's other major venture into television in the 1960s produced a victory for the technicians – over one member, at least. The Academy (augmented for the occasion with wind and brass) donned wigs, beards and frock coats to perform the 'Siegfried Idyll' in a film of the same name about Wagner's love affair with Cosima von Bülow. The producer, Anthony Wilkinson, had centred his film round the first performance of the 'Idyll', staged by Wagner for Cosima's birthday on Christmas Day 1870. The players were required to appear out of the gloom of Ealing Studios, tastefully sprinkled with fibreglass snow, stamp their feet and blow on their fingers in a manner expressive of extreme cold, mount the stairs to the landing outside Cosima's bedroom, and perform snatches of the 'Idyll' under the baton of Wagner, as portrayed by Alan Badel.

The trouble started, as Steve Shingles recalls, when it became clear that the set could not accommodate the whole Academy. In particular, the double bass was a problem – too unwieldy for the stairs, too large for the landing – and the morning was spent weeding it out of shots: to the question 'Where would you like the bass?', the inevitable answer was 'Er … well, perhaps the *next* scene…?' John Gray had been obliged to arrive at the studio at seven that morning, had spent some considerable time being made up, and started to feel that this was shabby reward for his pains. The first scene after lunch was the snow-strewn arrival at the house. He positioned himself (and the bass) carefully in front of the door where he was bound to be first in, centre stage, and on cue knocked loudly with the brass knocker provided and strode in, pleased. There was a loud and anguished cry of 'Cut!' – all sound effects, knockers included, were to be added later – and aggrieved but undaunted, John resumed his pole position at the door. This time he got halfway up the stairs with the bass before remembering that the steps petered out and that the landing on which the 'Idyll' was to be played was elsewhere. Callously, he was left up there to look down on Wagner conducting the rest of the band on a different set – and the film became known to the Academy as 'Where would you like the bass?'

The Academy's mixed fortunes on television did not deter them from broadcasting fairly frequently for BBC Radio. They did their first two Promenade concerts in 1965; Malcolm Latchem remembers the second particularly clearly as a concert shared between the Academy and the London Philharmonic Orchestra – of which he was also a member. The Academy opened the programme with a performance of the Mendelssohn Octet, and Malcolm then had three minutes before the next piece in which to struggle out of Academy tails and into LPO dinner jacket – to the amusement of Sir Adrian Boult, who murmured in passing, 'Plenty of time, dear boy, plenty of time. …' Meanwhile, the rest of the Academy hurried to Paddington to catch the last train to Totnes, and the Dartington Summer School of Music.

* * *

Dartington is regarded by many of the Academy in much the same light as St Martin's – as a kind of spiritual home, where the orchestra developed a sense of unity and gave some of its most exciting concerts, broadening its repertoire and consolidating its style. The Summer School was founded in 1948, at the suggestion of Artur Schnabel, by one of his pupils, Sir William Glock (later Head of Music at BBC Radio), with John Amis as organising secretary and Beatrice Musson as registrar. For the first five years it was held at Bryanston, but since 1953 it has been held at Dartington Hall, using the fourteenth-century Hall and its beautiful grounds for four weeks every July and August.

From the start Dartington was different. Unlike some summer schools, aimed at the specialist who goes to pursue his own particular interest, it was designed more as a miniature festival. Concerts and classes, lectures and workshops exist side by side; every aspect of music is represented, with performer and non-performer equally welcome. In the words of Charles Tindall-Lister, one of its most faithful supporters, 'Dartington is a kaleidoscope; there's something different happening all the time, the same people in different combinations producing different results, a new pattern forming.' From choir practice in the Banqueting Hall at 9.15 am, the Summer School student can go to an eleven o'clock lecture on a musical or non-musical subject, or an instrumental coaching session or work-

Stephen Shingles and John Amis on the lawn at Dartington

shop; after lunch he can choose between a master class, an orchestra rehearsal, or a composition class; and with more than three hundred students in residence each week, there are unlimited opportunities to play chamber music throughout the day, which ends with a concert by visiting professional musicians.

Over the years, these concerts have been of international standard; Dietrich Fischer-Dieskau gave his first English recitals at the Summer School, and Dame Janet Baker, Gerald Moore, George Malcolm, Alfred Brendel, and the Amadeus Quartet have all been Dartington 'regulars'. The teaching there is equally high-powered: Sandor Vegh, David Munrow, Manoug Parikian and André Tchaikovsky are among the artists to have taken master classes or workshops; visiting composers and composition teachers have included Hindemith, Britten, Copland, Stravinsky and Peter Maxwell Davies (now the Summer School's Musical Director).

However, the majority of the students attend the Summer School to participate as well as listen. All enjoy the chance to discuss the music they play and hear – over breakfast, lunch and supper (communal and noisy), over coffee on the lawn, round the swimming-pool, on the tennis court, and after the concert in the pub. Audience gets the chance to meet performer on the same level, without the distance imposed by rostrum, evening dress and dimmed lights; the performer gets the opportunity to experience appreciation and meet criticism at first hand.

It was this side of Dartington that appealed to the Academy. Neville was to say of the Academy, 'We play for love or money – rarely for both', and at Dartington, with its conspicuously low fees, it was not for money. At the invitation of John Amis, a friend of Neville's from the days when they shared a house in London, the group made its first appearance at the Summer School in 1964 and was to return annually until 1970, with a special appearance in 1973, the School's twenty-fifth anniversary year. Neville had himself visited the School in its earliest years, in the duo he had formed with Thurston Dart. It has been a feature of the School to avoid nineteenth-century repertoire, after Schubert at least, and to concentrate on music earlier and later – Neville and Thurston Dart, for instance, played works by Purcell and the twentieth-century American composer, Walter Piston. These musical tastes coincided

In concert in the Banqueting Hall (soloists – Iona Brown, Alan Loveday and Carmel Kaine)

neatly with those of the Academy who, in their thrice-weekly concerts, played a large proportion of their seventeenth- and early eighteenth-century repertoire – the Handel Opus 6 concertos, Bach's Brandenburg Concertos and the 'Ricercare' from 'The Musical Offering' (this at every concert one year, by special request of John Amis), and concertos from Vivaldi's 'L'Estro Armonico'. At the same time they were extending their repertoire, with the encouragement of Argo, beyond the baroque and into the twentieth century.

At Dartington, for the first time in their career, the Academy were playing together for more than two days at a time – usually for at least a week, sometimes for two. The players used the opportunity to learn new works in ideal conditions, practising them intensively and airing them before an audience, to perfect their interpretations before committing them to record. Thus the Summer School was one of the first audiences to hear the results of the Academy's search for new repertoire. Rossini's String Sonata in C, written by the youthful composer with a comically showy part for the double bass, regularly brought the house down; Richard Strauss's 'Metamorphosen' reduced the audience to tears; and the Academy's playing of Tippett's 'Fantasia Concertante on a Theme of Corelli' moved John Amis to walk, overcome with emotion, out of the rehearsal room and into a plate-glass window. (Sir William

Glock was not always as enthusiastic: on the occasions when the Academy and John conspired to programme a work not to his taste – 'Metamorphosen' was one – he would declare it 'a Horn-of-Plenty night', and boycott the concert in favour of an excellent meal at the restaurant of that name.) On the day Sir John Barbirolli died, the Academy, by way of a tribute, played the two 'Aquarelles' of Delius, novel repertoire for them but a worthy memorial.

The orchestra accompanied the Summer School choir in its weekly concerts of works ranging from Purcell's 'Fairy Queen' to Vaughan Williams's 'Serenade to Music' – and it was here that Neville made some of his first appearances as a conductor. He took the choir and orchestra through Purcell, Pergolesi, Vivaldi, Haydn, Mozart, Schubert and Britten, in a frank and fearless fashion that amused and impressed the majority of the singers as much as it outraged a minority, unused to being informed that they built up to a crescendo as subtly as workmen slapping undercoat on a wall. Charles Tindall-Lister remembers a tendency to refer to the tenors as violas – but he also recollects a performance of Britten's 'St Nicholas' after which the choir refused to take a separate bow, preferring to leave the credit to its conductor.

Neville's first appearance as a conductor

*Dame Janet Baker and
George Malcolm at
Dartington*

It was at Dartington that the Academy most often met their
friends, two of the closest being George Malcolm and Dame Janet
Baker. George appeared with the Academy both as soloist and, less
usually and as an exception to his general rule, as continuo player.
He always looked forward to working with them – 'There was this
wonderful feeling of co-operation: their phrasing, and the way
they'd make, for example, an unrehearsed *rubato* together, entirely
unanimous, made me ashamed for the harpsichord – it's so difficult
to get really smooth and beautiful phrasing like that, even with a
pedal-equipped instrument.' There was, however, one grumble –
the harpsichordist's perennial complaint that he cannot be heard.
Philip Ledger tells the story of the conductor who remarked of the
harpsichord, 'If I can hear it I don't like it, and if I can't hear it I don't
see why I should pay for it.' Nobody would say that the Academy
did not *like* the harpsichord, but George on occasion felt that they
were simply playing too loud, and said so; he remembers overhear-
ing, before a Dartington concert at which they were to play a Bach
concerto together, Neville addressing the players on their way to
the platform, in menacing tones: 'You've *never* played as softly as
you're going to play now.'

As continuo player, George was content to blend with the orchestra. The Academy's continuo players were to a large extent chosen by the cellos and bass: they looked for a harpsichordist whose playing was accurate and sensitive, prone neither to lagging nor to hurrying, and willing to complement the bass line rather than dictate it. In George they found an ideal partner, and he is proud of the team he made with them – 'One of the best I've come across, if I may say so. They were the most marvellous continuo players, listening all the time to the soloist and to me, and totally engrossed in the music: they would practise intonation together for hours.' Occasionally there would be dissent; George has heard himself referred to as 'the Liberace of the harpsichord' and recalls, 'John Gray used to say that whatever we were playing I managed to turn it into a harpsichord concerto – by Mendelssohn.' But in general Ken, Denis, John and George made an amicable and successful team, and the Academy, asked to list the musicians with whom they most enjoy working, invariably include George.

Nevertheless, Neville had no inhibitions in giving George, by way of a joke, unmarked continuo parts for pieces which the strings had already worked out in detail together. John Amis remembers, 'The strings would be clued-up, coming in at the point of a bow. They'd suddenly drop to a *pianissimo* and George, without the marks to warn him, would come in BANG – "George! Please don't make so much noise!"; or a little bit later they'd have decided on a tremendous *fortissimo* and George would be left tinkling away to himself – "George! Couldn't you give us a bit more there!"' Goaded beyond endurance, he waited to take his revenge and hit on a concert whose first encore was to be taken from Gluck's music for the ballet 'Don Juan'. The movement in question was for strings alone, *pizzicato* throughout, and George listened as the strings rehearsed. He then went away and composed a part for himself, extemporising on the familiar tune 'Over The Hills And Far Away', but in faultless Gluckian style. John Amis remembers the concert:

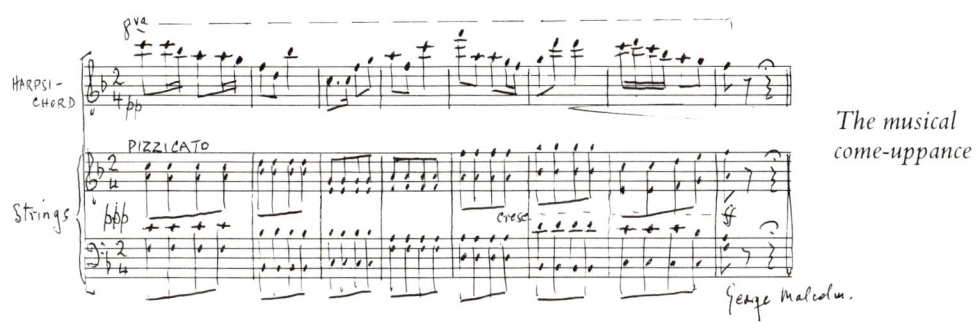

The musical come-uppance

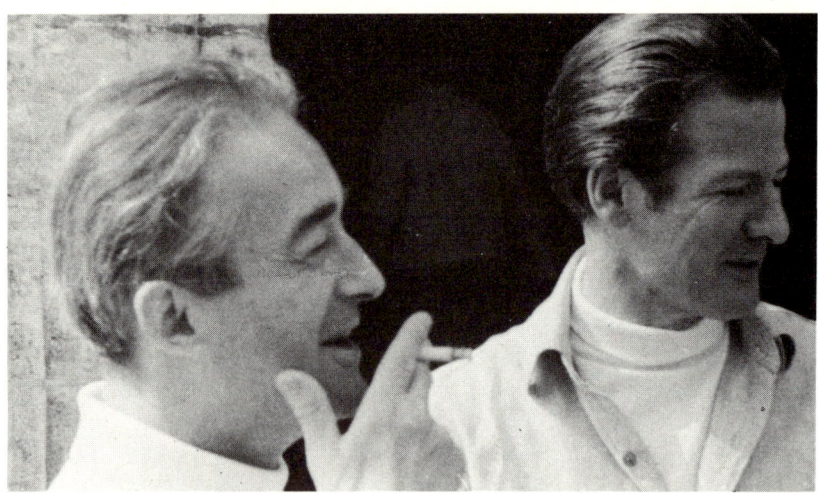

Dartington guerillas – George Malcolm and Neville Marriner

'They were, of course, expecting George to be sitting there with arms folded; but while they were going plink-plonk-plink-plonk, plunk-plink-plunk-plink, he suddenly let fly with his wonderful invention, a marvellous line, and corpsed the lot of them – the biggest musical come-uppance I've ever seen.' George's only comment, made with some satisfaction: 'At least you could hear the harpsichord for a change.'

This was the start of a protracted war of practical jokes, all more or less messy, waged over several years at Dartington. John Gray remembers a preliminary skirmish: 'There was a very nice chamber organ in the Banqueting Hall with silver pipes, which George was due to play. Before he'd had a chance to see it, Neville extracted the eight-foot rank of pipes, and George had to survive on what was left. He kept on grumbling about this curious organ – and of course, when he found a pile of silver pipes in the corner. . . .' Guerilla warfare was brought to a truce only with the episode of the chicken pie. Neville, arriving hungry at Dartington after the kitchens had closed for the night, was offered a piece of chicken pie by George. He appeared to accept it gratefully, but on retiring for the night George found the pie, in a half-consumed condition, waiting in his room. He duly returned it stealthily in the morning during the choral rehearsal – only to find it, by now considerably less attractive, in his music when he went to practice. Not to be outdone, he

66

wrapped it in a parcel with birthday paper, attached a little note reading 'From an admirer in the audience', and had it presented to Neville after that evening's concert, while he was deep in conversation with Sir William Glock. Flattered and unwary, Neville opened it with enthusiasm, and when the pie, now smelly, was revealed in all its glory, George knew to expect redress. 'I was leaving Dartington early the next morning to go straight to Yehudi Menuhin's festival in Gstaad, and I kept my room locked from that moment onwards. But when I unpacked my bag in the hotel in Gstaad the following day, there inside it was the chicken pie. I still don't know how he did it.'

Dame Janet Baker's concerts with the Academy were less fraught with peril. Among the music they performed together were Bach cantatas, Handel arias, and Sir Lennox Berkeley's 'Four Poems of St Teresa d'Avila'. She remembers their work together at Dartington with particular pleasure: 'For the kind of singer I am, that kind of music-making, in that size of hall with that number of players is perhaps perfection. It is interesting that it is often on the smaller scale that one's hopes and expectations are exceeded in music; composers like Handel and Bach, for example, create a structure you can comprehend: the field is smaller, you can look over the hedges, you can grasp the scope of the whole thing.'

Her feelings about the Summer School were not unmixed – 'It was a bit like going back to school, all that communal eating' – but she greatly enjoyed the more relaxed side of Dartington life. She was much in demand on the tennis court – 'I enjoyed playing with the Academy – there was no quarter given, and it seemed so marvellous to be doing something *normal* after all the music.' The 'normal' aspect of the School was taken at full advantage by the Academy. Steve Shingles remembers rushing hot from the tennis court, where he and the second viola Kenneth Essex had just finished a strenuous game of singles, to arrive breathless and sweaty at the orchestra's final rehearsal with the choir for the week's choral performance: the sopranos were vastly amused at the sight of the viola section, clad still in shorts, with violas in one hand and tennis racquets in the other.

Earnest music-making was similarly undermined by the Annual Cricket Match between Academy and Summer School staff (at

which the task of wicket-keeping again fell to Neville, on the grounds that broken fingers would not at any rate prevent him from conducting the choir). Several of the staff showed a tendency to take the game seriously, which was not reciprocated by the Academy: final honours were usually about even, and the match was a good excuse to retire to the pub – either the Summer School's own club, the White Hart, or the Cott Inn, twenty minutes' walk away through the medieval tilt-yard and gardens behind the Hall. The White Hart had a lamentable disinclination to stay open beyond 10.30 pm, and the Academy were notorious for arranging programmes to end not a minute later than 10.20, giving the players time to hurry off the platform, out of the Banqueting Hall, where the concerts were given, and into the bar for last orders. The ping-pong room was another nocturnal haunt: Alan Loveday, by then a regular member of the Academy, was a particularly skilled and fanatical player – many remember him half-demolishing the room's windows in the course of a spirited match with musicologist Hans Keller.

The time the Academy spent at Dartington, often with wives and families, helped to develop a strong sense of identity as a group; Steve Shingles recalls, 'The atmosphere was marvellous – those long walks back from the Cott through the gardens, and parties round the swimming-pool with people's children splashing in and out, and coffee on the lawn in the sun, with everyone chatting and Charles Davis, the Summer School's unofficial photographer, going round taking pictures.' (The flautist William Bennett remembers Dartington's open-air activities with less nostalgia: it was over a lunchtime glass of cider in the courtyard of the White Hart that he was stung on the lip by a wasp the day he was due to play Brandenburg Concerto No. 5.)

By 1967, the mid-point of the Academy's Dartington career, the composition of the group, disturbed by the loss of Norman Nelson, Simon Streatfeild and John Churchill (who had all emigrated to Canada) had begun to settle down again. New members had joined, and at the majority of dates the faces would be the same – among the violins Neville Marriner, Hugh Maguire, Iona Brown, Malcolm Latchem, Anthony Howard, Trevor Connah, Raymond Keen-lyside, Roy Gillard, Diana Cummings, Andrew McGee, and Ursula Snow; among the violas, Stephen Shingles, Kenneth Essex, and Margaret Major; the cellos Kenneth Heath, Denis Vigay, Joy Hall and Michael Evans; and John Gray, the double bass. Several players who were to become regulars joined at Dartington: both Alan Loveday and Carmel Kaine were at the Summer School giving solo recitals when the Academy fell short of fiddles and they agreed to stand in. Alan, as an old friend of Neville's from the Hop-kins–Loveday–Marriner Trio days and an expert on the baroque style in violin playing, had originally been asked to join the Academy in 1958; but as the invitation came on a day when he had already turned down invitations to join two similar groups, his reaction was, 'Not *another* string orchestra', and his entrance was deferred by seven years. Carmel, in preparation for the 1967 Vienna International Violin Competition, had brought her programme down to Dartington to play it through to Frederick Grinke: she went straight from the back of the Academy's second violins to win the competition.

Another player to make his début at Dartington was Anthony Jenkins, the Academy's second viola since 1970; that year he was brought in as the fourth of five violas in Richard Strauss's 'Metamorphosen'. Fresh from the Royal Academy of Music, much younger than most of the other players, nervous, and anxious to

Below, *The Academy at Dartington*

Anthony Jenkins

make a good impression, he went to his room as soon as he arrived, and practised his part long and determinedly; unfortunately the window was open, and in the next room Steve Shingles (due to play the first viola part) was taking his customary afternoon siesta in the manner of an experienced professional. After a brisk exchange on the theme of practice mutes and their desirability, peace was restored, and the evening's performance was a particular success. The Academy also acquired an embryo recruit at Dartington without realising it. Nicholas Kraemer, working for the holidays in the Summer School kitchens in 1965 and 1966, was greatly impressed by the orchestra's performances (to this day he can remember everything they played). He was seized with determination to play in the Academy – and was to become one of their regular continuo players in the decade to come.

7

Sex and Travel

During the Dartington years, the experience the Academy were acquiring – widening their repertoire and developing a corporate identity – was bearing fruit in the recording studio. In the words of Mike Bremner, 'Life is unfair: it is often the artists who through making records have had the opportunity to *listen* to themselves and improve accordingly, that are given the chance to make *more* records.' With Argo, Mike and Harley, the Academy were given the chance both to improve and to expand. Over the five years of the first contract, they were able to put into practice all their theories on the technical and musical aspects of chamber playing, analyse the results, and profit from the lessons learned. Recordings became the centre of Academy life, providing at last the necessary continuity of work to keep the members together on a regular basis, and by 1970 their recordings of string music from three centuries had prompted H. C. Robbins Landon to describe them as 'the finest chamber orchestra in existence'.

Success on this scale takes some explaining, and early photographs of the Academy in the recording studio provide a clue. The orchestra occupies centre stage – but in the background one can usually identify Mike Bremner and Stan Goodall, the balance engineer who succeeded Kenneth Wilkinson on the majority of Academy recordings after 1968. Mike, Stan and Wilkie were really part of the Academy at sessions, part of a team aiming at perfection – of style, performance, and recorded sound. As critic Peter Gammond commented in *Gramophone Record Review* three years after the Argo contract had been signed: 'The dedicated record collector, the person interested in repertoire as well as performance and quality recording, has come to expect a guarantee of pleasure and satisfaction along with each new

A team aiming at perfection – Stan Goodall, Kenneth Wilkinson and Mike Bremner

disc added to the growing list of successful collaborations between Neville Marriner and his Academy of St Martin in the Fields and the Argo Record Company. Here is the perfect and dedicated recording partnership in action, musicians and promoters carefully and enthusiastically probing the repertoire with high-standard perform-ances of accepted pieces interspersed with judicious sorties into the unknown, and everyone given assurance of the very best of today's recording facilities at their disposal.'

Committing a performance to disc involves a three-way process of communication. The recording producer is the middle-man between artist and engineer, ensuring that the musical ideas of the one can be translated into the technical vocabulary of the other. The Academy have never underestimated the importance of the techni-cal side of this equation, recognising their good fortune in having, first in Wilkie and then in Stan, engineers with the 'green fingers' required to record orchestral performances successfully. Both combined the necessary grasp of the theoretical and technical prob-lems with the flair and intuition which can – and should – make balance engineering a creative rather than a purely mechanical exercise. The Academy's Tchaikovsky record couples the 'Souvenir de Florence' balanced by Wilkie, with the Serenade for

*Mike Bremner
and
Neville Marriner*

Strings balanced by Stan – who remembers the sessions as the first on which he had ever gone solo. Wilkie had been called away to Cambridge at short notice and handed the record over to Stan, then the tape-operator, for completion. The record, a testament to team-work, was later to win an Edison, one of the recording industry's more prestigious awards.

The engineer's job is first and foremost to capture the sound of a performance as freshly as possible – a review of an early Argo/Academy recording suggests what can be achieved: 'The sound is vividly realistic; the string tone has the rasp of resin but is never shrill or harsh, it is just the vivid sound of strings heard from the third row of the stalls in an acoustically bright concert hall.' One of the drawbacks of the gramophone record (at present) is that it is an exclusively aural medium. At a concert, as much as fifty per cent of the effect created may be visual: the eyes identify the section of the orchestra with the leading voice and the emotional force of the music is suggested by the physical vigour of the musicians' attack; to some extent the sounds actually heard are affected by a purely visual judgement. (David Attenborough has pointed out that of the five senses sight is the most powerful: if two conflicting messages are projected simultaneously, one aurally and the other visually, the visual message will generally predominate.) On a record, the engineer has to compensate for the absence of visual clues and stimuli; he has to suggest the things that the listener cannot see – underline an attack by a particular section, bring out an important solo, generate the excitement of a live performance. As Chris Hazell, Mike Bremner's successor at Argo, explains, 'It's like putting highlights in hair: you're not actually colouring the hair, but you're emphasising the original colour.'

The positioning of the microphones in the studio is obviously crucial in this process, and it is here that an imaginative engineer can make his presence felt. Stan had had no formal musical training when he started as an engineer; for the first few sessions with the Academy he relied on Mike to point out the seating positions of the various sections, so that he could place his microphones correctly. However, with the conventional placings mastered, he began to experiment. Drawing on his experience at pop sessions, he tried close-miking, particularly with the lower-range instruments. This gave a clearer, firmer bass line which compensated to some extent for the Academy's seemingly 'top-heavy' composition: with as many as twelve violins, six first and six second, more than two cellos and one bass might have been expected, but were rarely

Stan Goodall

75

employed. On the occasions when the Academy had need of brass, instead of stringing the instruments in the conventional way in a long line at the back to play into the orchestral mikes, Stan tried grouping them together with their own microphone, which gave him greater control over the often unwieldy brass sound. Timpani are equally hard to record with clarity, often emerging merely as a muffled thud in the background; for the precise sound essential to the Academy style, they need a dry atmosphere, so Stan devised 'the little hut' for the Academy's regular timpanist, Tristan Fry. Sitting in an open-ended rectangle of screens, on occasion roofed with a curtain, with his own microphone and electric fire, Tristan, by a careful choice of stick and playing technique, could produce a dry clear sound which was prevented by the hut from 'swimming' into the main orchestral mikes.

Stan gratefully remembers having the freedom to go out into the studio and make small changes, some entirely from instinct, without being obliged to justify himself to anyone. However, his experiments did not go unnoticed, and Neville was once heard to remark that Stan's 'suck-it-and-see' approach must have cost the company several thousand pounds in mike-moving time. This was compounded by John Gray, who had a habit of moving his mike from the allotted position, arguing about balance the while; no amount of pleading or threatening could make him stop, until the day he went to move the mike without checking that it had been earthed: 240 volts are an efficient deterrent, and Stan had no further trouble.

Once the microphones have been placed, the volume of sound that each is required to pick up is balanced by the engineer, after consultation with producer and artist. The sounds coming through the various mikes can obviously be combined in an infinite number of ways; but whereas some companies using multi-track techniques make any adjustments necessary to the balance later, Decca/Argo techniques generally entail fixing the balance at the session, and all judgements have to be made on the spot. (These can be on the arbitrary side: Stan remembers being worried during the recording of the Bach Suites that he was not bringing out the sound of Thurston Dart's harpsichord with sufficient clarity – only to be told, in the grandest Dartian manner, 'The harpsichord, my boy,

Adjusting the balance

should be seen and not heard – don't give it another thought.')

The engineer's job in the control room is made much easier if the orchestra is balanced successfully by the artists in the studio. Neville has an acute sense of the internal balance of an ensemble – developed during his days in the Martin String Quartet – and is able to sort out musically problems which would otherwise have to be solved mechanically: 'less from the fiddles, please, and I'd like to hear more cello at bar 68' can satisfactorily replace 'push up the faders on the right-hand side'. By obtaining the desired balance in the studio, Neville leaves the engineer free to concentrate on his primary duty of reproducing the feel of the performance – and it was here that Stan's flair was most obvious. In Neville's words, 'Stan has an instinct for the sound that will make a recording special; he knows what he wants, and he knows when he's got it – he has a knack of creating an element of magic.'

The problems of capturing an atmosphere, even of rendering a performance faithfully, can be lessened (or multiplied) by the acoustic with which the engineer has to work. The studio's acoustic affects everyone – the engineer because he has to manipulate it,

77

allowing for echo or compensating for the lack of it; the players because they have to adjust their playing – lighter or heavier vibrato, softer or harder tonguing – to get the best out of their instruments; the producer because he is responsible for monitoring the overall sound of the performance. The acoustic must be carefully chosen to suit the type of music to be recorded. No single venue is likely to be suitable for all recordings – Mike Bremner is reported to have complained of one studio that it did not take the key of E major at all well – and Wilkie insists that the secret of successful recording is to take what each particular hall has to offer – warmth or echo, 'bloom' or dry clarity – rather than attempting to regulate every aspect of the sound mechanically.

Many things can affect the acoustic of a hall – the type and thickness of the paint on the walls, the hardness of the plaster, the resonance of the floorboards, the texture of the furnishings, and so on. Humidity, or the lack of it, can have a particularly marked effect: as Neville says, 'It's like bowling seamers: success can depend on the weather.' Though he was mocked for his pains, it was an example of John Gray's extreme professionalism that on arrival at sessions, when he felt it necessary, he would extract a large sponge from a gargantuan hold-all, repair to the cloakroom, damp the sponge and push it into the bass, to maintain the constant level of humidity that the instrument needs for full resonance.

Conditions outside the studio are equally important. One of the venues most frequently used by Argo in the early days was Kingsway Hall, with its warm, rich sound which can make a chamber group sound like a symphony orchestra. Its one drawback is the constant threat of noise from London Transport – and even that can be put to good use. During the recording of Vaughan Williams's 'The Lark Ascending', with Iona Brown as the soloist, all was going well; Iona and the Academy were playing beautifully, and Mike and Stan had virtually made up their minds – this was what Wilkie always described as 'the magic take'. Then, right at the end, as Iona's final note was fading away into nothingness, a tube train rumbled under the hall. Hearing it through the headphones, Stan turned to Mike, his face contorted in agony: 'Just the wind in the trees, Stan,' muttered Mike – and that is how the record ends, with 'the magic take' and the lark ascending to the faint rustle of wind-blown leaves

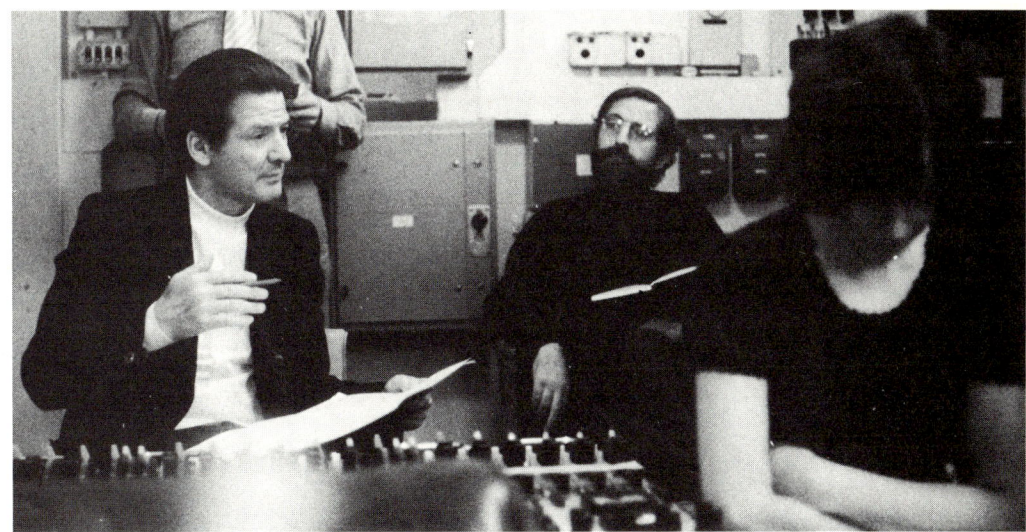

Listening to a play-back in the control room – Neville Marriner, Mike Bremner and Carmel Kaine

on the Piccadilly Line.

The engineer must also be familiar with the sound in the control room, where 'takes' are played back: misleading sound there can result in a recording which badly misrepresents the performance actually given. Wilkie often brings with him a record he knows well, to play in the control room at the start of sessions in an unfamiliar hall, in order to gauge the effect the acoustic will have on subsequent play-backs. Stan has on occasion resorted to more extreme measures: during one set of sessions at Rotherhithe, where the control room is large and cavernous, he arranged for a plywood partition to be built, halving the room and creating a more reliable acoustic. While the divider was being erected behind him Stan was intent on making adjustments to the mixing console, and it was not until the workmen had gone that he noticed the absence of a door.

Even without technical hitches on this scale, the first fifteen minutes of a session are generally the most difficult. A recording studio can be a hostile environment, not conspicuously conducive to music-making, with its booms, cables and arc lights, and the producer's first task is to humanise the situation – to reassure the performer that he is not simply playing to a microphone and a set of dials. The producer acts as both audience and critic. According to Mike, 'First one says to the performer "How super, you *are* playing

79

*Watching the dots
– Mike Bremner
(with Simon
Eden in the
background)*

well, life is wonderful, have a cup of tea", or words to that effect;
then later, when he comes into the box to listen, you act as another
pair of ears. . . . You don't try to impose your own conception of the
piece, it's *his* performance people want to hear, but where you think
you can help him improve it, you make suggestions – and all the
time one is trying to generate enthusiasm and spontaneity, in the
teeth of the machines and the wires.'

Psychology is of paramount importance in recording. On
occasions when the Academy were not getting the results they
wanted, largely through problems in their own playing, Stan's
favourite ploy was to go into the studio and fiddle ostentatiously
with a piece of non-essential equipment (usually the closed-circuit
television monitor), soothing jangled recording nerves by assuring
the players that *now* everything would be all right. Mike was
equally wily: 'Needle is part of the job – but it can be applied nicely
or nastily.' Steve Shingles remembers with admiration Mike's tactful handling of the orchestra: 'If the producer keeps interrupting the
music to correct every wrong note as it happens, the players get
fed-up – so Mike would perhaps let something go on although it
wasn't quite right, and then say, "Well, could we – just for safety,
because we had something wrong with the microphones – do this
little bit again . . . ?" He knew when to stop you and when to let you

go on.' When he thought it necessary, however, he was not afraid to halt proceedings altogether. Early on in the sessions for Mozart's 'Eine Kleine Nachtmusik' the players, possibly rather stale and jaded at the end of a long bout of recording, were finding it hard to concentrate, and expensive session time was ticking past without any usable takes being achieved. Mike decided on a bold approach and stopped the session to send the players off for an unscheduled cup of coffee. Twenty minutes later, cheered by their unexpected good fortune, they returned to finish the record with time to spare. Given that the producer is responsible for the financial viability of each recording, so that too many extra sessions or a series of flops could cost him his job, it was a brave experiment; Mike remembers reflecting on this responsibility during awkward sessions – 'It concentrates the mind wonderfully.'

On the technical level, the producer's job is to 'watch the dots', making sure that every note is on tape; with a multiplicity of takes of varying lengths, recorded at different times, and often in the wrong order, it is easier than it might seem to miss a bar or two and discover this only after the sessions have finished. After the sessions have been completed the producer is then responsible for editing the music recorded – and it was here that Mike's musical training at the Guildhall School of Music stood him in good stead. During recording he would mark the usable takes, discuss them with Neville and, once they had reached agreement on which to use, prepare the master tape. It is not always easy to decide which takes are most suitable for a recording. Opinion frequently differs as to whether it is preferable to use a smaller number of longer takes – which will convey more vividly the sense of a complete performance but may include the occasional error – or to use as many takes as are necessary to ensure a note-perfect performance, inevitably a more artificial procedure but one which avoids the irritation of preserving wrong notes for posterity. The Academy always try for a complete performance made up of as few takes as possible (the players are particularly proud of their performance of Richard Strauss's 'Metamorphosen', recorded with only one join), but long takes are not always easy to achieve, and one of Neville's attributes is his ability to maintain the standards and atmosphere of a concert performance for take after take – often in the most challenging circumstances. During the recording of the Bach Suites in December 1970, the studio was plunged into inactivity at irregular intervals by power cuts: John Gray remembers removing to a café on the corner whenever this happened, to be hauled back when the electricity was restored, 'to record another hour's worth'.

The producer's third responsibility is the choice of repertoire to be recorded. As Mike describes it, the planning of Academy repertoire was done on the most informal basis; ideas usually came best in the pub with Neville after sessions. To run a specialist label like Argo is to walk a knife-edge between repertoire so esoteric that nobody will buy it, and run-of-the-mill repertoire recorded in direct (and damaging) competition with the big companies. Harley and Mike were obliged to identify the profitable Argo artists and the commercial repertoire, and use their profits to finance experiments which might or might not pay off. The Academy was initially one such experiment and, despite glowing reviews, their early records did not make a profit. By 1966, Mike was seriously considering terminating the exclusive contract. It was only his faith in the quality of the orchestra which encouraged him to persevere and make one more record and, following up a suggestion by Peter Gammond in *Music on Record*, he chose four of Rossini's string sonatas as the ideal vehicle for a virtuoso ensemble. Rossini himself dismissed the pieces as 'those horrible sonatas which I composed on holiday near Ravenna with my friends... at an early age' (thought to be sixteen); but when the record came out in 1967, it caused a minor sensation. Mike had struck a chord with the record-buying public: the music was unfamiliar, having previously been dismissed as 'juvenilia', and no one was used to hearing music of such technical difficulty played with such panache, and by an entire chamber orchestra rather than an acknowledged virtuoso soloist. The reviews were outstandingly good – and this time critical acclaim was matched by international sales. The record received one of the 1967 Audio Awards (instituted by the magazine *Gramophone Record Review* to denote 'recordings of outstanding merit'), and it guaranteed the Academy's survival as Argo artists. It was appropriate that the named soloists should have been two of the orchestra's earliest members – Kenneth Heath and John Gray.

The Rossini was one of the first of many Academy records to be

*Kenneth Heath
and John Gray*

praised equally for performance and for recording quality: it was acknowledged by critics and the Academy alike that 'the men in the goldfish bowl' of the control room deserved a large share of the credit for a successful performance on record. Co-operation was the keynote of Academy/Argo sessions. It is an obvious advantage for producer and engineer to work together consistently, and Mike and Stan became a close enough team for a mysterious shorthand in communication to suffice. The cry of 'Whooom, Stan, give me some whooom' would encourage a sudden, subtle but perceptible increase in volume as the last notes of a piece died away in the microphones, giving a lift to the finish of the record. 'More mystery and magic, Stan' would entail cutting out all the microphones except those right at the fringes, for a remote and delicate sound. Stan attributes their rapport to the fact that they are both Geminis –

*Neville Marriner
at the mixing
console*

'warm, co-operative and loveable'. Be that as it may, both were unquestionably perfectionists, aiming less at a definitive recording to stand for all time than at a record which would encapsulate the excitement and artistry of one particularly good performance; for Mike it was not a question of thinking 'This has got to last for years', it was 'This is a most important *moment*'.

The team was helped towards its objective by having in Neville a performing musician with a thorough understanding of how to make records. It is a frequent complaint of recording producers that musicians see no difference between performing in concert and performing for records; they prepare a work for the concert hall and then expect to reproduce it unchanged in the recording studio. Neville has always taken the view that if one chooses to work in a particular medium, it is only reasonable to acknowledge the special demands of that medium and develop techniques to deal with them. From the first he appreciated that to make a piece work on record requires different techniques.

The process starts with the preparation of the music in meticulous detail. Slight imprecisions that might pass unnoticed in the

concert hall become obvious and aggravating when heard over and over again on record; to guard against them and to safeguard the clarity which is the Academy's hallmark, Neville made a practice in quick passages of turning crotchets into quavers with quaver rests, compensating for the tendency of the recording process to lengthen sounds. On the same principle he would usually take a piece at a slightly quicker pace for a recording than he would for a live performance, to give it added sparkle and presence. He might also make slight adjustments to the instrumentation of a piece to suit the recording. For example, he sometimes emphasised the brilliance of the top line by adding one or two extra violins; for the Rossini sonatas he provided for six firsts and six seconds, but arranged for two in each section to play either as firsts or seconds, whichever had the lead, for a more positive upper string sound. He was keen to avoid monotony in the continuo sound and used an unusual variety of continuo instruments, on the principle that Vivaldi, Bach and their contemporaries would have used whatever was available – harpsichord, cello, organ, bassoon, theorbo or chitarrone; even John Gray's violone, bought so that he could experiment with

Meticulous detail – Mike Bremner, Robert Tear and Neville Marriner

85

bowing techniques, was commandeered for the recording of one of the Vivaldi 'La Stravaganza' concertos.

The rest of the players (particularly the section principals) were also closely involved in every aspect of the recording. As their work for Argo became more frequent, they learned to tailor their playing to the demands of the recording studio. Denis Vigay explains: 'I'm afraid it doesn't really work to play exactly as you would in the concert hall – at least, not on the cello. You get all kinds of little squeaks and clatters, and sometimes the bolder, more powerful playing just doesn't come off; it's as though the microphone will only take up to a certain volume, and after that you lose quality, you get a forced sound. I find I have to have a very gentle touch.' To ensure that they met recording requirements consistently, the Academy adopted the 'test–take' technique, using the first take of each session as a trial run to monitor their performance as revealed on tape – 'Is it too loud, too soft, too fast, too slow, too coarse, too shrill, are the dynamics correctly gauged, is the balance right?', and so on.

The democratic approach to performance meant that any inter-pretation suggested at this 'test–take' stage was comprehensively discussed and analysed before it was recorded; Mike has remarked, 'Neville looked more like a referee than a director on occasions.' Then during recording, if any player made a mistake which he felt should not be allowed to pass, he would personally take responsi-bility for stopping the take; as John Gray has pointed out, 'As partners in the finished product, we were all anxious to save time.' Finally, when a take was completed, the large majority of the players would crowd into the control room to listen to the play-back, and to discuss the finer points of tempi, articulation, phrasing, dynamics, balance, and even instrumentation.

Several producers and engineers have remarked with gratified surprise on the Academy's unusual eagerness to hear and discuss the results of their efforts. But over the years, with session time ever more expensive, to prevent debate prolonging itself unmanageably it became necessary for one person (usually Neville) to have the final say. Yet the Academy still tended to regard themselves as 'all chiefs and no Indians', and it was important that the last word should be tactfully put. Neville had a talent for keeping the peace,

and for making sure the atmosphere was amicable whatever the problems. With the constant pressure of deadlines to be met, tempers frayed, and he developed a knack of anticipating tension and defusing it. One producer, Christopher Bishop, remembers, 'He was extremely shrewd in gauging the temperature of a session: if a fiddle was flat, there were several ways of dealing with it, depending on how friendly the atmosphere was at the time – it was rarely "Bishop says you're flat", more often, "I think we're all sharp *except* that fiddle at the back."'

Given this degree of involvement and interest among the players, it was fortunate that Mike was a firm opponent of the 'ivory tower' school of producing, seeing it as part of the producer's job to come down into the studio and discuss what he is doing with the performers – when he can; for at the faintest hint of temperament from the recording team, there was a good chance that they would find themselves locked in the control room by the orchestra. (Chris Hazell also remembers spending the odd lunch hour incarcerated.) But practical jokes and hilarity were normally confined to the breaks. One of the Academy's chief assets is their ability to switch from noisy relaxation to complete concentration the minute the red light goes on. Mike remembers: 'When we were just rehearsing,

Crowding into the control room – Iona Brown, Carmel Kaine, Richard Studt and Christopher Hogwood (foreground), *with Neville Marriner, Cecil James, Malcolm Latchem and Mike Bremner* (background)

87

there was so much laughing and tomfoolery going on that you'd think "They can't be serious" ... until the red light went on – and you could practically *feel* the concentration, everyone strung up and determined. Then the red light would go off, and everything would explode again. I think it's very English, this mixture of extreme seriousness and entire relaxation – and it's one of the unique things about the records we made together.'

As the Academy/Argo partnership progressed, the repertoire broadened – Dvorak, Grieg, Wagner, Richard Strauss, Prokoviev, Elgar and Tippett followed Rossini – and the awards started to come in, for Handel Concerti Grossi, Mozart Divertimenti, Tchaikovsky, Stravinsky and Bartok. But perhaps the most spectacular and characteristic of its successes was Vivaldi's 'The Four Seasons'. Produced by Mike, with Stan as balance engineer, and one of the Academy's own members, Alan Loveday, as soloist, it has become the Academy's best-selling record to date, with a sales curve resembling that of a pop record, heading for the 750,000 mark.

'The Four Seasons' was recorded in the venue with which the Academy were to be most closely associated during the 1970s – St John's, Smith Square. The recording had originally been scheduled to take place in Kingsway Hall but, five days before sessions were

Kenneth Heath's painting of St John's, Smith Square, presented to Stan Goodall with the inscription, 'For Stan in admiration of the "sound" you make here'

due to begin, disaster struck. After what is reputed to have been a particularly vigorous sermon by the Reverend Donald Soper, the ceiling of the hall collapsed. All other regular venues were booked, and Mike and Stan spent a nervous weekend scouring London for a studio. Almost at the last moment, St John's was suggested to them by David Booth-Jones, a member of the committee responsible for its restoration: St John's, which overlooks the headquarters of the Trades Union Congress and of both Labour and Conservative Parties, had been severely damaged during the war, and as an alternative to demolition had been restored, though still consecrated, primarily with concerts in mind. But at the time of the 'Seasons' recording in 1969 it had only just been opened; Argo had made no recordings there before, nothing was known about its acoustical properties or those of the control room, and the traffic circulating round the church threatened to be a problem. Mike and Stan spent a morning whistling, clapping and humming snatches of Vivaldi in an attempt to assess the sound – and on the basis of Stan's

Recording in St John's, Smith Square

89

gut feeling, Mike took the decision to use it. The equipment was lugged over from Kingsway in furniture vans, manœuvred into the control room, hastily assembled, and the sessions began. Ten years later, Mike recalled, 'We were all guessing – we simply did not know how it would sound; it could all have been totally unusable for all we knew. But Stan has a gift – deep down inside he knew he couldn't be far wrong, and he wasn't. It was marvellous.'

'The Four Seasons' is reputed to have been the second-best-selling music of the eighteenth century, and is certainly one of the most-recorded pieces of the twentieth – so the decision to make yet another version was, in its way, a gamble. (The fact that this decision was made in the pub opposite Kingsway Hall may have had something to do with it; Mike remembers that Neville had just hit the jackpot on the one-armed bandit, and a general air of optimism prevailed). Vivaldi based each of his concertos on a sonnet (it is possible that he wrote the sonnets himself) printed in the original solo violin part, and in translating the poem the musicologist and critic Stanley Sadie (editor of *The New Grove Dictionary of Music and Musicians*) had taken pains to make clear the connection between each event in the text and the musical passage depicting it. Neville prepared the performing edition accordingly, as a fantasy 'Seasons', heavily underlining the pictorial nature of the work. The howling winds and cracking ice of 'Winter' were conjured up by chill *ponticello* effects in the strings, and the barking dog of 'Spring' was impersonated with the greatest verisimilitude by the viola of Steve Shingles (who has been heard to mutter, 'They ought to give me a licence, I've played the damned dog so often'). *The Sunday Times*

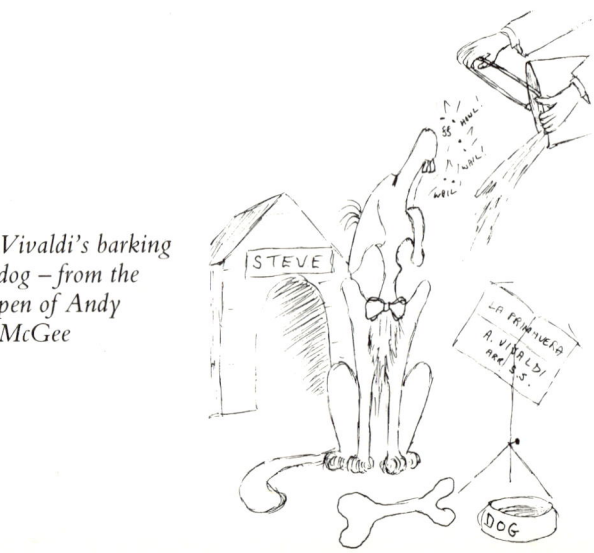

Vivaldi's barking dog – from the pen of Andy McGee

Simon Preston

commented: 'A performance of such freshness could jar conventional ears. It is programmatic to the point of idiosyncracy – the obtrusive viola for the barking dog in "Spring" is literally shocking' – and there were indeed some disapproving sniffs from critics.

Happily, this did not deter the record-buying public, and the 'Seasons' had immediate and world-wide success. For no apparent reason it excited particular admiration in Japan, where it sold 30,000 copies in the first three months of release; on a trip to Japan some years later, Neville was startled but flattered to find that the Academy's interpretation was being followed phrase for phrase by several ensembles, one of whom had even taken the trouble to work out and copy the continuo line note for note.

This continuo line played a vital part in the theatrical effects the Academy were seeking. It was realised by Simon Preston with originality and imagination (in his own words, 'thoroughly Dartian'); the alternation of harpsichord and organ to mirror the changes of atmosphere suggested in the poetry found particular favour with the critics, and the Academy have always attributed much of the record's success to Simon's inventiveness. (Other harpsichord players, presented with his marked-up continuo part for the piece, have not always been equally enthusiastic: Nicholas

Alan Loveday

Kraemer remembers, 'I kept up the pretence of doing a Prestonism at the beginning of "Winter" – the bit of Beethoven he used to put in – but I did my own version of it for my pride's sake.')

The other obvious reason for the record's success was the playing of Alan Loveday. For Mike Bremner, Alan approached the baroque ideal more closely than any other violinist. His pure, icily intense tone suited the music perfectly, without being in any way lacking in emotion; and since his performance of the work with the Academy at Kenwood five years previously, the interpretation had been allowed to germinate slowly. His playing has enormous projection, and he played most of the solo part sitting down – the poetry of the occasion being shattered only once, when a pneumatic drill started up outside. Alan did his best to ignore it, but after ten minutes of waiting for the din to subside, he could stand no more. Puce in the face, his ears (according to Mike) protruding with rage, he leapt up, stuck his fiddle under his arm, swept out of the church and, with his face an inch from the offender's, enquired belligerently, 'Do you like sex and travel?' – to which the unwary drill-operator, puzzled, replied, 'Yes, squire.' Alan's terse and Anglo-Saxon riposte brought howls of approval from the Academy, by now gathered on the steps of the church – and from that moment on, they heard not a single extraneous sound.

8

Permanent Fixture

By the time the first Argo contract came to an end, the relationship had established the Academy as one of the world's foremost recording orchestras. The timing of their recording career could not have been more fortunate. The development of stereo, coinciding with the Academy's formation, gave them the considerable advantage of being able to obtain a truly realistic sound on record, and with their early specialisation in seventeenth- and eighteenth-century music, they had caught the baroque revival on the way up. As the critic Geoffrey Crankshaw has pointed out, by the early 1960s much of the spadework in educating public taste towards the baroque had already been done, and economic conditions favoured concert-giving with smaller forces; a demand had been created which the Academy were ready to supply – both in concert and on record.

The Academy have always been conscious of their 'cart-before-the-horse' approach. Normally, for a group to be taken on by a recording company, it must already be a going concern in the concert hall; the Academy were the first to reverse this procedure and develop a concert career almost entirely on the strength of their recordings. Works chosen in conjunction with the recording producer would be put into the concert repertoire and prepared and perfected in live performances in readiness for the sessions. The Academy have always been content with their record-oriented career: and when Neville won the *HiFi News & Record Review* Audio Award in 1970 (the first to be conferred on an individual rather than a record), it was for his 'services *to the gramophone*'.

Thus by the start of 1969 'the Academy of St Martin in the Fields' was a familiar (if sometimes garbled) name on record – John Amis was to write of 'the pleasant daily bombardment on the public ear

The 1971 Audio Award presentation – Neville Marriner passing the Award to Raymond Leppard (centre)

by the BBC' – but the Academy themselves were considerably less well-known in person. It was largely to remedy this that they promoted three concerts for themselves in the Queen Elizabeth Hall on London's South Bank, on successive Sundays in January 1969. This was an experiment on a far grander scale than the Wigmore Hall episode; in ambitious programmes, the orchestra mixed Bach, Handel and Vivaldi with Mendelssohn, Wagner, Britten and Stravinsky, divertimenti and concerti with suites and cantatas, and the soloists included John Ogdon, Heinz Holliger, Sheila Armstrong, John Wilbraham, Frans Brüggen and Simon Preston.

In retrospect, the Academy like to measure the extent to which the venture served its purpose by comparing it with two other South Bank appearances, one immediately preceding and one following it. Seven months before the January series, they had given a concert in the Queen Elizabeth Hall which was shared with the King's Singers. This was promoted by the Hale Arts Trust, an organisation founded to help young musicians establish themselves, and was a repeat performance of an earlier experiment. In 1967 David Booth-Jones, one of the Trust's co-founders, had arranged a joint concert at Hale Park, his family home just outside Salisbury, at which the Academy and the Singers had performed alternate numbers. Denis Vigay once said he felt from the start that the Academy and the King's Singers were headed in the same musical direction, with the same vitality and desire for precision. They also enjoy the same jokes, and this early concert (which Iona

94

Hale Park

Brown remembers as one of the first Academy performances in which she took part) was a highly successful occasion – the general merriment not marred even by the rain which forced the concert from the portico of the house into the church across the Park in Hale village. The audience overflowed into the porch, and Molly, on the 'Family Hold Back' principle, remembers hearing the concert from her seat on a wet gravestone outside (possibly that of Thomas Archer, the architect of Hale – and also of St John's, Smith Square: hence David Booth-Jones's interest in the restoration of St John's and the life-saving suggestion that 'The Four Seasons' be recorded there).

It was this success which encouraged David to present the combination of Academy and Singers to a larger audience on the South Bank, and the concert – the King's Singers' official London début – took place in the Queen Elizabeth Hall on May Day, 1968. The programme was a curious mixture: sixteenth-century church music, negro spirituals and pop tunes from the King's Singers (radiant in a form of turquoise tunic since discarded as platform wear) were interspersed with concerti grossi from the Academy, and the concert finished with combined forces in a sequence of carols by Sebastian Forbes. Also implicated were Barry Tuckwell, playing a Cherubini Etude, and Simon Preston, an old friend of the Singers from his days as the organ scholar at King's, playing organ works by Hindemith and Handel.

The hall was full, and the audience looked down on the letters

95

HAT along the front of the platform, picked out in purple heather gathered by David that morning in the New Forest and woven into the Trust's insignia. After the concert there was a champagne reception in the foyer, followed by a large dinner at a Kensington hotel, and then the King's Singers went back to Brian Kay's flat to await the morning papers and their first London reviews. The concert had been a success; the Academy had greatly enjoyed it, and had played with their usual skill and style. But when *The Times*'s review came out, to the slight irritation of the players it was headed 'Singers of Resource' – and after a mildly flattering reference to the orchestra's recording reputation, the reviewer concentrated single-mindedly on the King's Singers. As an occasion it had been memorable, but as an aid to prestige, limited.

Considerably more morale-boosting as far as the players were concerned was the concert they took part in immediately after the January series in 1969. This was a harpsichord concert arranged by Thomas Goff, with the number of soloists rising to four for one piece. Simon Preston was one of the four, and he remembers rehearsals in Tom Goff's drawing-room: 'Harpsichords everywhere, budgerigars flapping about ominously, and the Academy squeezed out into the hall.' But the occasion is treasured by the orchestra as the day Ginger Rogers came to the dress rehearsal and Her Majesty The Queen Mother to the concert – and not a singer in sight.

Five highly successful appearances in twelve months on the South Bank had, each in its own way, helped the Academy to develop by the middle of 1969 a clear-cut public image. This was crystallised in an article written at the time by John Amis, who applied to the orchestra Roland-Manuel's phrase *'une assemblée d'hommes libres'*. Neville himself remarked in an interview with Peter Gammond at about the same time, 'The way to hold the best players together is to offer them freedom, not money – the freedom to combine playing in the Academy with the pursuit of their other interests – chamber music, teaching, or research.' The Academy continued to be part-time – the players were spending little more than three months of the year together in total – and retained the feel of an oasis in the midst of routine symphony orchestral work. Their resistance to the idea of the orchestra becoming a 'daily-bread'

*The trio on the
bass line – Denis
Vigay, John
Gray and
Kenneth Heath*

enterprise was behind the decision not to offer contracts; all the
players were (and continue to be) booked for each date separately –
meaning that no one was obliged to play any date he had not
specifically chosen to play.

The other, more obvious aspect of the players' freedom – the
absence of a conductor – engendered a strong sense of self-
discipline. Individual players were extremely jealous of standards
for the group as a whole, and this was reflected in their own playing
standards. Ken Heath typified this attitude, and Hugh Maguire
remembers him as 'an incredibly conscientious and devoted cellist.
He would never play without a great deal of practice beforehand,
like a ballerina needing two hours on the barre to loosen her muscles
– until he'd done his arabesques and pirouettes he wasn't happy.'
Denis Vigay remembers him on tour practising before breakfast,
and recalls the trio (so much admired by George Malcolm) that
cellos and bass used to make, 'constantly experimenting on the bass
line – very satisfying'. John Gray was similarly fastidious about
intonation – his own, and that of the orchestra as a whole – and
never hesitated to point out lapses from the standard required. In the
words of Christopher Hogwood, who worked closely with him for
several years on the continuo line, 'Tact wouldn't get in the way of
truth'.

Tact not getting in the way

The Academy continued to argue their way to interpretations: Simon Preston remembers, 'In the Academy there would always be some come-back ... there was dialogue all the time from all the sections, especially the principals, which seemed to me a fantastically good thing.' Trevor Connah remembers Neville 'losing patience with my everlasting questions', and John Gray was once described as the Academy's 'Speaker of the House of Commons'; it was from these two that much of the dialogue originated. Steve Shingles was likewise vocal: Christopher Hogwood recalls, 'Steve was a great one for stopping the show to make general musical points ... when I first joined, much of the Academy's character came from the middle lines – that marvellous viola section, which really carried responsibility for its line.' With every player free to offer an opinion and in charge of his own contribution, the playing was both more convinced and more assured; in the words of a critic from *The Daily Telegraph*, 'The conductorless ensemble can go direct to the sense of the music without having laboriously to translate gestures back into sound. We hear freedom as well as virtuosity in the easy brilliance of these violins.'

This freedom bore fruit because of the quality of every player in the Academy: they had both the ideas on how a piece should be played and the technical skill to implement the ideas. Reviewers continually remarked on the strength of the Academy's line-up – *The Daily Telegraph* wrote, 'Its violin section is so strong that the sixteen players are not grouped in the printed programme as 1sts and 2nds but are all named in one alphabetical list'; and Edward Greenfield observed, 'If any chamber orchestra has a more distinguished membership than the Academy, I have yet to hear of it. Where else could one find so high-powered a group of first violins, orchestral leaders sitting elbow to elbow?' Among them were Hugh Maguire, leader of the BBC Symphony Orchestra, Andrew McGee, leader of the LSO, and Ronald Thomas, leader of the Bournemouth Symphony Orchestra. Of those who were not orchestral leaders, several came from well-established quartets – Malcolm Latchem, Colin Sauer, and Michael Evans from the Dartington String Quartet, Raymond Keenlyside and Margaret Major from the Aeolian – bringing with them the quartet technique of responsive listening which has always characterised the orchestra. Others, like Alan Loveday and Iona Brown, had solo careers – but it was an important feature of the Academy that all members should be *capable* of playing solos and should be given the chance to do so as often as possible: the opportunity to alternate a supporting line with

Steve stopping the show – Neville Marriner, Stephen Shingles and John Gray

Come-back from the first violins – Neville Marriner, Alan Loveday and Iona Brown

the solo part was one of the things which attracted young players to the Academy. All the violinists at one time or another took the solo parts in Handel and Vivaldi concertos – in the early days of touring, it was customary for 'The Four Seasons' to be shared among four players – and the decision as to who was to play a solo was not infrequently left until the last moment. Alan Loveday remembers the start of the sessions for Vivaldi's 'L'Estro Armonico' when Neville stood up and said, 'Right. Who wants to play this one? We need four violins.' The principals of the other sections also appeared as soloists on record – Kenneth Heath and John Gray in the Rossini string sonatas, for example, and Stephen Shingles in recordings of the Telemann Viola Concerto, Mozart's Sinfonia Concertante K. 364 (with Alan Loveday), and Michael Haydn's Duo Concertante for Viola and Organ (with Simon Preston).

The democracy of *'hommes libres'* was given shape and direction by Neville's leadership from the front desk. John Gray explains: 'Because he was playing, he was able to turn round and say "No . . . try a faster bow stroke, further away from the bridge, *this* part of the bow, *this* sort of sound" and demonstrate – it's a marvellous way of getting a homogeneous style.' The net result has been described by

100

George Malcolm, as an inside observer: 'Neville had the most phenomenal control over an orchestra as a leader that I've ever seen – a quite unique faculty; it's difficult enough for a conductor to do something like an unrehearsed *subito pianissimo* for the whole orchestra, but I've seen Neville do it from the front desk just by a nod of the head or a lift of the eyebrows.' Because the players had all contributed to the interpretation of a piece, they were the more willing to follow Neville in his direction of it. When Simon Preston was appointed cathedral organist at Christ Church, Oxford, he applied to the cathedral choir the methods he had seen Neville use in concerts and recordings with the Academy: 'I soon realised how difficult it is to get that balance of discipline and dialogue; you have to know the people very well, and a great deal of mutual trust is involved.' It was to the feeling of trust within the Academy that John Amis was perhaps referring when he wrote, 'It is not so difficult to form musical fours and make perfect sonic drill – but to get technical perfection *and* to give an ensemble a heart and a spirit, that really takes some doing. That is what Neville Marriner has done, with the wholehearted co-operation of his gifted colleagues in the Academy.'

Neville Marriner leading from the front desk (with Carmel Kaine and Iona Brown)

The Academy were by now applying their performing techniques to an increasingly broad repertoire. Their early reputation was for 'brushing the dust off old music' as a specialist baroque ensemble. Later it was suggested that, with their recordings of teenage works by Mendelssohn and Rossini, their forte was for endowing seemingly insignificant music with respectability by sheer skill in performance. This suggestion became untenable as the Academy moved, aided and abetted by Argo, into the standard chamber orchestral repertoire of the nineteenth and twentieth centuries. To satisfy Argo's requirements for an interesting and well-balanced repertoire, the orchestra branched out into a wide variety of music – Dvorak's Serenade for Strings, Grieg's Holberg Suite, Vaughan Williams's 'Fantasia on a Theme of Thomas Tallis', Bartok's 'Music for Strings, Percussion and Celeste', Shostakovich's Concerto for piano and trumpet, and so on – mustering additional strings, wind, brass and percussion where necessary.

Finding the same standards of performance and interpretation in Bach and Bartok alike, critics started to comment in some surprise on the Academy's versatility: in a 1969 review of their work, an *Observer* critic recommended as the best versions available their recordings not only of the Handel Opus 6 concertos, but of Elgar's Introduction and Allegro and Stravinsky's 'Pulcinella'. John Amis remembers his misgivings on hearing that the orchestra was to tackle Richard Strauss's 'Metamorphosen', a highly romantic work and one of his own personal favourites. 'I thought, "But they don't know anything about that kind of music", and in a pitying sort of way I hurried to the sessions, to try and forestall the more obvious howlers. I needn't have worried: they took to it like ducks to water, and it's one of the most convincing versions of the piece I've heard.'

What was startling was that throughout the diverse repertoire a consistent style was emerging. Listeners came to expect certain distinctive characteristics, the first of which was still precision. Neville has remarked, 'The Academy's playing is designed to sound like a wrist-watch as compared to an alarm clock – clean, clear and focussed. It only takes one player to be poorly prepared for the performance to be muddied; in the Academy, everyone plays *everything*.' The desire for clarity was to be found in every section. It was perhaps most remarkable in the violins, given the difficulty of

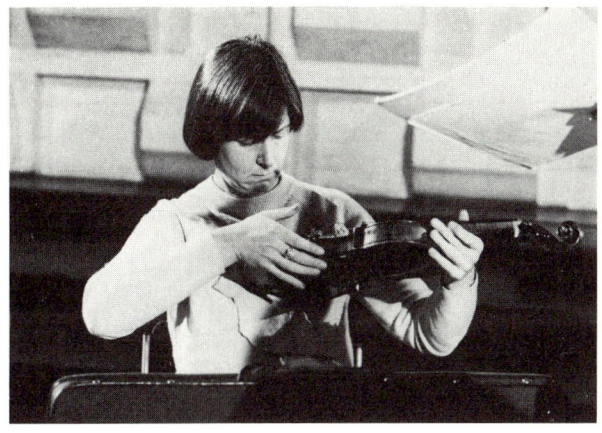

Marilyn Taylor

persuading a dozen outstanding players, each with his individual ideas and technique, to produce a single unified sound; when Marilyn Taylor joined the Academy in 1971, she remembers being struck by the violin section as 'a collection of terribly good musicians who were most unlikely to be playing together'. But it was equally important in the lower lines, particularly in the violas where the dark sound that the instrument sometimes makes would have clogged and confused the texture; Neville considers Steve Shingles' playing, with its bright tone and precise intonation, to have been of prime importance in fashioning the Academy's style.

Academy performances were also easily identifiable for their rhythmic vitality – and it was here that the bass section was crucial. By shortening their articulation, cellos and bass gave lift and direction to the overall sound: John Gray in particular avoided the sonorous organ-like tone that the double bass is often made to produce, and underpinned the ensemble with a springy, buoyant bass line. Vitality should not be confused with sheer speed – although the Academy were to become famous (in some quarters, notorious) for their often unnervingly brisk tempi; one critic has referred to 'tightrope string playing ... miraculously poised', and another pointed out, in *Records & Recordings*, that if one were simultaneously to play the Academy/Marriner and New Philharmonia/Klemperer versions of the Bach Suites, 'The Academy of St Martin's would be packing away their instruments as the NPO began to play No. 4.'

Pace, precision and rhythmic vitality alone can verge on the mechanical – in Neville's words, 'If you're not careful, it's like being locked in a sewing-machine factory' – and the Academy were careful not to sacrifice sensitivity to technique. The unanimous desire for a 'straight' sound ruled out ripe vibrato and exaggerated dynamic lunges ('Just like some voluptuous woman, lurching at you,' Neville was once heard to mutter testily), but the fact of emotion being controlled does not make it any the less intense. 'Warmth without sentiment' was the aim (Geoffrey Crankshaw's phrase), and in reviews of recordings of Richard Strauss, Barber, and Bach's 'Art of Fugue', critics wrote of 'an achingly beautiful performance', 'a climax of unparalleled power', and 'a profound feeling for the music shining through every glorious moment'. Most importantly, the playing conveyed the pleasure that the players took in performing together. In the true 'academy' spirit, they were still seeking to enjoy themselves as much as to entertain others – and enjoyment generates enjoyment: *Gramophone* wrote of their first Mozart recording, 'The way Marriner's group plays the Divertimenti is likely to make you smile with pleasure (and a Divertimento, after all, is meant to divert).'

Enjoyment generating enjoyment – Malcolm Latchem and Richard Studt (with Roger Garland in the background)

It has often been said that the Academy style is unmistakable –
that a thirty-second snatch of a record on the radio is enough to
identify it. (It seems to be obvious even at one remove – George
Guest remembers sending his daughter for violin tuition to Howard
Davis, a regular Academy member, and being able to detect the
Academy influence after the first lesson.) Neville worries that to be
so easily recognisable is to be predictable – and there have always
been reviewers who have found the Academy hallmarks an irritant.
Several seemed simply to suspect the technical skill, and used
'polish' and 'refinement' almost as terms of abuse; others were
troubled by the possibility that a consistently lively and buoyant
style might tend towards 'lightweight' music-making.

Whatever its strengths and weaknesses, the Academy's style by
1970 stemmed to a large degree from the editing of their music: the
group's attitude to performance, its tastes and its techniques could
increasingly be written into the music itself. For this reason, the
orchestra has always guarded its scores and marked parts carefully –
from them the *appearance*, if not the spirit, of the Academy approach
could be quite convincingly reproduced. Editing was becoming
primarily Neville's responsibility. As the pressure of work grew,
the prolonged and detailed rehearsals of the early days became
impracticable. With an increasing number of players involved,
many of them not founder members, it was unreasonable to expect
rehearsals to continue to be unpaid, and this drastically reduced the
time available. Less rehearsal time meant less debate: it was no
longer possible to thrash out every bowing, every phrase and every
dynamic communally, and discussion began to be confined to
meetings between the principals to decide on the most important
points of interpretation, leaving Neville to mark up all the parts in
detail later.

As he has said himself, this meant that his personal tastes came to
influence the Academy's style more noticeably than before,
although the markings that he was putting in were based to a large
extent on the principles of interpretation that had been hammered
out in those years of corporate editing. He talks of 'the Academy
style', not 'the Marriner style', and of himself as 'the arbiter of a
common taste'. 'In a lot of cases, there was simply no need to argue
about things any more. We'd decided how we liked our Mozart, for

example: I could mark up the music, and the original members would recognise a continuity of all the things we had discussed – *these* notes are short, we don't make crescendos *there*, we finish trills like *this*. When we came to record the complete Mozart symphonies, we'd only played four or five regularly, but I was able to mark the style straight into the other thirty-six or so, and it gave us both a consistent set of interpretations and one with which everyone agreed.'

With a clear-cut public image, a distinctive style, a regular system for preparing their music and a growing library of their own editions, the Academy seemed on their way to becoming an institution. One critic was to refer to the 'uncannily unanimous delight' with which he and his colleagues had received a selection of Academy records – and one immediately obvious result of the group's growing reputation was that it became a great deal busier. With the extension of repertoire, the pool of players on which the orchestra drew was becoming larger. The Academy still stuck to the principle of choosing only musicians with whose playing they were familiar, but the list of 'possibles' was lengthening so that, with personnel changing slightly all the time, they could take on the increasing amount of work being offered without impinging on the freedom of the players and subjecting them to what Furtwängler once described as 'the hoar-frost of routine'.

It became clear that more formal organisation on a larger scale was going to become necessary. Often the expanded Academy could not fit into the drawing-room in Cornwall Gardens for rehearsals, and the volume of paperwork was becoming more than anyone could reasonably be expected to handle unaided. The first step towards rationalising the orchestra's increasingly complex operations came with its incorporation in 1970 as a limited company – 'The Academy of St Martin in the Fields Orchestra Limited' – with the five section principals (Neville Marriner, Trevor Connah, Stephen Shingles, Kenneth Heath and John Gray, later to be joined by Malcolm Latchem) as the company's directors. Unavoidable for tax and accounting reasons, the incorporation had the unfortunate consequence of creating a hierarchy where previously there had been none, and the divisive effect was felt for several years – overcome eventually, as one player has pointed out, 'by the music: the playing was of such a high standard, people just wanted to go on being involved with it. Even when the family feeling was dented, there was still a terrific professional spirit.'

The other major change came with the decision to employ paid management. Molly herself continued to work for the Academy without payment, but she acquired a paid helper (or rather a series of helpers) in an attempt to check the flow of paperwork. The first was Elizabeth Williams, whose principal function was the booking of players. Though Molly continued to handle the concert management side of the Academy's work, she handed over to Liz the card index of players and the task of booking the musicians required for each date. At that time, Liz was sharing a flat with four other girls, and she remembers the problems players had in ringing her to accept or refuse dates: 'The phone was never free, and eventually I had to give people the number of the shop directly below the flat – a Scandinavian craft shop, run by my landlord. I told them to ring only in the evenings when I was home from work, so I'd be able to run down and answer the calls when the shop had closed for the night. But of course I came to grief when they started ringing during the day. . . .' She was followed by Barbara Cooper, previously a reader for the publishers Chatto & Windus, who set about the formidable task of cataloguing the Academy's music: her index remains the kernel of the system, though the music itself has quadrupled in terms of shelf space. Her other tasks included restraining the cats during rehearsals, and waking Simon Preston in time for the Oxford train on those occasions when he had been practising on the Festival Hall organ and had stayed overnight at Cornwall Gardens.

The jobs of both Liz Williams and Barbara Cooper, regardless of their peculiar hours, were part-time, as was that of their successor Christine Johnson, whose previous experience working for the LSO was to prove invaluable to the Academy in arranging their first world tour. However, the moment came when, with box files of music bursting out of the Marriners' flat and the kitchen table buried under a heap of Academy paperwork, it was clear that the Academy needed a more permanent paid administrator and their own office. Neville's career outside the Academy was developing rapidly, absorbing more and more of Molly's time and taking them both abroad for several months of the year. The Academy's work-load was now too heavy for the orchestra to be run from a distance: there had to be someone in England at the centre of things all the time, and the Academy advertised for help.

As Molly was to write in an article for the *St Martin's Review*, 'The Academy's luck worked again. They found in Sylvia Holford a manager who is not only highly efficient, extremely hard-working and devoted, but an excellent musician as well.' She had been working in the BBC's orchestral management office as the 'fixer' for the BBC Symphony Orchestra, which was to stand her in good stead with the Academy; but she had been attracted to the new job by the 'part-time terms' originally offered in the advertisement, which would leave her free to continue her freelance work as a pianist (some of it now as a *repetiteur* to Joan Sutherland). She had also, suitably enough, appeared herself at one of John Churchill's lunchtime recitals at St Martin's.

Although Sylvia's job when she first started was described as that of 'part-time secretary', neither part of the description remained true for much more than six months. Her initial responsibility was simply to book the players and arrange the concerts: Molly still looked after the music, and there was no promotion side at all. But then the office, minus the music library, moved across London to Sylvia's flat in Aberdare Gardens, the booking sheets got longer as the Academy began to tackle small symphonic repertoire, and the job became neither part-time nor strictly secretarial. As Sylvia says, 'Having the office in the flat may eliminate rush-hour travel, but it does mean that I'm on call twenty-four hours a day – there's no such thing as Sunday' – and the final nail in her part-time coffin came with VAT. Every payment had to be recorded, carefully itemised, on a proper invoice with the Academy's name, address and telephone number printed on it, and the payee's VAT number filled in at the top. It was Sylvia's job to compile the players' VAT numbers – and an embarrassing duty it was, inasmuch as it involved sorting the sheep earning £5000 and more a year (and thus liable to registration) from the goats *not* earning £5000 a year: needless to say, the borderline goats did not want to admit it. Eventually she evolved a means of keeping VAT in its place, aided by the Academy's accountant, David Dunbar – although she confesses that he had his doubts about her ability to handle even the simple finances of the early days, after the Academy had thrown a party and he found that she had put the drinks bill in the 'Music' column by mistake.

The Academy's agent in Germany, Hans Ulrich Schmid, has spoken of Sylvia's work for the Academy as having 'that mixture of professionalism and enthusiasm which is not too often to be found in our present musical world'. The professionalism is the result of her own experience on the concert platform; her first-hand knowledge of preparing and presenting programmes has given her a ready understanding of the needs of musicians on tour, and she is consequently often able to short-circuit potential difficulties. The enthusiasm helped her to survive the trials of having the office in her study – 'The Academy have had to build me some more cupboards, because the VAT invoice books were just bursting out all over the place: and I must say, the orchestra's tea-urn is a wretched nuisance in the hall – people keep catching their ankles on the tap.'

The wall behind Sylvia's desk is covered with little messages to herself – such as 'Lord Give Me Patience ... But Hurry' – and working for the Academy has made her, as she says, a workaholic. Her title is now General Manager, and the word 'General' covers the multitude of curious managerial duties all too familiar to Molly

Sylvia Holford at her desk

– wrapping the orchestra in rugs for recording in chapels, rescuing players accidentally locked in the lavatory five minutes before a concert, and putting her musicianship to good use writing out individual parts for the National Anthem for the benefit of those players who are somehow not sure how it goes. Nevertheless, in her words, 'I enjoy it all, believe it or not – except the VAT. In this business you have so many marvellous friends, and I live amongst the most wonderful sounds all the time – I'm very lucky.'

9

£5-worth of Doghouse

One of the major preoccupations for Sylvia and Molly alike has been the management of the Academy away from home. The majority of the orchestra's public appearances have always been abroad, and the players now spend anything up to three months a year touring all over the world. This reflects the international character of the orchestra – though its style may be English, the players have included Canadians, Australians, New Zealanders, three Welshmen, one Czech, one Russian and one Japanese.

The Academy's first appearance in Europe was at the Flanders Festival in Bruges in 1967 when they appeared both as a solo ensemble and accompanying King's College Choir during the Festival's 'Handel Week'. (It is interesting that the person who originally suggested inviting them should have been the owner of a record shop – Frans Vanagt of the 'Music Cottage' in Bruges – the Academy's reputation, as always, being based on recordings.) Apart from the pleasures of visiting Bruges and feasting, with Frans, at the famous Hotel Duc de Bourgogne, the orchestra also gained valuable exposure to the European critics and agents who congregate at the Flanders Festival, and this was in part responsible for the first tour of France – *le tour gastronomique*, as it came to be known.

The fortnight's tour through the provinces of France, accompanying the pianist Philippe Entremont, was perfectly enjoyable from the artistic point of view, but the Academy, accepting a distinctly Gallic order of priorities, were obliged in return for a princely meal allowance to run the gauntlet of a series of hotels which were less than *de luxe*. In the foyer of the first, Molly, sent ahead to reconnoitre, burst into tears of apprehension. Her fears

were justified: more than ten years later that hotel is still remembered as the one where Ken Heath's tea leaves, thrown last thing at night down the communal lavatory just off the landing, came up the next morning in the bidet in his room (as he remarked, 'The more you think about it, the worse it gets'). Molly also treasures the moment when, trudging for the n-th time from room to reception to register a complaint, she came upon John Gray standing sadly and in darkness on a chair in the corridor holding above his head an electrical device with a short lead, plugged into the light fitting. On inspection it proved to be his egg-boiler: dispirited, he had hoped to cheer himself with a coddled egg. The hotels did not markedly improve after this, but the situation was saved by dedicated and memorable application of the meals allowance; travelling, like an army, on its stomach, the orchestra has probably never since eaten consistently as well, or as much.

The excursion came to a suitably chaotic end when, after a ten-hour bus journey, the orchestra arrived at Boulogne at one o'clock in the morning, tired, cold and miserable, clutching their fortnight's earnings – to be asked, 'Have you any French currency, messieurs?', and subsequently informed that such currency as they had could not be taken out of the country as cash. With francs falling from every pocket, the orchestra was obliged to surrender its wages to Neville, who stayed behind waiting for the banks to open in the morning. As the ferry pulled away from the quay, leaving behind it

112

Neville and Molly with, in the foreground, Hans Tecker and Jan Rubinstein

a lone figure with a Gladstone bag full of francs, the players were less than reassured to see a neon sign flickering gently over his head bearing the word *C.A.S.I.N.O.*

The Flanders Festival and the French tour helped the Academy to make their mark, but it was in Holland that their European career first took root, largely through the efforts of Hans Tecker and Jan Rubinstein at Phonogram, the company which undertook the distribution of the Decca Group's records in Holland. Hans remembers clearly the day in 1962 when he heard their first 'Recital' record. At a subsequent sales conference to promote the record, he spoke glowingly of the (then unknown) Academy, comparing them favourably and at length with one of Phonogram's own ensembles – too favourably for a senior member of the staff, who remarked caustically that this 'Academy' still had to earn their keep. Hans was determined to ensure that they did; for six years he vigorously championed the Academy cause – and in 1968 he found an ally in Jan Rubinstein, who joined Phonogram in that year. The two of them brought an original approach to their publicity campaign, arranging for photographs of the orchestra to be taken in the open air at Dartington, around the grounds and on the steps of the Banqueting Hall; Jan has commented, 'We captured the Academy just as we wanted them – relaxed, lively, and ready to make music at the drop of a hat.' The informal touch was a novelty for 'serious' orchestras at that time, and the record-buying public warmed to the

113

Academy's unconventional image, especially when it was coupled with their well-publicised 'democratic approach' to music-making. Jan explains, 'Holland was desperately trying to become the most democratic country in the world, and in musical life, too, people were looking for a new way of doing things – the Academy provided an example.' Hans has suggested that the orchestra's name was a bonus: 'Although everybody who had constantly to type the name cursed its length (myself included) ... its typical British flavour held a special attraction to our rather anglophile country.'

The close relationship between the Dutch and the Academy (marked on the orchestra's side by their recording of four composers with Dutch connections, under the title 'A Tribute to Holland') was cemented by the Dutch recording industry's presentation to the group of the first ever 'hat-trick' of Edison Awards – in 1968 for the Mozart Divertimenti K. 136–8, in 1969 for the Tchaikovsky Serenade for Strings, and in 1970 for the Bartok Divertimento. These prestigious awards (won in previous years by artists of the calibre of Beecham, Schwarzkopf and Karajan) were the first tangible signs of international recognition for the Academy. The high point as far as the players were concerned was the invitation to give

The informal touch – outside Dartington Hall (left to right – Alan Loveday, Neville Marriner, Iona Brown, Stephen Shingles, John Gray, Ross Pople, Kenneth Heath, Gerald Jarvis, Trevor Connah, Colin Sauer, Colin Staveley, Roy Gillard)

114

the 1969 Edison Grand Gala Concert in Amsterdam's Concert-gebouw, after the presentation of the Awards – the previous year's concert having been given by the New York Philharmonic Orchestra under Leonard Bernstein. The orchestra was flown over to Amsterdam in the early afternoon and given an excellent dinner; Trevor Connah remembers the restaurant muzak, as he spooned up his turtle soup, including (as a gesture to classical music) 'A Whiter Shade of Pale' – happily not a portent. The concert (notwithstanding an earlier press conference at which Neville had been introduced to the assembled journalists as 'Mr Merryman') was a considerable success, with a programme including Bach's Brandenburg Concerto No. 5 – with Leonhardt, Rampal, and 'Merryman' as soloists. As a final encore, the Academy played the waltz from the award-winning Tchaikovsky Serenade, and brought the Gala Concert to a triumphant conclusion – on a flagrantly bungled last note, mercifully drowned in thunderous applause.

The first Edison, bringing the Academy to the attention of a wider European audience, also brought them an invitation to make their first tour of Germany under the auspices of Hans Ulrich Schmid, the Academy's principal agent in Europe. Herr Schmid has

Outside the Concertgebouw (left to right – John Gray, Marilyn Taylor, Roger Garland, Christopher Hirons, Anthony Jenkins, Stephen Shingles, Peter Thomas, Kenneth Heath, Malcolm Latchem, Neville Marriner, Alan Loveday)

115

*Stephen Shingles
with Alfonso
Aijon, the
Academy's
Spanish agent*

written, 'You may be amused – as I am when reading this after so
many years – that at that time I did not dare to present them under
their proper name – which seemed to be too long, and I had the
feeling nobody would have any idea what it really means! How
time has changed! Indeed, we named them in short words "London
Strings", and today I must say, I am ashamed because this name was
not too full of fantasy.'

Herr Schmid and other agents are the motivating force behind
tours: they book the orchestra for a given period and then fill that
time with a series of concerts arranged directly or with local
promoters. They generally arrange flights, hotels, and travel within
the country – and, in the Academy's case at least, the most generous
hospitality. As the Academy's reputation has grown, so has the
number of countries to which they have been invited – all the
countries of Europe, several Iron Curtain countries, Japan,
Australia, Hong Kong, New Zealand, the Philippines, and both
North and South America.

Each tour is different, coloured by the places the orchestra visits,
but all share similar problems. The progress of an Academy tour
can be seen, certainly from the management point of view, as a type
of obstacle race, with the same hurdles to be cleared in different
languages every time. The first always presents itself right at the
start of the tour – at the airport. Getting the players into the plane is a

problem: Iona in particular has a dislike of flying which verges on aerophobia, and others, though willing enough, are nerve-rackingly unpunctual. Sylvia has frequently resorted to a Japanese-style system of flags and a piercing cry of 'Ready!' (usually the signal for the players to file on to the concert platform) to shepherd the orchestra through a crowded airport and on to the right plane in time for take-off.

This procedure pales into insignificance in comparison with the effort involved in getting the instruments on to the plane. Ever since the Academy started to tour, Molly, Sylvia, Neville and the rest of the players, singly and collectively, have waged with the airlines the war of the cello. Patently, cellos, unlike violins and violas, cannot be carried as hand luggage: equally obviously, to the owners at least, they cannot be put in the hold at the mercy of sub-zero temperatures and baggage handlers. As one player put it, 'If you had twenty-five thousand pounds' worth of Chippendale writing desk with which you earned your living, you wouldn't want it bounced round Gatwick on its end.' They must, therefore, normally travel with their owners in the plane, where they take up, and pay for, one seat each (although one airline, by a curious mental process, has declared that two cellos take up three seats). It was the demand of one particularly humourless and inattentive ticket clerk that the sex of each and every ticket-holder be filled in on its Departure Card that led to 'Mr and Mrs Cello' being added to every Academy flight roster (although Mr and Mrs Cello, for all their full-price tickets, are consistently denied dinner or a drink – a bone of contention

Mr and Mrs Cello en route to Italy with Denis Vigay

between airlines and inexplicably greedy Academy members).

The double bass, faced with the same problem, but capable of occupying as many as five seats, often loses the battle and goes in the hold (although those airlines confident of their catering have been known to lock it in one of the lavatories). This led John Gray to construct a mammoth temperature-proof armour-plated case for his bass: Denis remembers, 'It looked like a pregnant lady, and it took six of us to carry it.' On one Spanish tour, the usual argument was presented; John having lost, the bass was then consigned to the hold – but the triumph of the airline staff was short-lived when all their efforts to get it through the doors failed. Nor could it be manœuvred into the passenger cabin – so while the Academy flew the two hundred miles to the next stop, John and the bass went by road.

Instruments continue to present a problem after the flight, especially if the players are then required to travel by train. German trains are particularly difficult to negotiate, stopping at stations for infinitesimal and inflexible periods. Getting an army of players, suitcases and instruments out of a railway carriage takes time (Roger Garland holds the record, having cleared a German carriage in thirty-six seconds), and in the early days it was not unusual for the less sprightly of the players to be carried off protesting to the next station. Over the years, the Academy have evolved measures to deal with this problem: they now divide into two squads, the first of which rushes on to the platform the instant the train stops to catch instruments and baggage hurled by the other contingent through hastily opened windows, a practice that tends to be unpopular with fellow-travellers in mid-January.

The next problem is to find the hotel and check in, double bass on the ground floor wherever possible. Having learnt from their early French experiences, the Academy now always insist on being booked into reasonably comfortable hotels – a justifiable expense, ensuring that over a long tour the standard of the concerts is not threatened by tired and crabby performers. In the early days of touring, it was taken for granted that, for reasons of economy, players would share rooms; of late, notions have become grander, and sharing is now regarded as a considerable hardship. This softening of attitude was scorned by Ken and Steve when it first became

118

apparent; they spent the first part of one tour making disparaging remarks to this effect, which abated only when they arrived at a hotel to find that they had been booked to share the matrimonial suite. For probably the first time in the suite's active life, it had someone sleeping on its pink-carpeted floor.

Left, 'Green side up' – the punch line: Trevor Connah, Stephen Shingles and (receding) Neville Marriner; right, Alfresco – Stephen Shingles and Kenneth Heath

Travel within countries is usually by coach, and during these journeys, often lasting six or seven hours, the players have got to know each other extremely well. The bus generally constitutes the bulk of the orchestra's social life on tour. Over the years, coaches have been the scene of flourishing bridge and poker schools, chess marathons, fervent 'Master Mind' tournaments, running repairs to music (and, on occasion, musicians), Andy McGee's cartooning, and Trevor Connah's card tricks. Trevor's forte, however, is the joke tailored to the six-hour bus journey; at least once a tour he would recount the immortal 'Green side up' – an epic known to last a hundred miles or more, with embellishments from bystanders. Journeys have occasionally been prolonged by individual absent-mindedness: there was a memorable day's cricket in the Blue Mountains of Australia while the bus went back for Nicholas Kraemer's music. But usually time passes quickly enough, helped along by such unlikely diversions as a brutally contested crochet competition, precipitated by Carmel Kaine's offer of a bottle of the local wine for the least discreditable effort. (The inches produced

119

were awarded as a booby prize to Christopher Hirons for the most discreditable effort.) It is important that the driver should be an ally, or at least neutral: a bottle of schnapps or some other suitable spirit, included under the heading of 'incidental touring expenses', normally helps preserve an *entente cordiale*.

Long journeys often make meals a problem, and the players have evolved their own arrangements for eating in transit – the 'nosebag system', as Steve calls it. Some are restrained and wholesome – involving nuts, cheese, raisins and yogurt – others less so. The communal 'nosebag' of Ken, Steve and John featured a travelling primus and what Christopher Hogwood describes as 'the hard-core garlic-eaters' kit – from where I sat behind the bass section, the fumes were overwhelming'. For special occasions, even more elaborate meals would be prepared to be eaten in the hotel rooms. Molly remembers one particularly magnificent German feast prepared by Ken, Steve and John and set out carefully on the balcony of their room, packed in snow to chill the wine and preserve the food. While they were out sightseeing, she clambered nimbly along the balconies to where the alfresco meal sat in state, and removed every single course: 'The mystification was most gratifying.' Her efforts to *provide* food for the Academy were to be less successful: arriving late one afternoon in Stockholm, with a concert to follow in the evening, the players found that no food was available in the hotel. As the sole possessor of a small amount of Swedish change, Molly hurried in search of a vending machine she had seen from the bus. Decorated with a picture of two apples and a banana, it had seemed promising; but in return for her Kroner, the machine delivered, much to her confusion, an unnervingly explicit pornographic magazine – and the players went hungry.

To the outsider, it might occasionally seem as if the bus journeys and the eating arrangements constitute a tour's *raison d'être*, so much energy do they absorb. However, the concerts present their own problems. Finding the time and place for adequate rehearsal is one: the Academy have always been scrupulous in trying to ensure that their live performances maintain the standard of their records, and this requires a great deal of rehearsal, both before a tour and during it. Molly remembers an early tour in the course of which someone bought a (then rather advanced) battery-operated tape recorder.

Nicholas Kraemer

The players took to recording each concert and playing the tape back afterwards in the bus returning them to the hotel. 'They'd be clustered round the thing, swaying about in the back of the bus, practically in tears of despair as they identified their imperfections, and there'd always be someone saying "We'd better go over that bit tomorrow".' But with concert halls often not ready until the last moment, finding somewhere to practise can be a problem.

Finding adequate instruments to practise on can be another. The principal victim is always the continuo player, at the mercy of the local promoter responsible for supplying the harpsichord. Nicholas Kraemer's solo début with the Academy in Australia, where he was to perform David Lord's Harpsichord Concerto, was jeopardised by an instrument rendered playable only after a day's hard tinkering. 'It was my first concerto, it was a live broadcast, I had been told the Queen's Representative was going to be there – and I hadn't been able to practise. Molly was wonderful – she offered to cut my hair for me to give me something else to think about while I was waiting to go on.' Chastened by a series of disasters, the Academy now take on tour not only a harpsichord, but also its owner, Malcolm Russell, to maintain and tune it.

The bass player is also at risk: one year, John Gray, tired of fighting airlines, tried using instruments provided locally. The experiment was initially a resounding success: when he arrived at the Hans Rosbaud Studio in Baden-Baden, he found no less than six basses lined up on the platform for him to choose from, each with a different bow and several kinds of mutes and rosin. At the other end of the scale, the bass provided in a small Spanish town was so bad that the scheduled Rossini String Sonata, with its prominent bass solo, had to be taken out of the programme. Denis Vigay remembers it as 'an unbelievable instrument, the strings whiskered and green with age – John listened to the concert from the audience, and I spent it playing the cello down an octave to fill in the non-existent bass line'.

Halls themselves may turn out to be less than satisfactory – acoustically odd, for instance. Christopher Hogwood looks back with disfavour on a concert given in the ballroom of a hotel in Singapore: 'The room was heavily carpeted, and the ladies were fanning themselves so vigorously with their programmes that the band was two minutes into the slow movement of the Bartok Divertimento before they heard a note.' The dressing-room in a hall is always a prime concern – 'Is there hot water?', 'Is there anywhere to hang the tails?': it may be too cramped – or insufficiently secluded. Denis, much aggrieved on this score, remarks, 'It's not unusual for them to give us a little room with bright lights and no curtains so that the audience, pouring past to their seats, are presented with the spectacle of the orchestra in the altogether as part of the performance.' (On one occasion Neville was obliged to receive a handsome tribute, prepared by the organisers of a concert, clad only in underwear, socks and all the dignity he could muster, when the donors in their eagerness chose to present it five minutes after the concert had finished.)

The platform may be too small to accommodate fifteen bowing actions, however well co-ordinated. When one leg of the bass stool slipped off the edge of a platform in Germany, John was hurled to the floor: his bow caught the adjoining music stand on the way down and precipitated a chain reaction in the violas. Denis recalls, 'I didn't dare look, and Ken had his eyes shut as if the end of the world had come: the fiddles' faces were a picture – and of course, the violas had ground to a halt completely.' Alternatively, the platform may be large enough but not level, and Trevor remembers with joy an occasion in Switzerland where George Malcolm was playing continuo for the Academy: 'During a couple of bars' rest, I happened to be looking in his direction – when all of a sudden the harpsichord ran away from him. He made a lunge for it and wrestled it back – but, overbalancing in the process, teetered on the back legs of his chair before crashing forward again on to the harpsichord. But George, being George, kept on playing throughout: some of the band only realised what was happening when the legs of the chair hit the platform for the second time.' Too smooth a surface can be equally awkward; cellos and bass need a floor on which the end-pin of the instrument can get a grip. Denis points out, 'If you get a nice new hard wood floor with a high gloss, you don't like to whip out your penknife and start gouging away – but honestly, sometimes it's that or disaster.'

However, all complaints about halls are silenced by the thought of open-air performances and the attendant hazards. In the margin of Sylvia's schedule for a tour of Yugoslavia in the height of summer, with concerts arranged in medieval village squares and monastery courtyards, is pencilled the single word PIGEONS. It still makes her laugh to remember a more recent open-air effort in Athens. The concerts were scheduled to take place in the Odeion Herodion, a beautifully preserved second-century amphitheatre on the Acropolis. The players, looking forward to performing in this romantic setting, were bitterly disappointed when the first of the two concerts was rained off, and they were determined to play the second at all costs. The price was high: on the following night the rain stopped, but a high wind was whistling round the columns, and rehearsals were interrupted at ten-second intervals as one section after another scaled the terraces to retrieve its music. Grimly determined, the Academy

Andy McGee's memories of music on the Acropolis

*The Academy
rehearsing in the
Odeion Herodion*

went ahead with the concert – albeit slightly depleted in numbers.
Sylvia explains, 'We simply had to have anybody who could be
spared to hold down the music. It must have looked ridiculous – ten
players with ten people crouching at their feet in full evening dress to
keep the music on the stands. We were almost too embarrassed to go
on – but people didn't laugh too much.' It was a compliment the
orchestra was able to repay: during rehearsals Sylvia had gone up into
the terraces to check the orchestral balance and had had an unwel-
come surprise sitting down on the cushions provided, now sodden
from the previous night's rain. The players, informed of this mishap,
had difficulty containing themselves at the interval as they watched
the audience of five thousand rise from their seats into the cool night
air and, as one, distastefully crane over their shoulders and pluck at
their nether garments.

These and the other hazards involved in giving a series of concerts
in unfamiliar surroundings, one a night for three weeks or more,
punctuated by thousands of miles of bus journeys, affect the quality
of the performances surprisingly rarely. Christopher Hogwood
remembers the high degree of concentration and tension on tour –
and the element of being on trial all the time, a combination of the
players' own pride in performance and Neville's determination to

maintain standards. 'If a concert ever did drop below standard, Neville was very quick to notice and to say "Right, auditions tomorrow" – he was only half-serious, but I saw people going away and practising.'

Neville applied the same standards to himself; when, as the soloist in a Handel concerto grosso, he missed an entry by a split second, Christopher remembers, 'He was tight-lipped for two days, really mortified.' After five years of a career that consisted increasingly of conducting, and playing the violin only with the Academy on tour, Neville had realised that he must concentrate on the one to the exclusion of the other. He remarks, 'I had become the kind of violin player I wouldn't care to employ', and he announced his retirement as a player in 1975, during a tour of Germany, by presenting the orchestra with a case of champagne during the interval of a concert in Wuppertal. The players went out for the second half and Neville's last appearance as director in slightly merry mood, and decided to try and catch him out at the end by starting a different encore from the one they had prepared. Waiting for him to forge embarrassingly ahead with a firm down bow while they were daintily *pizzicato*, they were sorely disappointed when he noticed in the nick of time and went *pizzicato* with the best of them: 'He always was too damn quick,' lamented David Takeno.

Sometimes it is the problems which beset a concert, or the surmounting of them, which make the occasion. Molly remembers with real pleasure the last concert of the Academy's 1972 World Tour – a performance of Bach, Britten and Vivaldi in Yokohama. Sitting backstage, she was puzzled during the 'Simple Symphony' by an ebb and flow of helmeted officials; by the interval it was clear that the hall, or at least the library attached to it, was on fire. The audience was evacuated, and though the fire was quickly put out, the electricity supply to the hall was cut off. Undaunted, representatives of the orchestra's local agents in Japan, Kambara Music Office of Tokyo, hurried to nearby houses to borrow torches, and the concert continued in blackness, with only the music illuminated by torches held by volunteers over each music stand. The piece was 'The Four Seasons', and Carmel, playing 'Summer', remembers it as one of the most moving performances of her life. 'The man

125

Ronald Thomas

holding the torch for me didn't move a muscle – it was *extraordinary*, and when we finished, the people, still sitting in darkness, just wouldn't stop clapping.' When the lights went on, they revealed an audience of approximately double its original size. According to the Kambara office staff, 'Many onlookers had come in. All sorts of people were found there – firemen, construction workers half naked and with sandals on, grandmothers carrying babies on their backs etc. – not the type of people likely to be seen in concert halls. The Academy gave the pleasure of music to so many people, the half of which were not at all expected.'

Molly also remembers that during the necessarily prolonged interval, the players, unimpressed by the drama, continued to call for tea, and this she tried to provide, in the midst of hoses, smoke and firemen. Management takes on a new dimension on tour, as Denis remembers: 'I don't think Molly can have got a wink of sleep on those early tours – she was always finding sticking plaster for this person, a new light bulb for that person's room, making sure that everyone had got their cases and that the music stands hadn't been left behind, and listening to everybody's worries as well.' Making sure that everyone has the right concert clothes is a constant concern. Molly recalls one occasion when, between rehearsal and con-

126

cert in Hong Kong, Ronald Thomas went to inspect the violin collection of a local Chinese doctor, taking with him for safety's sake not only his own Guarnerius violin but also his tails for the evening's performance. He left the clothes, though not the violin, in the doctor's brand-new Jaguar – and when his host, inadvertently slamming the front door of his house, locked them out of both house and car, Ron, with half an hour to go to the concert, was left without tailcoat, trousers or dress shirt. The doctor was understandably reluctant to force open his new car, and Ron, hastening to the hall, borrowed the requisite garments from Tony Jenkins, who was not playing in the first piece. Unfortunately, the two are not built on the same scale: Tony spent an uncomfortable first half sitting backstage in a raincoat, from which pale British legs and black socks coyly emerged, mesmerising the Chinese stage-hands; and Ron, in Chaplinesque trousers, took some very uneasy bows.

The task of looking after the orchestra is sometimes shared by the local agents and promoters and, if the circumstances warrant it, by British Embassies abroad. Hospitality is usually more than generous, and some of the high points of Academy tours have been the parties given for the players round the world. In Hong Kong they were wined and dined in the best colonial style by Harry Weinrebe, the founder of the Hong Kong Conservatory of Music. An old friend of the orchestra since its Dartington days, he was instrumental in bringing the Academy both to Hong Kong and to Japan,

Neville Marriner with Harry Weinrebe, the founder of the Hong Kong Conservatory of Music

Valkoog – David Takeno second from right

where he mounted a vigorous and effective publicity campaign. This included a Press conference for the directors which was held, to the accompaniment of Academy records, in a large department store, and the distribution of beer-mats and cigarette packets emblazoned with the 'Four Seasons' record sleeve.

In Warsaw a party was thrown for the Academy by Jerzy Maksymiuk and the Polish Chamber Orchestra, an ensemble which Neville particularly admires. In Sydney the players were taken to lunch by Argo's Australian representative in a revolving restaurant at the top of the city's tallest building. In the Dutch village of Valkoog, where the Academy were to give a concert to celebrate the 500th anniversary of *another* St Martin's, the entire orchestra was transported to the church in a fleet of veteran cars. Andy McGee remembers with embarrassment the moment when David Takeno asked what *this* little knob did and the owner, politely demonstrating, brought the whole cavalcade to a halt. 'We had to be towed the rest of the way . . . and I thought the Japanese knew about cars.' In the Hague, the British Ambassador held a reception for the presentation to the Academy of a Gold Disc for 'The Four Seasons'. In Buenos Aires the Academy actually per-

128

formed in the Embassy – not without misgivings. Rehearsing in a room at the front of the building, the players, finding the atmosphere stifling, had opened all windows and shutters; Embassy personnel, passing the door, remarked on how pleasant it was to see the room so light and airy. When asked if this was unusual they replied, in true British fashion, that *they* always kept the windows closed to avoid being shot at.

In trying to respond to their welcome, the Academy have had the odd communication problem. One early failure was a speech of thanks Neville made, with considerable effort, in French – to a Flemish audience. 'You'd have thought everyone in the hall had died.' His command of the language proved marginally more useful in Aix-en-Provence, where he was conducting the Academy in *The Marriage of Figaro*, their first venture into live opera. Arriving for the first night, he found his way barred by an obstinate doorman. 'All bona fide ticket holders and guests were in dinner jackets, and with me in my tails, I think he thought I was some sort of pushy head waiter. I kept explaining that I was the conductor, but I might just as well have been claiming to be a bus conductor – it took every French word I knew to get him to let me in.'

Sylvia would have been grateful even for a limited Polish

The 'Four Seasons' Gold Disc; left to right – *Sir John Barnes (the British Ambassador to The Hague), Stan Goodall, Neville Marriner, Willem Barents (Phonogram's managing director), Hillary Watson (Decca's export manager), Harley Usill*

129

vocabulary to deal with the episode of Colin Sauer's Stradivarius. The Academy were on their way to give two concerts in Warsaw, for which a prodigious amount of organisation had been required. Sylvia had had to prepare a detailed list of the orchestra's instruments – name of maker, date made, insured value etc. – and her heart sank as she watched a singularly hostile customs official scanning this minutely. 'As he came to the Strad, you could see him thinking – "1699 – nearly three hundred years old? – well, with a grotty old instrument like that he's bound to want to sell it and buy a new one. Let's make sure he can't" – and he lifted up his rubber stamp and was about to plaster it with prohibitions. How do you explain to a customs official, in a language you can't speak, that a Strad is better *not* covered in green ink?'

However, the reception the Academy have had abroad has been worth all the trials and tribulations – and the players remember with particular affection their audiences in Poland. Nicholas Kraemer recalls the first concert in Warsaw as the most moving in which he has ever been involved. It began at the rehearsals, where he met a Polish music student: 'I have a passion for apples, and I'd brought some with me; I offered them round, although it was the middle of the morning and I didn't really expect anyone to accept. But the girl stared at them for a moment, asked "Isn't that a Cox's Pippin?", and took one with real gratitude. I had to go then, to rehearse one of the pieces: when I came back an hour later, she was still eating it.' The Polish audiences seemed equally starved of contact with Western music and musicians, and the hall was packed. 'There wasn't a square inch of floor space, and people were five deep against the walls and up the aisles. They wouldn't let us go, the encores went on and on – we felt as if we were deserting them when we finally left.'

As several players have remarked, to do a tour like that, with that kind of audience, and then come back to England and give a Sunday afternoon concert in a cavernous auditorium to three men and a dog is really to know you are home. It is a commonplace of the music business that it is always easier to be foreign. While not exactly without honour in their own country, the Academy have greatly enjoyed the special treatment they are given abroad – the parties, the flowers (kept alive in a bucket at the back of the bus), the presents (once, in Holland, a whole and unpackable Edam each), the sight-

Neville Marriner with a Japanese reception committee

seeing, even, occasionally, the bus journeys. As Celia Nicklin puts it, 'I love touring because it's such a holiday – so much more interesting than doing the dusting.' For those left behind with the housework, the Academy's trips abroad can be something of a red rag. Families are not forgotten, and large sums are invested in postcards and long-distance telephone calls – but often to little avail: as Steve Shingles has been heard to mutter on several occasions as he returns disgruntled from the hotel telephone kiosk, 'Well . . . that's another £5-worth of doghouse.'

10

Stand Where We Can't See You

After the success and recognition the first ten years had brought, it would have been reasonable to expect the Academy to cling tightly to the formula they had hit upon – touring and recording the music for small string orchestra with which they had made their name as a fraternity of '*hommes libres*'. An outsider at the sessions for their recording of Stravinsky's 'Apollo' might, therefore, have been surprised to see this normally well-drilled and professional ensemble get off to its fifth ragged start in as many minutes, and to hear its oboist Roger Lord remark with some asperity, 'Nev – if you're going to conduct, would you mind standing somewhere where we can see you ... or somewhere where we can't.'

Neville was conducting the Academy for the first time, and although, as Edward Greenfield has pointed out, he dispensed with the baton and conducted with his bow 'to show his essentially democratic spirit', his early efforts fell on stony ground. The change from seated director to standing conductor was a highly significant one for all concerned. For the players it meant that the Academy was no longer as secure a refuge from conductors, and their democratic approach seemed in jeopardy. Their image of themselves was (and in some ways still is) as a group of fifteen string players – six first violins, four seconds, two violas, two cellos and a bass – with or without a harpsichord, everyone equally involved and concentrating at the highest level (hence Steve Shingles' standing joke that the day the Academy record Beethoven's Ninth Symphony is the day he will retire). The Academy had enjoyed demonstrating the dispensability of the conductor, and it was with reluctance that they came to accept the (occasional) necessity for one: in Neville's words, 'There had to be an *awfully* good reason for conducting.'

The initial reason was the impossibility of directing some of the rhythmically more complex chamber works from the front desk by what Alan Loveday has called 'the nodding and smiling technique'. However, the principal reason was the need to extend the repertoire beyond the chamber range. The Academy, first and foremost a recording orchestra, had discovered that the number of records they needed to keep themselves in business was increasing. To win a wider public they had to give concerts, but the 1969 Queen Elizabeth Hall series, though a critical success, had made the point yet again that, for them, concert-giving was uneconomic: the public expects from an orchestra in concert something resembling the standard of its performances on record – which in the Academy's case entailed a quantity of rehearsal time that made every concert, however well-attended, a loss-making venture. To balance the books and pay for public appearances, they had to make more records – and to make more records they had to widen the repertoire available to them. They began to tackle small classical symphonies – and with the larger forces this required (a full complement of woodwind, trumpets and timpani), the orchestra became too large to control effectively from the front desk. As Neville commented, 'You *could* probably do these pieces without a conductor, if

An early conducted session in St John's, Smith Square

133

The nodding and smiling technique

you had enough rehearsal time, by discussion and with practice – but no one would ever give you the time to make this kind of experiment.'

The decision to accept a conductor was made easier for the Academy by the fact that in Neville they had one within their own ranks. It was in the mid-1960s that Neville had begun to think about conducting: 'When you start learning the fiddle, you want to be Heifetz; then as you go on, you find the position is filled, and you're not going to make it as a soloist, so you take a job in an orchestra. But I wanted more influence on the performance than I could ever have as leader of the second fiddles – and I found that in the Academy. Then in the end I started to find the repertoire for small chamber orchestra limiting – it's a long canvas, but it's a narrow one – and I looked towards the larger symphonic field.' Temptation was put in his way by Pierre Monteux, then the principal conductor of the LSO, who suggested to Neville that instead of waving his bow at the Academy from the front desk, he should 'stand up and conduct like a man'. When Monteux followed this up with an invitation to his Maine summer school for conductors, Neville accepted with alacrity. His experience under Monteux, and some time spent conducting the Northern Sinfonia Orchestra, were instrumental in his appointment in 1969 as the founding conductor

134

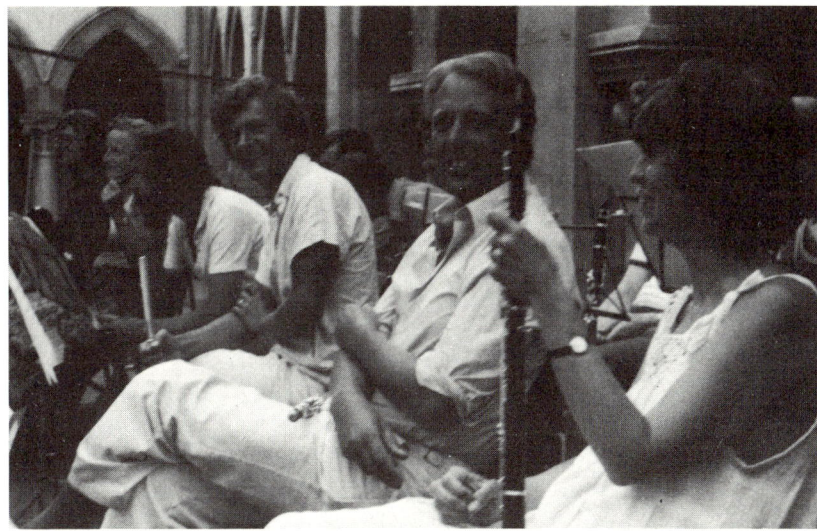

Academy wind players – Christopher Nicholls, William Bennett and Celia Nicklin

of the Los Angeles Chamber Orchestra. 'I didn't even pack my fiddle,' he remembers, 'and from then on, I knew it *had* to be conducting first.'

When the Academy started to record the new symphonic repertoire under Neville's baton, it was with a new recording company – Phonogram, on their Philips label. It had become clear that however high the standard of the records Argo was producing with the Academy, as a small company it could not offer more than five or six records a year, and this was not enough to keep the orchestra financially secure. As Mike Bremner explained to *Music Business Weekly* in 1970, 'Thanks to Argo, [the Academy] have become one of the most important of today's recording orchestras, and our relations with them have never been better'; but, as he also explained, 'We could not handle the whole of their available recording time. . . . We wanted at all costs to maintain their existence, and so we agreed to release them from exclusive contract so that their extra time, not needed by us, could be put to good use, both for the Academy and for recording in general.' With the Argo/Academy link on a non-exclusive footing, the Academy became free to accept a contract offered by Phonogram, which gave them the opportunity to double their output of records.

The architect of the Academy's career on the Philips label has

*Erik Smith and
Neville Marriner*

been Erik Smith. A fellow student at Monteux's conducting school and an old friend of both Neville and Molly, Erik had already worked with the Academy as a Decca producer on records of harpsichord concertos by Haydn and J. C. Bach (with George Malcolm as soloist), and the Handel Opus 6 concertos. With excellent chamber groups already on the Philips label, Phonogram did not want another baroque orchestra, and much of the nineteenth- and twentieth-century chamber repertoire had already been recorded by the Academy with Argo. Erik saw the orchestra's potential as a symphonic ensemble in classical and early romantic repertoire, and his suggestion that they record for Philips was made specifically with the larger orchestral repertoire in mind.

His first large-scale project with the group made this clear. 'The Rise of The Symphony', issued in 1971, was a set of four records, each illustrating a particular composer's contribution to the development of the symphony. The set's main aim in musicological terms, as Erik described it, was to 'make out the case for playing the symphonies of the eighteenth century with the sort of chamber orchestra that might have played them at the time – six to eight violins in each section, three violas, three cellos and two double basses – where fullness of tone can be combined with complete clarity and grace with vitality'.

While some critics questioned the actual choice of symphonies – J. C. Bach's six Opus 3 symphonies, Haydn's Symphonies 52 and 53, Mozart's Symphonies 35 and 40, and Beethoven's First and Second – all welcomed the chance to hear the works performed by this smaller ensemble. *Records & Recordings* commented on the performance of Mozart's Symphony No. 40: 'What a rare pleasure it is to have this wonderful score so finely played and to be able to hear the wind instruments penetrating the string sound with exactly the right degree of clarity,' and, on the Beethoven symphonies, 'It is a real treat, in these intensely vital, affectionate but never affected performances, to hear such details as the timpani flourishes and woodwind scale in the coda of the First Symphony's finale.' Reviewers also remarked on the care taken to obtain accurate texts. This was the first recording ever made of the J. C. Bach symphonies, and the score was specially prepared from the first edition by Erik Smith. Similarly, for Mozart's 'Haffner' symphony, Neville used the then recently published facsimile of the autograph score, differing in several interesting respects from the standard editions.

'The Rise of The Symphony' was of fundamental importance to the Academy in establishing beyond doubt that there was a place for them in the symphonic field. These were their first *mature* Mozart symphonies, their first Haydn symphonies, and their first Beethoven recordings of any kind, and the set served as a springboard into the classical repertoire. Over the next ten years the orchestra was to complete the full cycle of Mozart symphonies, make inroads into those of Haydn, and add to the First and Second symphonies of Beethoven a recording of his Fourth which was described in *Records & Recordings* as 'coming uncomfortably close to exuding an aura of perfection'. There are current plans to complete the Beethoven cycle with recordings of the remaining six symphonies – including, *pace* Steve Shingles, the Ninth.

One of the assets of a major international recording company is the capacity to finance large-scale projects, and the Academy have been encouraged to take full advantage of this, with a considerable proportion of their work for Philips taking the form of major symphonic cycles which have made them increasingly familiar to the public as a small symphony orchestra. Cycles give musicians the chance to immerse themselves in a composer's thought and follow his development, and Neville has found this a particularly satisfying approach to recording (although he occasionally wonders who can afford the 'presentation heaps' that result). For the complete cycle of Rossini overtures, for example, the Academy started with the earlier works, written for an orchestra small enough to fit into the most cramped of theatre pits. As Erik points out, there is a small theatre in Spoleto which has a plaque to the effect that Maestro Rossini was present when one of these works was performed; it was customary for the composer when present to lead the orchestra, either from the keyboard or from the first violin, but on this occasion there were two eminent musicians in these posts whom he did not wish to offend, and he seized the double bass and directed the performances from the back – the inference being that a theatre of this size could only accommodate the size of orchestra that would have a single bass. *Hi-Fidelity Magazine* wrote of this small-scale Rossini, 'This record simply obliterates the competition. Thanks to the chamber orchestra-sized string section and the quality of execution, every wind line in these works emerges with the full import Rossini clearly intended' – and reviewers were equally enthusiastic when the orchestra moved on to the larger 'symphonic' overtures – *William Tell*, *La Cenerentola* and others. The set was completed by means of a persistent search for the scores of works known by name but rarely performed – *Torvaldo e Dorliska*, *Edipo a Colone*, *Maometto II* and others. Erik recalls, 'It was extraordinarily laborious – some only existed in manuscript, one or two were kicking around in the depths of the BBC, others we found by hook or by crook in Italian libraries; one – Sinfonia "al Conventello" – turned up in 1979.'

The material for the Academy's cycle of Haydn symphonies posed no such problems, but here Erik faced the difficulty of selection. It was never the intention to produce a complete set of all 104 catalogued symphonies, in direct competition with the Dorati/Philharmonica Hungarica set. Equally he could see no point in presenting an entirely random assortment, and he was looking for a guiding principle by which to assemble a number of symphonies. He hit upon the idea of singling out those of Haydn's

symphonies with well-known nicknames and coupling them in related pairs – 'Surprise'/'Miracle', 'Mourning'/'Passion', 'Horn Signal'/'Hunt', 'Drum-Roll'/'Military', 'Oxford'/'London' and so on. He tends to be apologetic about this approach – 'Not a very *artistic* notion.' However, the nicknames have caught the imagination of the record-buying public, and do throw interesting sidelights on their subjects – if not always terribly accurate ones: as Robin Golding pointed out in his review, the 'miracle' from which Symphony No. 96 takes its name (the first-night audience's narrow escape from a falling chandelier when they rushed forward to applaud the composer) actually occurred at the first night of Symphony No. 102, which confusingly has no nickname at all. The 'Surprise' symphony, No. 94, is more precisely named, after the unexpected *fortissimo* outburst in the sixteenth bar of the slow movement, of which Haydn himself is said to have remarked, obviously with some glee, 'The ladies will jump here'.

At the heart of the larger-scale repertoire that the Academy have recorded for Philips lie the works of Mozart. This has been primarily at Erik's instigation; a recognised authority on Mozart, Erik devised and produced the Academy's first Mozart record after 'The Rise of the Symphony'. In August 1764, Leopold Mozart, while in London with his children, fell prey to 'the national disease which they call a cold'; though he believed that with this affliction 'the best thing to do is to cross the Channel at once: many people have immediately felt better on so doing', as second-best he repaired to rural Chelsea for six weeks' recuperation. The eight-year old Wolfgang occupied himself during his father's convalescence by filling a manuscript notebook with little compositions – forty-three in all – and it was these that the Academy recorded at Wembley Town Hall in 1971, under the title 'Mozart in Chelsea' (otherwise known, to the Academy at least, as 'Smith in Wembley'). Erik believed that this 'London Notebook', first discovered at the end of the nineteenth century, was a collection not of keyboard pieces (as had been generally assumed) but of sketches for instrumental works. To prove his point, he orchestrated the compositions for strings and wind, as 'a labour of love and intuition, rather than academical analysis', and was rewarded with high praise from *Records & Recordings*: 'I doubt whether Mozart, if he were able to hear this side of the record, would guess that the instrumentation was not his own.'

The Academy continued with Mozart's music for wind and strings in a complete set of the wind concertos. The principal characteristic of the set was its resolutely chamber-music approach, each soloist taking pains to keep within what one critic described as 'the true Mozartian balance of first among equals'. The concertos were written by Mozart as virtuoso pieces for specific soloists – Ignaz Leutgeb, for instance, a fellow freemason in Vienna and, when not playing the horn, a purveyor of cheese. Critics commented favourably on the easy interplay between soloists and orchestra, carefully gauged and clearly illuminated. This close rapport may well have been due to the fact that the soloists were either wind players who had appeared regularly in the Academy – Neil Black, Michael Chapman, and Alan Civil – or soloists with whom the orchestra had worked before – Claude Monteux, Jack Brymer and, for the Flute and Harp Concerto, Osian Ellis. All the wind players joined forces for the Sinfonia Concertante in E flat (K. 297b), in a performance described by John Warrack as 'characteristic of the set as a whole in its understanding of the emotional weight of the music', and in 1974 the set won for the Academy a Wiener Floetenuhr award, presented by the Vienna Mozart Foundation for the year's best Mozart recordings. The prize itself, a clock which plays tunes by Mozart, was described a trifle ambiguously by one reviewer as 'definitely *ein echt gemütliches Geschenk aus Wien*'.

The largest of the Academy/Philips Mozart projects has been the complete cycle of symphonies. The recordings began in 1970 with the two symphonies included in 'The Rise of The Symphony', and were to span the next ten years. 'The Early Symphonies' (Nos. 1–20, minus the spurious Nos. 2 and 3, plus eight which escaped standard numbering, four expanded from overtures, and the 'Neue Lambacher') were released in 1974, and 'The Late Symphonies' (Nos. 21–41) followed in 1980. Here the Academy were given their most obvious chance to explore the work of a single composer over a long period. Neville, who prepared all the editions, commented at the time, 'When Mozart started out, he was very close in style to the early eighteenth century. But as you follow the symphonies through, you can *hear* his attitudes changing, you can feel the sweep of the whole series. Our aim is to produce a set of the symphonies which is consistent in thought and technique, so the Academy style will be apparent throughout – but it will be responsive to the music, and as Mozart's style develops, our style will develop too.' One of the most obvious differences between the orchestra's handling of the early and late symphonies was in the use of continuo. Neville took the view that in the earliest symphonies Mozart would have expected the middle harmonies to have been supplied by a harpsichord, and that continuo only became unnecessary when Mozart started composing independent parts for the second violins and the violas, thereby strengthening the middle line. Accordingly, he used harpsichord continuo (realised by Nicholas Kraemer) in the seventeen earliest symphonies for the first time on record, the only previous recording of the early symphonies having dispensed with continuo entirely. Critical reaction to this innovation was mixed – one critic found the harpsichord 'irrelevant and impertinent', another felt that 'the deft accents of the harpsichord add a great deal' – but the experiment did attract attention, and it was one of the features which earned the set several major awards.

Even after ten years, conducting the Academy remains more strenuous for Neville than conducting any other orchestra. 'In other orchestras, particularly symphony orchestras, players rarely pass comment. When you're conducting your friends, at the very least

Conducting friends (Neville Marriner, Kenneth Heath and Denis Vigay) your close acquaintances, they'll all tell you if they don't like something, and somewhat pungently, too. They still make me work for my podium.' However, his willingness and ability to conduct the Academy, and Philips's readiness to record them as a symphony orchestra, have opened up a new repertoire and a new direction. In Neville's words, 'We may, in our youth, have been a baroque group – but we've grown up with Mozart.'

11

Taste, Thought and Feeling

Parallel to the Academy's complete Mozart symphonies and wind concertos has run their cycle of Mozart piano concertos with Alfred Brendel. This project, initiated by Erik Smith, has been the orchestra's most significant large-scale collaboration with a soloist; as Roger Covell remarked in the *Sydney Morning Herald*, 'There may be a better combination of creative genius and performing talent than Mozart, Brendel and Marriner, but at the moment I can't think of it.'

It is the unity of purpose between soloist, conductor and orchestra – Brendel once described Neville as 'an extension of my right arm' – which has distinguished the collaboration. The relationship was cemented from the outset by a similarity of approach to the Mozart concertos. In Alfred Brendel's words, 'Every one of our interpretations is a unity, not just an accidental combination of soloist and orchestra. I regard our work together as a sort of extended chamber-music playing, where every player joins in a unified style: it's something that can't always be realised – it's not often one finds chamber orchestras of this level of accomplishment – and I must say, it has spoiled my taste for Mozart performances in general.'

Alfred Brendel has a particular affinity for Mozart: 'For some time in my life, Mozart was definitely *the* greatest composer – even now he's one of the four or five greatest.' He considers the piano concertos to be the peak of the concerto repertoire: 'There are so many marvellous ones; it's the occupation of a lifetime to deal with them, delight in them and try to get to terms with them. I am not so foolish as to think that one can ever do justice to a Mozart concerto: one can only try to get one's performance better.' His painstaking

Neville Marriner and Alfred Brendel

preparation of every piece he performs is legendary; he will not perform any work until he is totally convinced of every aspect of his interpretation, and he has spent on average six months preparing each of the fourteen concertos he has so far recorded with the Academy. As he says, 'I'm not a "sit-down-and-join-the-party" player – I'm simply incapable of playing a work practically at sight, I like to think about things.'

His first step is always to research the music itself, going back to the original sources to confirm that he has before him exactly what Mozart wrote. Then a few weeks before the sessions he and Neville meet to discuss the work. Although he is not opposed in principle to concertos directed from the piano, Brendel has no ambitions as a director himself, and prefers to work with a sympathetic conductor. As he says, 'I am not a conductor myself, and would feel unprofessional both taking the solo and directing the orchestra.' Together he and Neville work through solo and orchestral lines in minute detail, aligning text and interpretation. They share an unwillingness to be mesmerised by the text; neither is prepared to follow it slavishly, and both are ready to make small adjustments – doubling a line here, making minor emendations there – if they consider it necessary to make exact musical sense. Brendel explains: 'I play – and sing – to Neville how I think it should go and what I intend to do, and he tells me how the orchestra will play each passage, so that before we go to the sessions, where time is short and expensive, we know precisely where we stand.' It is preparation at this level of detail (which includes wherever possible a public performance before the recording) that has made it practicable to record each concerto in only two sessions.

Harmonious co-operation is made considerably easier by the Academy's attitude to accompanying, held since their earliest days. The soloist, whether he be a guest artist or drawn from within the orchestra's own ranks, must have the final say on the work's interpretation; the orchestra's job is to assist him in emphasising what he wants from the music. Dame Janet Baker, whose solo work with the Academy has now extended over nearly twenty years, has observed this in action: 'The way the Academy used to phrase seemed to me to bring out for the singer the right qualities of expression for the words. If one did what the instruments were doing, the words slotted into place; if you lightened the end of a syllable or made a *diminuendo* in a certain place as they did, the meaning of the word became more apparent.'

However, the orchestra's independence is not sacrificed: as an '*assemblée d'hommes libres*' and essentially a solo ensemble, they have not needed to rely for public exposure on commercially attractive

Alan Loveday, Neville Marriner, Dame Janet Baker and Iona Brown

145

'name' soloists, and have been free for the most part to choose as soloists only those musicians with whose aims they are likely to be in sympathy. Dame Janet considers their choice of vocal soloists instructive: 'All the singers Neville and the orchestra have used are musicians disciplined in the manner of working in *groups*, and likely to understand the Academy approach instinctively.' With this kind of understanding established, the need for compromise disappears, and all are free to express their own musical personalities.

The Academy's attitude is clearly apparent in their working relationship with Alfred Brendel. As Neville points out, 'These are *piano* concertos, not concertos for orchestra, and a soloist who has played the pieces dozens of times before is bound to have firm ideas: interfere with his conception of a work, and you risk damaging the conviction and confidence of his playing.' Brendel's ideas on Mozart are particularly clearly articulated: he has thought deeply not only about his own part but also about the orchestral lines, and his views are conveyed to the orchestra, sometimes directly, more often through Neville. As one player puts it, 'I don't necessarily agree with what he wants – but I admire the fact that he has the musical personality to *know* what he wants and to make sure he gets it.'

The Academy's first appearance with Alfred Brendel was at Mill Hill Music Club in June 1971, where they performed the concertos K. 414 and K. 453. In July the works were recorded, with Erik Smith as producer; K. 459 and K. 488 followed shortly afterwards and the cycle could hardly have had a more auspicious beginning – the first record was a *Gramophone* Critics' Choice, and Stephen Plaistow wrote of the second (in *Gramophone*): 'I thought [the recording] exceptional for its combination of taste, thought and feeling with the highest level of accomplishment from everyone concerned; for once, real style, as rare and precious as ever.' The pattern was repeated early in 1973 with the performance of K. 491 and K. 466 at Mill Hill, followed by recording sessions, after which a further performance was scheduled at the Cheltenham Festival. Brendel has a tape of this concert, specially recorded to remind him of an unnerving occasion. On the morning of the performance, the car bringing him to Cheltenham was involved in a head-on collision. Although he was not seriously hurt, by the time he reached the

146

rehearsal delayed shock had stiffened his muscles – 'I felt like an old man of eighty, capable of playing only from my fingers down.' The ministrations of a flautist turned masseur saved the performance: Brendel remarks, still surprised, 'It was not a bad concert – all things considered. . . .'

Recordings of K. 456 and K. 595 followed in 1974, and in the same year the Brendel/Academy relationship found visual record in two films made by London Weekend Television for its arts magazine programme 'Aquarius'. The producer was Humphrey Burton (now Head of Music and Arts at BBC Television), a friend of Neville's from LSO days and the executive producer of the 1965 Kenwood 'Four Seasons'. He explains: 'My intention was to record, for now and for posterity, a very fruitful partnership between the Academy and Alfred, both of whom I had admired a great deal. . . . My ambition was to show how an orchestra of very high quality soloists work together like chamber players with a musician who is in the tradition of Central European chamber music-making and has very strong views on how [the music] should go.' He set out to do this by concentrating on the Brendel/Academy recording of K. 595, prefacing a studio performance of the piece with a 'workshop' film charting the progress of the recording from the first session to the disc's eventual appearance in the record shops.

The first programme has been described by Brendel as 'a virtuoso performance by Humphrey'. It brought the television cameras into the Philips sessions at Brent Town Hall to show how a record is made, emphasising the commercial realities of the recording business by intercutting film of the slow movement of the concerto taking shape in the studio with shots of sales conferences and mass production machinery. In Humphrey's words, 'There is a savage juxtaposition of the necessary salesmanship that goes into pushing the record out into the shops, and the total dedicated delicacy and poetry of the performance.' His aim was to demonstrate how soloist, conductor, orchestra and technical staff work together towards the maturing of an interpretation and its encapsulation on tape, focussing on the human element: 'I tried to organise it so that the performers weren't concerned with the cameras. The cameras were running the whole time, and [the artists] didn't know whether they were on film or off. They didn't stage anything for us, and I didn't ask them to do anything again specially for us; we just took what was happening.' The artists were too preoccupied with making a successful recording to worry about the camera crew, and the film shows the grimace of one musician at another as a wrong note is played, Brendel's sticking-plastered fingers, and the occasional friction between soloist and orchestra, conductor and technical staff, even producer and cameraman. The result was authentic enough to provoke from the critic Michael Oliver the comment that 'The variety stage lost a great comic when Alfred Brendel took up the piano. Whether turning in pained silent outrage to investigate a noise in the studio, [or] conspiratorially misdirecting the orchestra behind Marriner's back ... Brendel is clearly the most accomplished silent comedian since Buster Keaton.'

For the second programme, players and cameras regrouped in the LWT studios to film a complete performance of the concerto. This formal 'concert' situation is perhaps the most difficult for television to handle successfully, the object being to provide visual images entertaining enough to keep the interest of an audience for whom the music (heard inevitably through television's relatively low-quality mono speakers) is not sufficiently compelling on its own. The major pitfall for the producer is the temptation either to present images so elaborate that they distract from the music, or to 'interpret' the music by underlining the rhythm with shots of appropriate Old Masters timed to follow the beat. David Attenborough, for four years Controller, BBC 2, has summarised what he looks for in the presentation of classical music on television: 'What I require is reticence and good manners, and a film which shows me roughly what the action is, who's playing what – that's all I wish to know.'

Humphrey's views are similar: 'When you're recording an actual performance, the music itself must be the thing you're serving; the human interest should never interfere with your appreciation of the music. You can perhaps allow yourself the smile of the conductor, at the end of the cadenza delivering the orchestra back into the fray, or at a particularly felicitous phrase from either orchestra or soloist – but on the whole the film must always be about the music.' Accordingly he concentrated on keyboard and hands: 'The hands are very expressive. I don't think it helps to see whether the sweat is pouring off the brow, or whether he's got an agonised or beatific expression.

I hate showing the full face . . . because it means technically that you can't also show the hands – normally I come round the side and look at the hands with the profile. . . . Occasionally I look over the top [of the piano] – I had a little mirror fixed up so that I could look down and see the hands spread out on the keys. . . . I tried to get the rapport between Alfred and Neville, so I took longer shots – of Neville moulding a phrase and of Alfred seeking to mould the phrase at the moment he stops playing – living every bar of the music himself.' It was a very good performance – Brendel owns to preferring it to the recording in some respects – and Humphrey's efforts to present it faithfully were rewarded with high praise from Brendel, whose intense aversion to television is well known. 'All television is torture, but this was *less* torture than usual.'

After a Promenade concert and an appearance at the Harrogate Festival together in 1975, Brendel and the Academy recorded one further concerto – K. 482 – and two of Mozart's Concert Rondos, K. 382 and K. 386. The edition of K. 386 was specially completed for this recording by Erik, with Brendel's assistance. As *Gramophone* commented, 'Erik Smith joins the formidable array of editors who have had a hand in restoring the piece to its presumed original shape (the autograph score was cut into pieces in the nineteenth century for use as greetings cards).' Irritatingly enough, soon after the record had been released, a complete original score was unearthed in the British Library (by Alan Tyson), and it is probable that this Rondo will be re-recorded.

The cycle continued in 1977 with a recording of the 'Jeunehomme' Concerto, K. 271, coupled with Mozart's Concerto for Two Pianos, K. 365, in which Brendel was joined by Imogen Cooper, making her first recording for a major international label. This was at Brendel's own suggestion: Imogen had studied with him for several years, and he regards her as 'far and away one of the best and most natural Mozart players among the younger generation of pianists' – she won the Mozart Memorial Prize in 1969. Their musical tastes are similar, and there was no difficulty in co-ordinating style; as *HiFi News & Record Review* observed, 'The performance is an exemplary one, the two soloists are completely in accord and respond, as Brendel always does, to the stimulus of Marriner's direction.'

The Academy in the recording studio with Alfred Brendel and Imogen Cooper

The double concerto, in common with the majority of Brendel's records over the last five years, was produced for Philips by Volker Strauss. In most Philips recordings, the functions of both balance engineer and producer are combined in a single *Tonmeister*. The dual responsibility for both sound and music is obviously a heavy one, and Brendel has stressed the importance of working with a *Tonmeister* in whom one can have complete confidence. 'Mr Strauss knows me as a musician very well. My ideas are more "horizontal" than "vertical" – my principal concern is for the line and for the development of the music; he shares my priorities, and he knows how I should like the end product to sound. He takes a lot of the burden off my shoulders.'

Over the years, soloist, conductor and *Tonmeister* have come to agree on the proper balance of piano and orchestra for their recordings – in Brendel's words, 'Something similar to good concert-hall balance. The piano should not be isolated from the orchestra, but equally it should not sound as if it is sitting behind the first desk of the fiddles.' They were given the chance to capture actual concert-hall balance when Philips recorded live the whole of the gala concert given in the Palais de la Musique et des Congrès de Strasbourg in aid

150

Jessye Norman
with the Academy
in Strasbourg

of the International Musicians Mutual Aid Fund. It was 27 January 1978, the day of Mozart's 222nd birthday; the programme was built round Mozart's *Idomeneo* and included two arias from the opera performed by Jessye Norman, with *obbligati* supplied by Alfred Brendel and Hugh Maguire. The idea was Erik's: for twenty years he has had his own first edition of the opera, bought with money earned as a producer for L'Oiseau-Lyre – 'At the end of the first month, Mrs Dyer gave me a bundle of pound notes, as a tip, out of a large paper bag – £28, a lot of money then, and I spent it on a first edition of *Idomeneo*.'

The concert was a considerable success. However, the fine acoustic of the Palais de la Musique, ideal for concert performances, has the disadvantage for recordings of reproducing extraneous noises equally vividly, and parts of the recording were not considered to reach a high enough standard to be put on disc. It was decided that some passages would have to be re-recorded, and after a quick supper provided by the organisers of the concert, conductor, soloists and producer returned to the hall. Meanwhile, the Academy had gone *en masse* to dine at a restaurant booked for them by Philips. Arriving at 11 pm, they were surprised to find it empty, but asked

151

for their booking for thirty-five. The manager, gulping slightly, led them to their seats and hastily furnished wine. Two hours and many bottles later, with food still not in evidence, the players realised the extent of his opportunism: they were in the wrong restaurant, and in the kitchen distraught staff were struggling to meet an unexpected order for thirty-five. They began, rather blearily, to express concern for the re-recording, and the food, once presented, was crammed down. At 1 am they headed back to the hall at speed.

The piano concerto K. 503 taken from 'Mozart Live', as the record of the Strasbourg concert was subsequently called, forms part of the Brendel/Academy box set issued in 1979, which assembled all thirteen of the solo concertos so far recorded and won a Wiener Floetenuhr, setting the seal on a partnership which, while of immense practical and musical value to all concerned, has always remained firmly within the Academy tradition of playing for pleasure.

12

The Rule of Three

Multiplication is vexation,
Division is as bad;
The Rule of Three doth puzzle me,
And Practice drives me mad.
Elizabethan manuscript, *c.* 1643

One obvious consequence of the symphonic repertoire opened up
to the Academy by the Philips contract was a substantial increase in
the number of players on regular 'call'. The Academy now have a
card index of sixty or more freelance musicians, each carefully
chosen by the principals, from whom Sylvia puts together the size
of 'Academy' required for each tour, recording or performance.
The protean 'Academy of St Martin in the Fields' have since the
mid-1970s performed music as diverse as Handel trio sonatas and
Schubert symphonies, and the wide scope of their repertoire, with
the consequent variety of forms in which they appear, has caused
some bewilderment as to the orchestra's true identity.

The confusion is more apparent than real. The bedrock of the
Academy remains the 'sixteen band', the fifteen string players plus
harpsichord who over the years have been the orchestra's nucleus
and its main touring group. This group is directed, as always, from
the front desk; since Neville gave up the violin, it has been led by a
number of distinguished players – Iona Brown, Manoug Parikian,
Hugh Maguire, György Pauk, Hugh Bean and Kenneth Sillito. The
sixteen band forms the core of the larger symphonic ensemble,
conducted by Neville, and it is also the group from which are drawn
the players who make up the third 'Academy' – the 'Academy of St
Martin in the Fields Chamber Ensemble'. Belying its unwieldy title,

153

The Academy of St Martin in the Fields Chamber Ensemble – Kenneth Sillito, Malcolm Latchem, Roger Garland, Andrew McGee, Stephen Shingles, Anthony Jenkins, Roger Smith, Denis Vigay

this is a small, flexible configuration, which plays string trios, quintets, sextets and octets, and, if the repertoire demands, varies its composition to include wind and brass – in performances of the Schubert Octet, for example.

With ensembles ranging from three to sixty, consistency of style is ensured by consistency of editing, and identity and performing standards are secured by the Academy's refusal to appear without a significant proportion of their key players. Neville still remembers an occasion in 1970, two years before the orchestra's first world tour, when he was telephoned from Australia by a promoter offering a six-week tour later in the year; the invitation could not have been more timely, coming at a stage when the Academy's international career was just beginning to gain momentum, but a glance at the diary revealed that only one of the principals would be free, and to Neville's extreme chagrin he was obliged to refuse.

Although the greater part of the repertoire recorded with Philips has been for the larger symphonic ensemble, the Academy have also recorded works requiring their smaller configurations – such as the version of the Brandenburg Concertos they made in 1971, with Neville leading from the front desk. The recording was part of an ambitious project hatched by Neville and Thurston Dart in the

mid–1960s over dinner at the Savile Club; Dart had announced his decision to combine playing with his teaching again, and he proposed that he and Neville should record with the Academy the major works of Handel, Bach, Corelli and Vivaldi. Neville recalls the approach on which they agreed – 'The technique of preparation and performance, one which we had ground out over twenty years, was set: Bob was to research for the umpteenth time existing manuscripts and earliest publications, I was to edit them into performing editions; we would review them together in their printed form, perhaps rehearse dubious conclusions with the orchestra, and then go to the studios. A matter of six months per *magnum opus*.'

The first *magnum opus* had been recorded for Decca in February 1968 – Handel's Twelve Grand Concertos, Opus 6. The Dart/Marriner edition conformed strictly to baroque performing practice in using double continuo – harpsichord played by Bob Dart with the concertino group, and organ played by Andrew Davis with the ripieno. There was then an ominous delay of two years before the second *opus*, the Bach Suites, was recorded for Argo in 1970, because Dart had developed what he referred to as 'a little tummy trouble'. His contribution to the recording was, in spite of his developing illness, still most significant. According to Neville:

'He came to the recording sessions as a continuo player, but as usual his insight and constructive criticism managed to transform our performances. His insistence on the quick dance tempi, his willingness to accept the changes of texture we proposed, and his technical resourcefulness in the purely practical business of making records was invaluable.'

The move to Philips brought the opportunity to take the project further with the Brandenburg Concertos, which Neville remembers as being 'perhaps closer to Dart's heart than any other music. He never believed that the immaculate score Bach prepared for the Margrave of Brandenburg was the whole story, and so for years he pursued earlier versions of Bach's work. The bitterness of the attacks on his essays in alternative instrumentation for some of the concerti did not deter him, and by December 1970 he had produced for us yet another version.' Dart's thesis was that the Margrave of Brandenburg, having asked for a cycle of concertos, was presented with a collection of works which were neither composed as a cycle nor strictly 'concertos' as Corelli or Handel would have understood the term, but chamber pieces, scored (except No. 1) for single players throughout, forming 'part of the larger repertory of chamber music which Bach wrote for performance on Sunday evenings during the winter at the ducal court of Cöthen'. Composed for the most part between 1718 and 1720, with No. 6 possibly the product of an even earlier period at Arnstadt (1703–7), when Bach received the Margrave's request they were collected up, polished, revised and copied out in that 'masterpiece of calligraphy', the Dedication Copy, and it was during this revision that several significant changes in instrumentation were made. Dart's intention was to reverse the process and recover the works in their original Cöthen form: among other alterations to the Dedication Copy, he removed the *violino piccolo* from No. 1 and one of the cellos from No. 3, used the original nineteen-bar keyboard cadenza in No. 5 and supplied organ continuo in No. 6. The most radical changes came in Nos. 2 and 4. In No. 2 he substituted a horn for the more usual solo trumpet, on the grounds that the key – F major – is not one in which Bach wrote for the trumpet anywhere else, whereas it *is* the key most often used for his horn parts. In No. 4 he gave the solo wind parts to sopranino recorders, interpreting the *fiauti d'echo* marked in the original score as instruments most closely resembling flageolets, and taking sopranino recorders as their nearest practicable modern equivalent. Erik Smith, who produced the Brandenburg recordings, remembers going up to Cambridge with Neville to discuss the project with Dart over tea in Grantchester: 'Although we weren't convinced that this was the way Bach – "the Old Man" to Bob – intended everything, it was obviously a function of the gramophone record to present this kind of argument; amongst all the conventional Brandenburgs it seemed interesting to offer this idea.'

Dart's 'little tummy trouble' – now cancer in an advanced stage – brought an air of urgency to the sessions which began in the last week of January 1971: Trevor Connah recalls Dart saying, in a heated debate during one session, 'Come on, chaps – let's get on, I haven't much time.' Neville was later to describe those sessions in an article for *Gramophone*: 'Bob looked grey and tired. On Monday he did not make the frequent journeys with us to the control room to listen to playbacks. On Tuesday he had a mattress by the harpsichord so that he could rest between takes. I put him into a car to take him to the London Clinic at 5.30 pm. That was the last time I saw him.' Concertos Nos. 1, 5 and 6 remained incomplete, and Stanley Sadie was later to write of his visit to Dart in hospital shortly before his death, 'He told me how deeply touched he was by the way that London's leading continuo players had rallied round to enable the sessions to be completed.' Dr Sadie observed in his review of the concertos, 'These distinguished players so far submerge the individuality of their own continuo playing that there is no suspicion of inconsistency.' The players were Raymond Leppard, Colin Tilney, George Malcolm and Philip Ledger, who responded at very short notice and considerable personal inconvenience to Molly's urgent appeal for help – a moving tribute to one of the great post-war figures in English music.

Trevor remembers Bob Dart saying halfway through the sessions, 'All my life I've been a voice crying in the wilderness . . . and now after twenty-five years I'm hearing my ideal performance.' He would have been delighted by the furore his 'ideal' Brandenburgs caused. The horn in No. 2 generally found favour with the critics, but the sopranino recorders drew from *Gramophone* the acid

157

Listening to play-backs of the Dart Brandenburg recordings (left to right – Malcolm Russell, Erik Smith, Neville Marriner, Philip Ledger, Kenneth Heath, James Brown, Barry Tuckwell, Neil Black)

comment that they would 'no doubt give pleasure to passing bats', and Edward Greenfield protested, 'When it comes to using sopranino recorders shrieking stratospherically in No. 4 in place of ordinary recorders or flutes, my ears seize up.' Dart's was a provocative scholarship. He never claimed to offer definitive solutions; having expressed his views with maximum vigour, he would, on the uncovering of fresh evidence, revise or repudiate them with equal force and, as George Malcolm recalls, 'from that moment onwards treat anybody who still held the views that he'd been preaching up to the year before as being almost criminal'. Christopher Hogwood suggests, 'His forte was the awkward question which no one else had asked ... it wasn't so much the answers, the dictates he came up with, but the fact that he asked the questions. . . . He was the most marvellous hornet.' It was in this perspective that Stanley Sadie summed up the significance of Dart's Brandenburg Concertos: 'It is only fair to say that some of his theories are somewhat tendentious, that they are not consistently based, that they beg a number of significant editorial questions. But all this is beside the point: Dart, who was a prodigiously gifted musician, thought in terms of what the music actually sounded like; and I think that many people who hear these records will find his views remarkably refreshing.'

Eight years later the Academy were to record their second version of the Concertos – this time with Neville conducting – in an edition based firmly on the Margrave's 'immaculate score'. The conventional combination of solo instruments was used – *violino piccolo*, flute, oboe, trumpet, treble recorders, violin and harpsichord – played by Carl Pini, Jean-Pierre Rampal, Heinz Holliger, André Bernard, Michala Petri, Elisabeth Selin, Henryk Szeryng and George Malcolm respectively.

Opportunities to work with soloists of this calibre, as both symphony and chamber orchestra, have been an important feature of the Academy's relationship with Philips. In addition to the Mozart piano concertos with Alfred Brendel, the orchestra has recorded Bach violin concertos with Henryk Szeryng and Maurice Hasson, recorder concertos with Michala Petri, and in 1978 a unique selection of songs from the 'Arie Amorose' orchestrated by Simon Preston and sung by Dame Janet Baker.

Dame Janet remembers the record as 'one of the most beautiful I've ever done. The "Arie Amorose" are volumes of songs which all students sing in auditions, and I thought this would be a marvellous opportunity to sing them as an adult, with all the years of experience I've had. I'd done the songs with piano or harpsichord all my life –

The 1980 Brandenburg sessions – Michala Petri, Elisabeth Selin and Neville Marriner

and when we got to rehearsal, suddenly there were the different colours: here was Simon's view of them, and very successful it was too. It put a totally different light on the pieces to hear them played by a group of instruments – a marvellous musical occasion. . . . Then Neville's father died that week, and my mother died also that week. The last thing I had done for the record before she died was "Amarilli, mia bella" – very beautiful and poignant. The day after she died I went to the sessions without a clue what was going to happen. I went into the lavatory to practise, and as soon as I tried to start singing, I couldn't, from emotion, and I thought "What am I going to do?" I could see myself standing up in front of all these people and bursting into tears. I went in; all the orchestra knew what both Neville and I had been going through – and somehow I sang perfectly normally, I can hear from the tapes that there's no difference at all. I remember thinking that if I'd had to sing "Amarilli" I would have been finished; fortunately we were on to pieces that were fairly extrovert and unexposed from the emotional point of view. . . . I've always dreaded that moment – something deeply emotional happening to me in the middle of something; I'd always wondered how I'd cope, but somehow because there are other people there who are professionals doing their job you get up and do yours. Here I was amongst friends – everybody understood, and that made it possible to carry on where in public it might not have been. That repertoire, and the way it was done, made it something quite unique in my life.'

Dame Janet and the Academy have over the years achieved a special unanimity of performance. In his review of their record of Bach arias, Geoffrey Crankshaw wrote: 'Gone completely are the tyrannies of bar lines, of square-cut phrasing, of runs mechanically executed. Instead we hear continuous melodic lines floating on a current of purposefully projected accompanying textures (all praise to Marriner for this) and inflected with unerring instinct into verbal significances and into the relationship between theme and melisma.' He also described it as 'the record of a lifetime' for the producer, Christopher Bishop, who had been instrumental in bringing the Academy to record for EMI after the Argo contract became non-exclusive in 1970.

Over the past ten years, the Academy have explored a wide

Above left,
David Munrow;
above right,
*Dame Janet
Baker;* left,
*Christopher
Bishop and
Neville Marriner*

variety of chamber orchestral repertoire on this label. EMI tended initially to use the orchestra principally to accompany solo artists, and under their auspices the Academy have worked not only with King's College Choir, but with Josef Suk, Elly Ameling, David Munrow, Barry Tuckwell, John Wilbraham, Dame Janet Baker and, in a memorable recording of Walton's 'Façade', Fenella Fielding and Michael Flanders. However, with Chris Bishop and his successor John Fraser, the Academy have also made several successful records, as a solo ensemble, of chamber repertoire ranging from the familiar Pachelbel Canon and Holst's 'St Paul's Suite' to the rarely heard orchestral version of Haydn's 'The Seven Last Words'.

In addition to the Academy's work for Philips and EMI, the special relationship with Argo has been maintained – through Mike Bremner until 1975, and since then through his successor Chris Hazell. Chris, who studied composition under Herbert Howells at the Royal College of Music, joined Argo in 1972 after the company had recorded one of his pieces (the children's cantata 'Holy Moses', performed by the King's Singers) and since Mike Bremner's departure for Phonogram Holland, he has produced the majority of the Academy's records for Argo. He remembers in lurid detail the complete Handel Keyboard Concertos, one of the earliest Academy recordings in which he had a hand, and something of a baptism of fire. Several of the concertos, with George Malcolm as the soloist, had already been recorded with Mike Bremner, using the organs of Merton Chapel, Oxford, and St John the Evangelist, Islington; the remainder were to be made at St Mary's, Rotherhithe, in the East End. To much general consternation, this organ, which is one of the few remaining large eighteenth-century instruments in England, was found on the first morning to be tuned to the old-fashioned pitch of A = 456 cycles per second, noticeably sharper than the standard modern pitch of 440. For the violins, re-tuning posed no special problem, but the wind players were, as Chris puts it, 'black in the face from blowing sharp' by the end of the first session, and with the organ becoming ever sharper in the August heat, Malcolm Russell, in charge of the harpsichord, lived in perpetual fear of its disintegrating before his eyes as he tuned it higher and higher.

The sessions were understandably something of a strain, and Chris remembers everyone gathering for sustenance during the intervals at a transport café over the road from the church. 'I went across one morning and there was George: someone had left a copy of the *Daily Mirror* on the table, and he was reading that, he had on an open-necked shirt, he was eating fried egg on toast with a great mug of tea, and he really looked the part. To walk in and think "This man's going to play Handel organ concertos in five minutes" – it just didn't seem right.' But however greasy George's preliminaries, they were effective; *Gramophone* commented: 'George Malcolm is uniformly superb, his technique equal to every demand.'

Another aspect of the Academy's repertoire which particularly interests Chris is twentieth-century English string music. By 1976 the orchestra had already recorded much of the string music of Elgar, Tippett, Vaughan Williams, Britten and Butterworth (released in 1977 as the box set 'A Festival of English Music'), and he set out to fill in some of the remaining gaps, with recordings of Warlock and more Vaughan Williams, including the Oboe Concerto (with the Academy's principal oboe, Celia Nicklin, as soloist) and the rarely heard Romance for Harmonica and Orchestra (played by the virtuoso Tommy Reilly). Music such as this provided something of an antidote. Chris recalls, 'The Academy had

Neville Marriner and Barry Tuckwell

Kenneth Heath's drawing of the offending organ at St Mary's, Rotherhithe

been doing a great deal of baroque playing just before we made our Delius record; after all that pristine playing, to indulge in the music of Delius – "Cooking the First Hero" and so forth – was a pleasure: you could see them swaying in their chairs. I think they miss it from time to time, the chance to have a really good soupy session.' They got the chance again at the end of 1979, when they recorded with Chris a collection of English folk tunes (among them 'John Peel', 'The British Grenadiers' and 'Summer Is Icumen In') which, with Leslie Pearson, he had both arranged and orchestrated. ('Rather a frightening experience,' he remembers, 'but the pieces seemed to come out all right, and it gave me a great kick to be doing something of mine with the Academy'.)

Chris has had to accustom himself not only to the Academy's exacting professional standards, but also to the members' elaborate sense of humour. He was not present at sessions early in 1978 at Kingsway Hall which were disturbed halfway through by the snores of a tramp who had wandered in off the street and fallen

164

asleep, lulled less by the music than by the warmth. However, he had been told at great length of Neville's successful attempts to embarrass Andy McGee with gibes about needy relations, and he should perhaps have anticipated trouble at the Academy's recording of Handel's *Acis and Galatea* in St John's, Smith Square, which he was due to produce the following week. The players had just started the first take of the sessions when the curtains behind them parted and a hideous, ragged, evil-smelling figure lurched out, coughing disgustingly as he weaved an irregular path through the orchestra, meths slopping everywhere. The session collapsed in disarray, with both Acis and Galatea beating a hasty retreat from the platform and the players embracing their instruments protectively; not until several drops of meths had found their way into Neville's coffee did the orchestra realise that the much-abused Andy, with the aid of a superior Hallowe'en mask and his gardening clothes, had exacted some measure of revenge.

In performances of Handel and other baroque composers, the authenticity of the Academy's style has always stemmed from their performing editions. These were prepared by Neville until the early 1970s when the time available to him for research was curtailed both by the Academy's increasing workload and by the development of his independent conducting career. The Academy therefore began

Andy's revenge

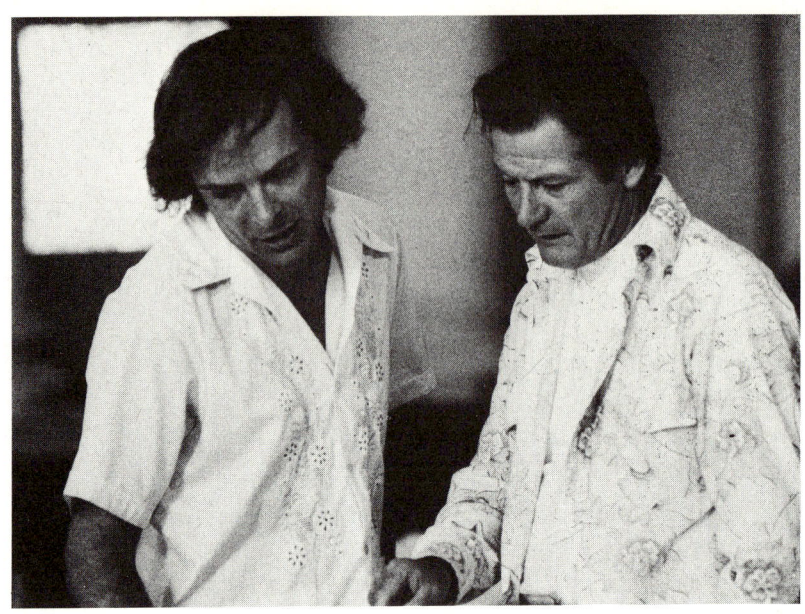

Christopher Hogwood and Neville Marriner

to employ musicologists to prepare the music for their baroque recordings (although Neville remained responsible for all other editions), and in the years since Bob Dart's death they have used editions by Christopher Hogwood, Jane Glover, Andrew Davis and Nicholas Kraemer. Nicholas remembers being delighted at Neville's invitation to edit Handel's Concerti a Due Cori and the overtures to *Arianna* and *Agrippina*, recorded for EMI in 1975. During his years in the Academy, he had had impressed upon him repeatedly the diligence of previous editors – from Michael Bowie and Simon Streatfeild to Bob Dart – and their hours spent burrowing in the British Museum; not to be outdone, he hastened to the archives. As he tells it, on his first visit the archives were shut, but from the next attempt he emerged dusty but triumphant – to find that the excavated scores were identical in all but the least interesting details with the readily available printed editions. Some allowance should, however, be made for the modesty of this account, since *Records & Recordings*, for one, described the new versions of *Arianna* and *Agrippina* as 'an outstanding contribution to the Handel catalogue'.

Apart from Hande's *Jephtha* and a new set of the Opus 6 concertos (both edited by Jane Glover) and Bach's 'Art of Fugue' (co-edited by Neville and Andrew Davis), the majority of the Academy's baroque editions since 1971 have been prepared by Christopher Hogwood. He has worked for the Academy on editions of Corelli, Handel, Bach, Telemann and Boyce, but their most significant collaboration has been on the concertos of Vivaldi. The baroque project which Neville and Bob Dart had discussed at the Savile Club had included Vivaldi's major works; Dart was already editing one of these works – 'L'Estro Armonico' (Opus 3) – when he died, and Neville passed on to Christopher some of the ideas he had sketched out, including the characteristically Dartian suggestion that the published version of 'L'Estro' was not at all what Vivaldi had intended. Christopher was intrigued: 'It was the first time I'd ever seen a slick modern orchestra, as I saw the Academy, interested in what Vivaldi may have actually wanted, and in the evidence for it. I was interested to see what it would be like to make a performing edition for the Academy' – and in particular, how easy it would be to accommodate their highly distinctive style to his own conception of the historical style. The 'L'Estro Armonico' sessions, held in October 1972, were the first to which Christopher had come as editor, and he remembers: 'Not knowing how the Academy felt about conductors, I tended to say things like "Just follow me, I'll show you how it's done." They did it, but Neville did come up afterwards and say "Er ... I think it might be a good thing just to *discuss* things as we go along ... and you probably don't need to beat time".'

The association continued with a two-record set of Vivaldi's concertos for wind and strings, his Opus 4, 'La Stravaganza' (for which the Academy were awarded the Grand Prix du Disc Classique Canada in 1976), and Opus 9, 'La Cetra'. The entire project – Opus 3, Opus 4, the concertos for wind and strings, and Opus 9 – was issued, with the best-selling 'The Four Seasons' of 1970, as a ten-record box set in 1978, to celebrate the 300th anniversary of Vivaldi's birth. In their work together, Neville, Christopher and the Academy had done much to advance the search for a true Vivaldian style. This search has now been taken further by the increasing use of 'authentic' instruments of the baroque period (in 1981 Christopher re-recorded 'L'Estro Armonico' with his own

*The Philips contract (*left to right – *Erik Smith, Stephen Wright, Ernst van der Vossen, Neville Marriner)*

Academy of Ancient Music), but the Academy's recordings of Vivaldi were innovative, particularly in their use of mixed continuo. In 'La Stravaganza', for example, harpsichord was used for the *tutti*, organ for the solo passages, and chitarrone (a large lute-like instrument, with a softer sound than the harpsichord) in the quietest moments; in 'L'Estro Armonico', the occasional use of theorbo or bassoon brought the bass continuo line into vivid focus. Some critics consider Vivaldi to be the composer to whom the Academy's approach is best suited: as Geoffrey Crankshaw wrote, 'Energy – always energy – this is the key to a man of supreme fascination.'

In 1975 the Academy signed a second five-year contract with Philips – the largest ever concluded with a chamber orchestra. The negotiations between Philips, Neville and the Academy brought into sharp focus the changes that had been gradually taking place within the orchestra – changes which were reflected in the resulting contractual arrangements. Neville signed two contracts with Philips: one, with Stephen Shingles and Kenneth Heath, in their capacity as directors of the Academy; the other an individual contract separate from the Academy, to conduct and record with symphony orchestras associated with Philips. This separate contract marked an important stage in the development of his conducting career, and over the next two or three years he came to limit his work with the Academy to recordings of the larger repertoire involving thirty-five or more players. The direction of the orchestra in recordings of baroque and other chamber works passed in consequence to Iona Brown, a member of the Academy since the mid-1960s and their leader on several European tours since 1974. Her appointment from within the orchestra's own ranks supplied the element of continuity in change which has been an important feature of the Academy's success. It had other advantages, as a Buenos Aires critic pointed out (in a review translated *con brio* by a South American friend of the orchestra) – 'If the United Kingdom is able to have the tremendous luxor (in accordance to some persons, not a luxor but a risk) of having a lady as Prime Minister, it's obvious that also an English orchestra can be directed by a lady. In the case of Iona Brown, you don't know if she's the director because of her musical talent or because of her beauty, since she's first level in both.'

Iona's solo work on the earlier Vivaldi sets had attracted excellent reviews, so it was appropriate that her first recording as director of the Academy should be 'La Cetra'. She was also the principal soloist on this recording, and *HiFi News & Record Review* commented: 'Miss Brown's faultless technique and superb tone add a great deal of lustre to the already brilliant solo figuration.' Under Iona's direction, the Academy have toured the world performing 'The Four Seasons', a favourite of concert promoters in five continents, and in 1980 they recorded the interpretation they had developed over hundreds of performances, with Iona taking the solo part. The

Iona Brown directing the recording of 'La Cetra'

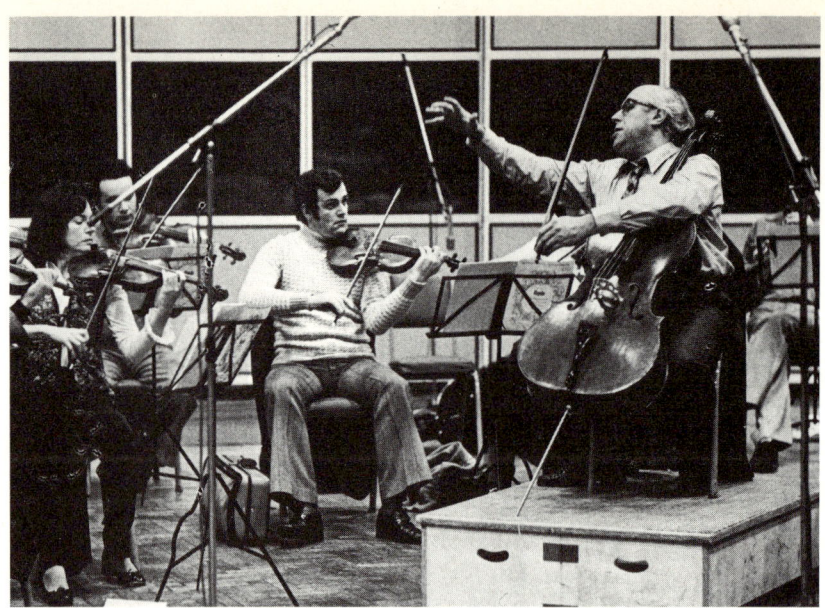

Mstislav Rostropovich directing the recording of Haydn's Cello Concertos (Carmel Kaine, Josef Fröhlich and Roger Garland in the background)

continuo line for this version was supplied by Nicholas Kraemer, who has his own reasons for remembering the slow movement of 'Autumn': it was one of those special occasions when one take suffices – fortunately for Nicholas, since, drenched by a cloud-burst at Hyde Park Corner on his way to St John's, Smith Square, he was obliged to play clad only in underpants and a borrowed jacket.

The most recent recording in the Academy's Vivaldi series has been Opus 10, six concertos for *flauto traverso* played by the young Danish recorder virtuoso Michala Petri, again with Iona directing. Iona's past work with soloists has included leading the Academy in a recording of Haydn cello concertos with Mstislav Rostropovich as both soloist and director, and directing them in a recording of eighteenth-century harp concertos with Marisa Robles (described by *Gramophone* as 'arguably the most life-enhancing harpist around'). With George Malcolm, Iona ventured into twentieth-century music in Poulenc's 'Concert Champêtre' (for harpsichord and orchestra) and the Concerto in G minor for organ, strings and timpani, which posed the most serious technical problems she had ever encountered. Iona sees her principal responsibility as director as being 'to liberate the playing . . . to inspire confidence and create a situation in which everyone can give their best' – but the circumstances in which the Organ Concerto was recorded conspired to make her task an arduous one. The recording was made in the Chapel of St John's College, Cambridge, and Tristan Fry, the

Iona Brown directing the recording of Poulenc's Organ Concerto

timpani soloist, recalls: 'The orchestra was in the ante-chapel – but the keyboard is halfway down the chapel on the left of the nave, and the pipes are right down the other end. It was simply impossible to hear the organ clearly: if it had just been distant, that would have been one thing – but it was far away *and* mangled. . . . With percussion instruments, you've only really got one go at an entry; for nearly every other instrument it is possible to creep in somehow, but on the timps you've really got to go for it – and in that concerto there's very little cover: unless you're dead on time and absolutely with the organ, it sounds *awful*. So George, Iona and I all had to wear earphones: for the rest of the band, who couldn't hear anything clearly, it was blind faith – an absolute madhouse.'

Like Neville, Iona has a busy career independent of the Academy as an international soloist. She made her début at the Proms in 1964, playing the Mendelssohn Violin Concerto under the baton of Sir Malcolm Sargent, and she has frequently appeared as the soloist on Academy recordings – with Neville conducting for Vaughan Williams's 'The Lark Ascending' and the Beethoven Violin Concerto, and in the dual role of director and soloist for Mozart's Violin Concertos K. 216 and K. 218. She has also recorded the concerto composed specially for her by David Blake – who was inspired to write the piece after hearing her with the Academy Chamber Ensemble in a performance of the Mendelssohn Octet.

It was pressure from her solo engagements which in 1980 obliged

Iona to step down from the leadership of the Chamber Ensemble, although she continues to lead the Academy in other figurations. The Ensemble had originally been founded in 1967 to perform the Mendelssohn Octet, at the suggestion of Eleanor Warren of the BBC, who preferred the work performed by a *genuine* ensemble of eight players, and not just two quartets fighting it out. The experiment was a success, and with Hugh Maguire as its leader, the group recorded the work for Argo in 1968. Though it was to make no further recordings until 1977, the Ensemble made sporadic broadcasts and live appearances in Britain throughout the early 1970s. The most impressive, in theatrical terms at least, was in 1973 at Levens Hall, a beautifully preserved Jacobean house in the Lake District, with its unique seventeenth-century topiary garden. By the interval of the concert it had become clear that the second viola, incapacitated by influenza, was not going to be able to return for the second half; so Trevor Connah slid across from fourth violin to second viola, leaving his fiddle for Roy Gillard, who stepped up from the audience where he had been sitting peacefully in civilian clothes – Trevor remembers the onlookers, unaware that Roy was an Academy regular, giving him a tremendous ovation.

The elegant rooms and magnificent furnishings of houses like Levens provide an ideal setting for chamber performances, and in the following year the Ensemble made the first of its several appearances at the Festival of Great Irish Houses. Held annually in June, the festival, organised by David Laing, is centred on four eighteenth-century houses – Castletown House, Headfort, Carton House, and Slane Castle. The programme for each concert is chosen and presented as though it were an entertainment provided by the family of the house for their guests, and the atmosphere is captured vividly in Philippa Garner's paintings – of the Ensemble in concert in the candlelit Long Gallery of Castletown House, and in rehearsal in Lexlip Castle. In 1976, the Ensemble played in Holkham Hall, Norfolk, to an audience which included Her Majesty The Queen Mother; the programme ended with a Brahms sextet, and Malcolm Latchem remembers Her Majesty at tea afterwards speaking with some authority about the music, and expressing a particular fondness for Brahms.

The repertoire for string octet is limited (the octets of Mendels-

The Academy performing the Mendelssohn Octet in 1967 (clockwise from centre – Hugh Maguire, Neville Marriner, Iona Brown, Trevor Connah, Kenneth Essex, Stephen Shingles, Kenneth Heath, Denis Vigay)

sohn, Shostakovich and Spohr being the ones most frequently performed) and the Ensemble soon found itself appearing as a sextet or quintet as well. As Malcolm (the Ensemble's second violin and since 1977 its manager) points out, with the sextets of Brahms and Martinu and the quintets of Mozart, Schubert and Boccherini to draw on, repertoire ceases to be a problem; and the players have always had the advantage of working together regularly, unlike many sextets and quintets, who may be assembled for one particular occasion and expected to perform as a unit after scant rehearsal. The Ensemble has always been composed of the principal players from the Academy's sixteen band, and its membership has changed with that of the larger orchestra. However, as in the Academy proper, continuity of style and approach has been maintained, and by 1977 the membership had settled down. Its composition – Iona Brown, Malcolm Latchem, Roger Garland and Andrew McGee, violins; Stephen Shingles and Anthony Jenkins, violas; Denis Vigay and Roger Smith, cellos – was to remain largely unchanged until 1980, when Kenneth Sillito took over from Iona as leader of the Ensemble, combining it with his work as first violin in the Gabrieli Quartet.

Since 1973, the Ensemble has undertaken regular European tours, principally in Germany. In the early days, its appearances formed part of concerts given by the Academy as a whole: the Ensemble normally played the second half, liberating the rest of the orchestra, one of whom remembers with great glee the players from the back desks splashing happily in a swimming-pool outside the hall where the principals were sweating through the Mendelssohn Octet. However, its growing reputation encouraged Hans Ulrich Schmid to offer it an independent tour, and since 1975 it has visited Germany at least once a year.

The Chamber Ensemble is important to the Academy, because it ensures that despite the growing symphonic repertoire, the principal players do not lose touch with the chamber music approach which has always distinguished the orchestra. The Ensemble extends the range of opportunities for 'Academy' concerts – many smaller festivals or promoters who would find it hard to finance the larger orchestra are happy to have the Chamber Ensemble instead – and in recent years, it has significantly enlarged the Academy's recorded repertoire. In 1977 Iona led the Ensemble in a recording for Philips of the Schubert Octet – and the success of this record, which won a Grand Prix de l'Academie Charles Cros in 1979, encouraged Philips to use the Ensemble for other projects. Since then it has recorded the Beethoven Septet and all of Boccherini's guitar quintets (with Pepe Romero), and, after ten years of performance, re-recorded the Mendelssohn Octet: Malcolm reflects, 'We must have played it two hundred and fifty times – but this performance was quite new; the work is one of the great masterpieces, but it's fresh every time.' Over the next two or three years the Ensemble will be recording the Spohr Octet, all the Mozart divertimenti for strings and two horns, both Brahms quintets, and the complete chamber works of Handel (to be issued as part of Philips's complete Handel edition for his tri-centenary in 1985).

'The Rule of Three doth puzzle me' – and in the early years of the symphonic and chamber ensembles, the Academy's versatility had its drawbacks: as Malcolm ruefully remarks, 'It was not unknown for promoters to ask "Where's the orchestra?" when the Chamber Ensemble arrived for a concert.' However, in 1975, when Neville was appointed for three years as the Artistic Co-ordinator of the South Bank Summer Music Festival, the Academy got the chance to dispel confusion and appear before audiences in the full range of their performing ensembles, playing music from all aspects of their repertoire. The South Bank Festival, held every August since 1968, is organised by the Greater London Council to provide two weeks of intimate music-making under the guidance of a distinguished musician: Neville's predecessors were Daniel Barenboim (1968–70), Gerald Moore (in 1971, for a special fortnight of 'South Bank Summer Song'), and André Previn (1972–4).

The Academy provided the basis of the programmes for each year's festival, and the choice of repertoire clearly illustrates the extent to which the orchestra had developed from its baroque beginnings. The themes running through the first festival were the chamber music of Brahms (a private tribute to Pierre Monteux, who as a young man had played quartets with Brahms), and the emergence of the concerto form. In their 1959 concert series at St Martin's, the Academy had illustrated the development of the baroque concerto; by 1975 they were equipped to illustrate the growth of the form in general, from its concerto grosso beginnings right up to the contemporary virtuoso solo concerto. In 1976 the music of Mendelssohn and Schumann predominated, and in the following year the 150th anniversary of Beethoven's death was commemorated. This final year of Neville's appointment was also the year of the Queen's Silver Jubilee, and with the festival forming part of the official celebrations, he pursued an English music theme.

During August, London is crowded with tourists, and during these three festivals multi-national audiences saw the many facets of the Academy. They saw the players with Neville conducting them in both symphonic and chamber orchestral works, and in piano concertos with Alfred Brendel; with Iona as director and soloist; displaying their strength in depth as the Chamber Ensemble and playing chamber music with guest artists (Steve Shingles particularly recalls performing the Beethoven Serenade with Salvatore Accardo and Lynn Harrell and a Mendelssohn quintet with the Vermeer Quartet); they saw Neville as a symphonic conductor with the New Philharmonia Orchestra, and the Academy performing with some of their closest friends – Dame Janet Baker, George Malcolm, Robert Tear, Alfred Brendel, and the King's Singers. And to complete the vexation of multiplication, another 'Academy' made its appearance – the 'Chorus of the Academy of St Martin in the Fields'.

13

How Charmingly Sweet You Sing

The Academy Chorus is a child of expediency – and Hans Ulrich
Schmid can justifiably claim to be its midwife. The English choral
tradition is much admired in Germany, and it was Herr Schmid's
office that recognised the potential of a tour made by the Academy
with an English choir. With the orchestra's enthusiastic support,
Konzertdirektion Schmid worked hard with promoters to arrange a
series of performances of Bach's B Minor Mass for January 1975.
The original intention was that the Academy should bring with
them a smallish choir (to match the touring strength of the
orchestra) composed of singers drawn from one of London's existing choirs. The proposal was put to the leading choirs in turn, but it
became clear that none was prepared to appear at less than full
strength, double or triple the required number. The tour, which had
taken more than a year to arrange, was on the verge of collapse
when Sylvia Holford, herself an experienced choral singer and
administrator, suggested that the Academy should supply their
own choir – and volunteered to found it.

The idea of an Academy Chorus quickly took root, and
developed far beyond the immediate requirements of the 1975 tour.
To have an affiliated chorus would open up a marvellous new
repertoire to the orchestra: to have their *own* chorus, specifically
trained to complement the Academy, would ensure a similarity of
approach and style in the works tackled. Sylvia, required to find a
chorus master willing and able to produce a choir with the
Academy sound, turned to Laszlo Heltay, in whose choirs she had
often sung and worked. Laszlo, who studied under Kodaly and
Bardos at the Franz Liszt Academy in Budapest (in the company of
Istvan Kertesz, Tamas Vasary, Peter Frankl and György Pauk), had

176

come to England in 1956 after the Hungarian Uprising. After several months spent going to language school in the morning to learn English and cleaning offices in Oxford Street in the evening to survive, he went as a postgraduate to Oxford ('I passed the English entrance examination with the lowest possible mark') where he formed two choirs – the Kodaly Choir of Merton College, of which he was the Director of Music for a time, and the Collegium Musicum Oxoniense which Sylvia was to run. This was followed by three years in New Zealand, as associate conductor of the New Zealand Radio Orchestra and conductor of the New Zealand Opera, after which he returned to England in 1967 to join the Phoenix Opera. In the same year he founded the Brighton Festival Chorus, and his freelance career as choirmaster and conductor began to flourish.

The Academy and Chorus of St Martin in the Fields

When Sylvia put the Academy's proposal to Laszlo early in 1974 he accepted with alacrity, and together they began the process of selecting the seventy-two singers for the January tour. From the first Laszlo took at face value the suggestion that the Chorus was to sing as the Academy played. He went to the orchestra's concerts, listened to their records, formed his own conception of their style, and chose his singers accordingly. He saw the Academy sound primarily as clean, precise and well-integrated, and so concentrated

177

Hans Ulrich
Schmid

less on individually startling voices than on good voices he knew
would blend. For this reason, many of the singers he chose were
amateurs: 'With professionals you have the task of overcoming
their individual training – the different techniques they employ, the
amount of vibrato and so on: they may sing brilliantly, but it's not
choral singing.'

Laszlo was looking for voices that were free of intrusive vibrato,
fresh and youthful. Katy Woolf, who joined the Chorus in 1977 as
an alto, and was recruited shortly afterwards to help Sylvia as
Concerts Manager with special responsibility for the Chorus, has
remarked, 'Laszlo's ear for who will fit and who won't is uncanny:
even when somebody turns up for audition with a filthy cold, he can
tell if they're any good underneath – and when they arrive, cold-
free, for the first rehearsal, they're wonderful.' Voices were thus
required to be of a certain weight and timbre; Laszlo once remarked,
'I could build an excellent choir from the rejects – but not to suit the
Academy.'

The other principal requirement was the ability to sight-read
accurately. The Academy Chorus was never intended to be full-
time; like the orchestra, it was to be called together as and when
required, to perform a particular work in concert or on record. Its
rehearsal time was correspondingly limited, and the ability to learn

Members of the Academy Chorus (Sylvia Holford, extreme left, front row)

quickly was essential. Katy, now a seasoned Chorus member, recalls her first rehearsal, where the majority of those present had already performed the piece and she was among the few new-comers: 'It was like the first day at school. I felt incredibly junior, and spent most of the rehearsal three pages behind, hanging on for dear life – I'd never been in a choir which expected so much from you straight away.'

Through long and painstaking auditions, Laszlo and Sylvia built up a card index of 'possibles', and many of the singers called for that first tour were to become the hard core of the Chorus. As in the orchestra, there was a nucleus of regulars, supplemented as the repertoire demanded – 'heavy' basses for the Mozart Requiem but not for Handel's *Israel in Egypt*, a preponderance of male altos for Bach but not for Haydn, extra sopranos and altos for the B Minor Mass with its doubled upper lines, and so on. The size of the Chorus was to range from forty-eight (for the smaller Handel works) to seventy-two – the strength required for that first German tour.

With the Chorus assembled for the first time, preparation of the work began – and a procedure was evolved which has been repeated for each piece the Chorus has performed. First Neville and Laszlo meet to discuss the piece and to prepare a performing edition. Laszlo has described this preliminary stage: 'We don't leave the room until

179

we are absolutely agreed on how we should tackle the work. Sometimes I take his views and sometimes he takes mine – our ideas are very similar, and there is argument but no real conflict.' It is at this stage that the styles of choir and orchestra are aligned and marked into the vocal and orchestral scores. As they go through the score, Neville explains how he wants each passage to sound and marks the style – bowings, phrasings, tempi and dynamics – into the instrumental score; simultaneously Laszlo marks the vocal line to match. 'If he adds an ornament to the first violins, I add it to the soprano parts; if he asks for détaché bowing, I ask for detached singing. Conversely, if I point out that a certain phrase must end for the Chorus on a short note because the last syllable of the word is short, then Neville marks in a short bow-stroke for the orchestra – and so on. There are very few choirs whose performance is matched so closely, note for note, with that of the orchestra.'

With the blend of texture, balance and phrasing considered and agreed, vocal rehearsals, taken by Laszlo with piano accompaniment, could begin. From the start he made it clear to the Chorus that the aim was an instrumental sound, by using in his rehearsals terminology that was frequently orchestral – 'Sing this note off the string', 'This phrase starts on an up-bow' – and often geared specifically to Neville's musical predilections – 'That's a long crotchet', 'This is a short quaver'. As in the orchestra there was to be little vibrato, no sudden bulging dynamics, and no scooping after notes, with clarity the main priority and the striving for precision extended even to pronunciation: 'German composers' Latin we sing in the German way, Italian composers' Latin in the Italian way.'

These requirements were exacting and rehearsals were arduous – and mandatory. Laszlo always insists that everyone should attend every rehearsal: he finds it impossible to gauge the balance for the performance if attendance at rehearsals is not regular. Nevertheless, despite the hard work, Sylvia looks back on those first rehearsals in 1974 with real pleasure. 'It was terribly exciting: Laszlo took seventy-two strangers – they all knew him, but they didn't know each other – and moulded them into a chorus in three rehearsals flat.' His approach to the Chorus did much to inspire the loyalty and sense of identity which has characterised it ever since. His ear for the source of a mistake is uncomfortably acute, but as one of his tenors,

*Laszlo Heltay
and Neville
Marriner*

Robert Key, points out, he never criticises offenders harshly in public: 'He may come round afterwards and tell you you're making a horrible noise, but he never humiliates you.' His professionalism and respect for each member of the choir have endeared him to them: Chris Hazell once remarked, 'In a chorus there is very little opportunity for the individual to show himself, and to keep people both entertained and interested is hard – Laszlo does it by sheer enthusiasm and by instilling in his singers the sense that they are the *best*.'

The Chorus, then, were thoroughly prepared by the time that they met Neville and the Academy for the first full rehearsal of the B Minor Mass – and were somewhat affronted when Neville insisted on giving them the notes on which to make their respective entries in the Kyrie. As Sylvia puts it, 'There's nothing more ruinous to the atmosphere than to be given a note just before you start, so we would always pick it up from the tuning of the orchestra and start out of the blue – but Neville, with his experience of choral conducting confined to the Dartington Summer School Choir, couldn't believe we could do it.' Both parties slightly shaken by this gap in communication, Neville and the Chorus proceeded with the rehearsal. His technique for conducting singers, developed at Dartington, remained unorthodox; as Eleanor Boulter, one of the

181

original altos, commented, 'The first time you hear the sopranos told to "bring in the washing, it's flapping about", you do blink, and it can be unnerving to be called a second fiddle' – and she remembers rehearsals with Neville conducting and Laszlo padding round behind the choir hissing advice and encouragement. However, as the Chorus watched Neville's handling of the orchestra, and observed how vocal and instrumental lines were fitted together, their misgivings melted away.

The first German tour was described by Hans Ulrich Schmid as quite simply 'a sensation', with reviewers united in their admiration of the technical skill displayed by Chorus and orchestra. However, being used to a far weightier style of Bach performance, they were divided on the question of interpretation, some expressing reservations about an approach which they felt to be frivolous. The *Rheinische Post*, for example, wrote, 'One cannot help feeling that Marriner had in mind more of a musical stage production than an interpretation,' and they complained of excessive speeds and exaggerated articulation in 'an emphasised unconventional performance ... which was often somewhat strange in style.' *Der Tagesspiegel*, however, remarked with pleasure on the pains taken by Neville and Laszlo to achieve a unified performance: 'The voices were produced so clearly, lightly and precisely, like instruments, that at times one could hardly distinguish who was "singing", the oboe or the tenors.' And to the eminent critic H. H. Stuckenschmidt, writing in the *Frankfurter Allgemeine Zeitung*, a performance in which the Chorus astounded the audience with 'a quick, soft staccato one has hardly ever heard before', was 'an important new step ... made towards a musically true Bach interpretation'.

Audiences were of one mind about the Academy Chorus. Sylvia has particularly vivid memories of the first concert: 'It's impossible to describe how exciting it was. I kept thinking of all those months of planning and auditioning, all Laszlo's hard work, Neville's first concert with his own choir – and then at the interval the applause simply *exploded*. We were bowled over ... but then when we came back for the second half they simply clapped and clapped ... and we sat down and they kept clapping, so we stood up again and they were still clapping – it was very moving.' And it was repeated for the rest of the tour, with audiences on their feet cheering, even

PRO MUSICA '74 '75

FREITAG, DEN 10. JANUAR 1975 · 20 UHR · KUPPELSAAL DER STADTHALLE

5. Konzert · Solisten-Zyklus B

J.S.Bach
Messe h-moll
The Academy and Chorus
of St. Martin-in-the-Fields

CHORDIREKTOR: LASZLO HELTAY

ARLEEN AUGER SOPRAN
HANNA SCHWARZ ALT
ROBERT TEAR TENOR
HANS SOTIN BASS

IONA BROWN VIOLINE	FLÖTE **WILLIAM BENNETT**
TESS MILLER OBOE	HORN **BARRY TUCKWELL**
MICHAEL CHAPMAN FAGOTT	TROMPETE **JOHN WILBRAHAM**

EINSTUDIERUNG U. LEITUNG **NEVILLE MARRINER**

Kartenvorverkauf im Pro Musica-Büro, Schmiedestr. 8 (Eingang Döll – Das Haus für Musik) Tel. 17673

*A poster from the first
German tour*

rushing the stage at one concert. Hans Ulrich Schmid remembers the tour as 'unforgettable, one of my most treasured memories'. It was also exhausting, with four performances of a long and gruelling work on consecutive days in different cities, and there was the occasional nerve-racking moment. Herr Schmid remembers one particular concert: 'Iona Brown was playing the violin *obbligato* in one of the arias when her string broke – her neighbour instantly handed her his fiddle, and she finished the bar without a break. I have often been asked how long the Academy rehearse this kind of cabaret act!'

The B Minor Mass expedition set the pattern for future touring with the Chorus. Even Sylvia, the Chorus's most loyal defender, concedes that a touring group which can number over a hundred people does pose logistical problems. The worst of the practical difficulties are solved by treating the Academy and Chorus as two parties. The singers are sent ahead of the orchestra whenever possible, to check in first at the hotel. A double-decker bus is hired for them to accompany the orchestra's more modest single-decker and, on arrival at each new venue, the management (Sylvia, Katy, and, in the early days, Julia Williams, another helper recruited from the altos) reach the concert hall well in advance of both choir and

183

Double- and single-deckers (Colin Sauer in foreground)

orchestra to check on seating arrangements, changing-room accommodation, lighting, acoustic and the other details that, if neglected, can sabotage a performance.

Even these precautions are not foolproof, and Chorus tours have produced some memorable near-disasters – such as the flight in January 1976 to Berlin, where Academy and Chorus were to perform Handel's *Messiah*. Travelling *en masse*, they virtually filled an entire aeroplane, the first to leave Heathrow that afternoon after a day of severe gales. Robert Key remembers the flight from Hamburg to Berlin as one of the most silent he has ever had with the Academy: the plane was obliged to fly at a regulation height which put it at the base of the storm clouds, and by the time it made the steep banking turn necessary to avoid an East German radio tower on its descent to Berlin, orchestra and choir were pea-green and more than a little anxious. But as Robert relates, 'It was an absolutely perfect landing ... and John Wilbraham got out his trumpet and started to play the ''Hallelujah'' Chorus: the whole choir joined in – we sang it from beginning to end – and the pilot came back, thanked us very much, and asked for two tickets for the evening performance.' Laszlo has particular reason to remember the aftermath of that flight; its late arrival left him only half an hour to

184

rehearse the Chorus and raise the spirits of the airsick singers. His initial attempts were less than successful: Robert recalls, 'After he had given us the full works – breathing exercises, jokes, everything – he was beginning to get desperate. So on the spur of the moment he stood on his head – and that's what he was doing when Herr Schmid walked in to see if "the artists" were ready.'

Left, John Wilbraham; right, Albrecht Deininger

For many of the Chorus, amateur singers with full-time jobs elsewhere, the Academy tours of Germany (and, more recently, Spain) are their holidays. Every year, before the first concert of the German tour, the choir members gather for a showing of the holiday snaps taken the previous year by Herr Albrecht Deininger, who supplies the organ for Chorus tours and travels with the Academy in Germany to tune and maintain it. The tours have a festive atmosphere: as Eleanor Boulter says, 'It hardly feels like work – a succession of good hotels, excellent company, the chance of some really exhilarating music-making – and six Academy concerts thrown in.'

Hospitality is offered as generously to the Chorus as to the orchestra; the members have much enjoyed the parties thrown for them by Hans Ulrich Schmid and, on one occasion, by Johannes Wasmuth at the Kaiser's railway station outside Bonn. (Bahnhof

Bahnhof Rolandseck Rolandseck, built for the Kaiser's private use on the way to his summer residence, has been converted in part by Herr Wasmuth into an arts centre, and houses a fine collection of paintings and sculpture.)

Sightseeing is restricted during the day by rehearsals (although the more determined take every opportunity), but after the concerts, a variety of revels is arranged. The Chorus bus has a saloon on the lower deck with a table bisecting it, where lavish 'meals-on-wheels' are prepared. Hotels are the scene of constant parties: to the Reverend Christopher Walker, for four years a curate at St Martin's and one of the Chorus's regular baritones, fell the doubtful privilege of the largest room in a Brussels hotel – soon known as 'the Vestry', and the focal point for all social activities. A prime mover in the Chorus's jaunts is Tristan Fry, both timpanist to the Academy and percussionist to Sky, whose records regularly appear in charts throughout the world. It is rumoured (wrongly) that Tristan instigated the trip to see the ladies wrestling in mud, but beyond question that he masterminded the excursion to the Bierkeller in Hamburg where, for the price of a *Stein* each, the resident band bedecked in *Lederhosen* allow themselves to be conducted in a

186

painfully limited selection of drinking-songs. Nicholas Kraemer remembers bitterly, 'John Wilbraham, being a brass player, knew all the tunes and got them to do it properly, but by the time I got out there, it was 2 am, they'd been doing it for seven hours, and it was what you might call an uphill struggle. I tried every nuance' – (Nicholas recently conducted the English Chamber Orchestra in Carnegie Hall to a packed house and considerable critical acclaim) – 'but they were very, very bored, and the bill was colossal.' Both Nicholas and Tristan were present at the disco in a Spanish monastery town where, 'We were vastly diverted by the sight of the young men of the town, dressed up as monks for a local festival, busily dancing in their cassocks to the music – until the monks started a knife fight and we had to beat a hasty retreat through the kitchens.'

In general, relations between choir and orchestra are of the friendliest; but on tour there is a tendency to bunching, with brass and timpani gravitating towards the Chorus bus, where barber's-shop quartets at the front and conviviality at the back combine to generate a degree of boisterousness. The rest of the orchestra, and the odd choral refugee, remain sedately in their single-decker, because it is usual, at the end of the tour, when brass, wind and Chorus go home,

*Sightseeing –
Morys Davies
and Robert Key at
Checkpoint
Charlie*

for the sixteen band to go on for a further week or fortnight's touring. There are occasional grumbles about the Chorus – as Celia Nicklin puts it, 'It is so *aggravating* when you're used to all fitting in the same lift on tour, and suddenly there are a hundred people milling around at reception and queuing for breakfast.' The larger-scale parties in hotel rooms have been outlawed – principally, it is fair to say, as a result of complaints not from the players but from the bus drivers; and on a few occasions the subject of late-night revelry has had to be discussed in depth. But as Sylvia explains, 'Audiences have very high expectations now; we have to put the music first – and there is little point in taking on tour people who can hardly *speak* the morning after, let alone sing.'

Riotousness apart, the Academy are proud of their Chorus; the players respect its technical skill and its careful adaptation to the Academy sound, and they appreciate both its enthusiasm and its loyalty. Denis Vigay has remarked, 'Having a Chorus has opened up some wonderful new works to us – and the singers take such pains, they have such zest. They've given us the most whole-hearted support' – and choral birthdays are often saluted with a lavishly ornamented rendition of 'Happy Birthday' as a small demonstration of gratitude from the musicians who have been described as 'the aristocrats of European string-playing'.

In the best Academy tradition, choral tours serve a double pur-

pose – that of giving orchestra and Chorus valuable public exposure and at the same time preparing works for recording. As Laszlo points out, a concert performance brings a work to life in a way that mere rehearsals can not: unsuspected difficulties come to light, the piece is presented from a new perspective, and the foundation for the recording is laid. The B Minor Mass was recorded in 1977 for Philips, with Margaret Marshall, Dame Janet Baker, Robert Tear and Samuel Ramey as the soloists. For this recording Academy and Chorus were well served by their *Tonmeister*, Vittorio Negri – about whom Geoffrey Crankshaw wrote, after attending sessions at St John's, Smith Square, 'I was struck by the air of dedicated enthusiasm manifested by all concerned. Negri's absorption of the Bach idiom was acknowledged by all, and his considerate but painstakingly detailed attention to balance, nuance and clarity did much to release the artists' own great gifts.'

During the B Minor Mass recording – in the foreground, Neil Black, Neville Marriner, Dame Janet Baker and Vittorio Negri

The first choral recording, however, had been made the previous year when, after a tour of Germany in January 1976, orchestra and Chorus had recorded what was to prove their greatest success, with sales approaching 250,000 by the end of 1979 – Handel's *Messiah*. It is the performance of which Laszlo is most proud, and it was one of the two issues selected by Harley Usill to celebrate Argo's twenty-fifth anniversary in 1977 (the other one being a spoken-word issue – *Watership Down* read by Roy Dotrice, with the Academy's recording

Laszlo Heltay and Chris Hazell

of three pieces by Butterworth used as incidental music).

Three separate scores were used by Christopher Hogwood in his preparation of the edition of the *Messiah* – the autograph score in the British Library; Handel's conducting score (now at St Michael's College, Tenbury Wells); and a late eighteenth-century copy, now in the Rowe Library of King's College, Cambridge, but used at one stage in its career to raise the organist's seat in a Dublin place of worship. The idea was to reproduce an actual performance, a version of the work which Handel would have recognised, rather than the 'mongrel' *Messiah*s more usually performed. The first performance of all – Dublin, in 1742 – was not typical because, for various reasons, it left out many of the numbers which have since become favourites. Accordingly, the first London performance, given on 23 March 1743 in the Theatre Royal, Covent Garden, was chosen as the model. This version included most of the well-known choruses and arias, but avoided the subjective approach of the conventional 'best-of-*Messiah*' hybrids. As Christopher has explained, 'It seemed worth making the point that there were *nineteen* different versions of the piece, and not just the standard one that has been handed down – all part of the Dart philosophy of making people sit up and ask questions.' In this aim he more than succeeded. *Gramophone* observed: 'Nothing could be further from the traditional performances in soot-encrusted Victorian town halls in the north where

190

Peter Simple's Alderman Sidebotham doubled the role of Chairman of the Tramways Committee with that of Chorus Master of
the local choral society. This is *Messiah* as Handel surely meant it to
be.'

The Academy had given Christopher's provocative edition a
performance to match. Chris Hazell remembers Neville saying at
the first rehearsal, '"This time we'll do it *my* way" – he wasn't being
arrogant, it was just that he'd done the piece so many times before,
and this time he knew what he wanted.' This was a light, quick,
clear style in both singing and playing, free from pretension and
pomposity. What he got came near to being, as Chris remarked, 'the
first *Messiah* to fit on two sides of a record'. Critics were sharply
divided. Some welcomed a new approach; others felt that Neville
had over-compensated for the thunderous nineteenth-century-style
*Messiah*s with choirs two hundred and fifty strong, and had gone
too far in the direction of what John Amis was to call the 'now-
you-see-it-now-you-don't school'. Geoffrey Crankshaw wrote,
'The process of emasculating Handel, which has recently gained
such startling momentum, is here carried a significant stage further.
On this showing he was brilliant, amiable, much concerned with
pretty effects, and quite deficient in the cosmic vision which ...
preceding generations of interpreters have contrived to find in him.'
As he has since said, 'I was sorry to do it – I think it was the worst
review I have ever given them – but I just don't think Neville had
got it right: it's a Rembrandtian score and a Rembrandtian view of
God and man, and I think it was treated as a rococo diversion.'
Physical support for his views came from an unexpected source,
during a performance of the *Messiah* at the South Bank Festival: as
Robert Maycock of *Classical Music Weekly* recounts, 'Midway
through Philip Langridge's positively sadistic singing of "Thou
shalt dash them in pieces", Neville Marriner's baton mysteriously
rent itself asunder and flew off into the heavens. I suppose the
patron saint of musicologists *might* have been getting restless.'

The Academy's performances of the piece have often fallen prey
to such disturbances. Arriving for one performance in Brussels
Cathedral, choir and orchestra were obliged to postpone their
rehearsal for two hours by the unaccountable absence of platform,
chairs, music stands, harpsichord and organ. A makeshift stage was

*Queen Fabiola
with Iona Brown
and Laszlo
Heltay*

hastily contrived, but the remaining hour was lost when what appeared to be the entire Belgian army arrived to set up six thousand metal chairs in the nave. Nor was the repeat performance the following year any more tranquil. Her Majesty Queen Fabiola of Belgium was at the concert, and the cathedral was packed, so when the two trumpet players and Tristan decided to go for a drink while waiting off-stage for their first entries (at the end of the first half and in the middle of the second respectively), they were obliged to leave by the vestry door after extracting from a verger a promise that the door would remain open. As Tristan relates, 'The trumpets' first passage was in "Glory to God", which they play off-stage, and I didn't have anything till the "Hallelujah" Chorus. So we went across the square, had a coffee, strolled back with twenty minutes to spare – and found the vestry door locked. There were about three numbers to go before "Glory to God", and mouthing "Let's not panic", I marched round to the front to see if I could find a way of letting them in. I had to fight my way down a side aisle, explaining all the while in *awful* French that I wasn't simply trying to get a better view, and as luck would have it, I emerged next to the Queen

– I'm told it looked quite funny from the Chorus. Unfortunately, by the time I reached the vestry, it had been raining hard for about five minutes, and I let in two drowned rats, just in time for them to whip out their trumpets and away.'

Since the *Messiah* and the B Minor Mass, the Chorus has made five records – Mozart's Requiem and his C Minor Mass, Handel's *Jephtha*, and Haydn's *Creation* and *Seasons*. For the Mozart Requiem, recorded for Argo in 1977, the soloists were Ileana Cotrubas, Helen Watts, Robert Tear and John Shirley-Quirk, and the sessions were enlivened by a flying visit from the Right Honourable Edward Heath, MP, accompanied by Robert Key, a Conservative parliamentary candidate at the last General Election. 'During one of the Mozart Requiem sessions I simply had to go to a meeting of the Conservative Group for Europe, of which Edward Heath is the President: I had said I was in a hurry to get back to recording sessions, and when he expressed interest, I invited him to come and listen. It was a lovely moment to see the choir's faces as we walked in – but I couldn't understand why Sylvia was looking less than impressed. It turned out that approximately ten minutes before, she had addressed the whole choir to explain in some detail why the Academy were unable to make a record of Christmas carols with Mr Heath – and then we made our entrance. I think she thought I'd fixed it.'

The most recent of the Chorus's recordings – and its first to be made using digital techniques – was Haydn's *Seasons*, made for Philips in 1980; the soloists were Edith Mathis, Siegfried Jerusalem and Dietrich Fischer-Dieskau. The work is long and difficult, and the sessions, held in St John's, Smith Square, stretched over three weeks, light relief being supplied in the later stages by Neville's appearance on BBC's 'Desert Island Discs'. This was the subject of much ribaldry, and rehearsals were punctuated by the cries of gulls and the programme's theme tune in many and various arrangements for strings and voice.

The Chorus has continued to tour Germany with Neville and the Academy – but in 1977 there was a new departure, with choir and orchestra going to Spain for four performances of Handel's *Israel in Egypt* with Laszlo as their conductor. While the concerts were highly successful, the tour suffered from what might best be

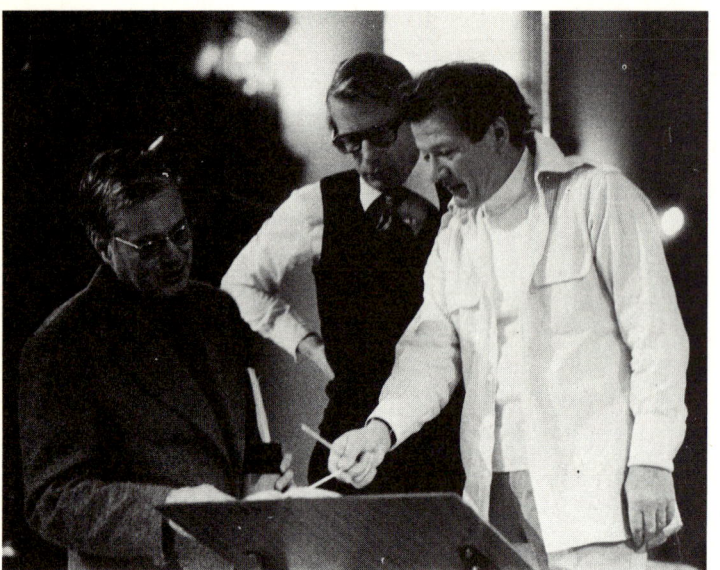

Left, *Dietrich Fischer-Dieskau, Erik Smith and Neville Marriner;* right, *Neville's desert island – Andy McGee's cartoon*

described as the odd administrative hiccup. The first hint of trouble came when Tristan, travelling on the day of the opening concert, arrived in Barcelona late and minus timpani, sticks and clothes, all his luggage having been sent, courtesy of London Airport, to New York. 'There had been a baggage handlers' strike earlier which delayed all flights for about six hours – the only good part being that by the time I reached the concert hall, they'd got past the "Where the hell have you been?" stage and had reached the "Thank goodness you're here" point. But of course I had not got the wherewithal to play the concert. The local promoters supplied me with some antique timpani, but I had to borrow an outfit to perform in, and finally appeared in black jeans – not my own – a white shirt, a clip-on bow tie, and Laszlo's smoking-jacket. I'd bought some clothes by the next concert, but my timps and sticks still hadn't arrived, so I bought a pair of drumsticks in a toy-shop in Palma de Mallorca and used these – to my cost: in the middle of the concert I did a huge drum-roll and the top came off one of the sticks. It flew in the air, hit poor David Takeno on the back of the neck and rolled under Iona's chair, emerging as if someone in the orchestra had laid an egg. The choir were beside themselves, but the audience seemed to think it was all part of the show.'

By the time the Chorus reached Cuenca, Tristan had regained his luggage; but his troubles were not over. 'We were playing at the monastery, which is set high on the hill overlooking the town – with no negotiable approach road. The coaches deposited us at the foot of the hill and left us to struggle up it on foot in concert dress. The basses and myself, with heavy instruments to lug, took twice as long as everyone else, and by the time we got there the rehearsal was over and everyone was having tea – as usual. When we came out for the concert there was a huge audience sitting there, and as we were waiting for Laszlo and the soloists, I thought I'd do what concert managers are supposed to do, and start the applause. So the minute they stepped on to the platform I burst out clapping furiously ... suddenly I became aware that no one was joining in ... at the rehearsal, during which I was pounding up the path, it had been announced that, because this was a monastery, there was to be no applause. The moral being "Don't miss rehearsals". But my pre-concert confusion was as nothing compared to the uproar at the end: there was this little fellow in the audience who had obviously been weighing up during the whole performance whether it was going to be worse to be excommunicated than to fail to show his appreciation – and he jumped up in the middle of Laszlo's second

*'Thank goodness
you're here' –
Tristan Fry*

195

silent bow and started applauding wildly. Whereupon he was pounced upon by five other people, and hustled away in disgrace.'

For the Academy Chorus, with seven successful recordings behind it and a loyal following in Germany, Belgium and Spain, the question now is one of future repertoire. This is determined primarily by the size of the orchestra and its character. The larger nineteenth-century choral works of Brahms, Verdi, Bruckner and Berlioz, for example, require a bigger orchestra than the Academy even at their largest can supply: as Neville points out, 'Once the regular players are outnumbered ten to one by extras brought in for the occasion – tubas and such like – it stops being the Academy, and becomes like any scratch orchestra.' The problem is by no means insoluble, as Laszlo is quick to explain – 'After all, we could record Handel and Bach for another twenty years' – but there is a risk that the singers, finding themselves repeating the same or similar repertoire too often, will grow stale, and he is keen to diversify. 'I think we should extend the repertoire through Haydn and up to Beethoven – but then we should have to jump the nineteenth century and the Romantic repertoire and go straight into the twentieth century. Much modern choral music is written for forces far larger than ours – but I can see no reason why we should not commission new works.'

14

No Token Gestures

Shortly before the 1975 South Bank Summer Festival, Neville summed up in a *Guardian* interview the Academy's attitude to *avant-garde* music (which he characterised as music which introduces electronic devices or non-musical instruments, or which brings in an element of random performance). 'The only strong stand I've taken this year is that there will be no token gestures to *avant-garde* music ... because I quite genuinely believe that for a string-based orchestra there is no *avant-garde* music which gives us pleasure to play, or gives many people pleasure to listen to.'

However, the fifteen string players at the core of the Academy, with their individual virtuosity and skill in ensemble, form an ideal performing group for the more conventional string repertoire of the twentieth century. Audiences at the South Bank Festivals heard them play works by Bartok, Bliss, Britten, Copland, de Falla, Goehr, Kodaly, Maw, Schoenberg, Stravinsky, Tippett and Walton, displaying their wide range of contemporary repertoire in concert.

Similarly, some of the Academy's most highly praised recordings have been of twentieth-century string music – Bartok's Divertimento in particular, Stravinsky's 'Apollo' and Prokoviev's 'Visions Fugitives'. Among the English composers whose works they have recorded, the Academy have a special affection for the music of Sir Michael Tippett. In 1970 they recorded his Concerto for Double String Orchestra, 'Little Music for String Orchestra', and 'Fantasia Concertante on a Theme of Corelli' (which was later used as background music for the film of Ronald Blythe's *Akenfield*). Some Academy members, including Neville, have known Sir Michael since their student days, when they participated

197

Michael Ayrton's painting of Sir William Walton (Capri, 1948)

in the concerts and recitals he organised as musical director of Morley College: as the *Guardian* has commented, 'Marriner and his team have grown up with Tippett's string writing: they make lightweight of its difficulties.'

At Sir Michael's invitation, the Academy appeared several times at the Bath Festival, of which he was the Director from 1970–72. The Festival gave them the opportunity to première, with George Malcolm, David Lord's Harpsichord Concerto, and in 1972 they gave the first European performance of Sir William Walton's Sonata for Strings. This was adapted especially for the Academy from his Fourth String Quartet (at Neville's suggestion – as Sir William has recently written, 'I left the adaption of my 4tet almost entirely to Neville'), and their recording of the piece was awarded an Edison in the following year.

The Academy have also explored the solo concerto repertoire with interesting results – recordings of Shostakovich's Concerto for piano, trumpet and strings, with John Ogdon and John Wilbraham as soloists; light-hearted works by Gordon Jacob, James Moody and Vilem Tausky for harmonica and strings, with Tommy Reilly as the soloist; and, over the past five years, a series of works for guitar and orchestra with the family of Spanish guitarists –

Celin, Pepe, Celedonio and Angel Romero – for whom several of the pieces were written. With Los Romeros they have concentrated primarily on the works of Rodrigo (his 'Fantasia para un Gentil-hombre', 'Concierto Madrigal', and 'Concierto Andaluz', as well as the familiar 'Concierto d'Aranjuez'), but in 1979 they made the première recording of Federico Moreno Torroba's 'Concierto Iberico' for four guitars and orchestra, in the presence of the composer who, at the age of eighty-eight, flew to London specially for the occasion.

Tommy Reilly, with Neville Marriner, Malcolm Latchem, Andrew McGee and Iona Brown

The Academy's opportunities to work with composers on new pieces have otherwise come almost entirely from festivals. An interesting exception was the Sonata for String Orchestra by Christopher Brown, winner of the 1974 Guinness prize for composition awarded by Arthur Guinness Son and Co. Ltd. in association with the London Borough of Brent. It was known in advance that the winning composition was to be performed by the Academy at Brent Town Hall in 1975, and in his programme note Christopher Brown explained that 'Though it was intended for use by string orchestras of all sizes, it was nevertheless the particular characteristics of the Academy that decided the shape and style of string writing of the finished work. This is evident in two ways –

Federico Moreno Torroba at the sessions for his 'Concierto Iberico'

considerable use of solos and multiple *divisi* effects (at one stage it divides into fifteen solo parts), thus making the work a showpiece for as many members of the orchestra as possible and also, mainly in the slow movement, the writing is more akin to chamber music than to the world of the large string orchestra.'

The 'band of soloists' character of the Academy has influenced the approach of most of the composers who have written specifically for the orchestra. In Richard Benger's Concerto Grosso, for example, performed at the Little Missenden Festival in 1969, all thirteen of the players are soloists at one point or another, in contrast to the eighteenth-century concerto grosso, with its carefully distinguished concertino and ripieno groups. Gordon Crosse, whose 'Symphonies II' they premièred at the 1968 City of London Festival, has written: 'I think now, as I thought then, that the greatest strength of the Academy was its working without a conductor. It meant that a piece was rehearsed and performed with the musical commitment of a string quartet. This, in theory at least (because twelve players are not four and don't live with each other), was the strength I was working to.' But he adds, 'I didn't find out for five years or so *how* (technically) to utilise this freedom without

200

making life unpleasant for the players,' and he subsequently withdrew the piece. The experience, however, was not wasted, as he explains: 'It is particularly unfortunate that when I wrote the "Symphonies II" for the Academy, I was in some turmoil as to where I was going, and the resulting piece was clearly *not* in the right direction. Despite the *excellent* performance, I promptly withdrew the piece.... Some of its material then found its way into my opera *The Story of Vasco* ... in the process of rehearsing the "Symphonies" I learned a great deal about writing for strings and wrote several pieces with rewarding string music in them over the next few years. But it is a great source of sadness to me that I made nothing of a wonderful opportunity to write for the finest (only?) group of string soloists around.'

Tackling new works is a difficult and time-consuming process for any orchestra, requiring close analysis of a usually complex score and long rehearsals. With a vast repertoire available to the Academy of music which is familiar both to orchestra and audiences (and hence more acceptable to concert promoters), they have been asked why they trouble to première new works. The overriding consideration is variety of repertoire, as Neville explained in an

The Academy with Los Romeros (Pepe, Angel, Celin and Celedonio Romero)

interview with Peter Gammond as long ago as 1969: 'We are beginning to commission new pieces now – contemporary pieces which are intellectually challenging – the sort of cerebral work that we need. We can't have an entirely emotional repertoire, because if you are planning a festival, for instance, you can't have a continuous wash of string sound. You've got to present variety to make a programme.' The latest of the Academy's commissions, initiated by Malcolm Latchem and Stephen Shingles, is the 'Metamorphoses for String Octet' written for the Chamber Ensemble by Richard Rodney Bennett. 'The work', Bennett explains, 'is based on Musgrave's String Quartet (1958), and consists of a series of strongly contrasted free variations in which Musgrave's opening phrase provides all the intervallic material.' It was premièred by the Chamber Ensemble, under Malcolm's leadership, at the Fishguard Festival in 1980, and the work forms an important addition to the string octet repertoire.

The Academy's most consistent contact with new music has been through the Cheltenham International Festival, where they have premièred six new works in the past ten years. The first festival to take place in England after the Second World War (held five weeks after the cessation of hostilities in Europe), the Cheltenham Festival has over the past thirty-five years commissioned something approaching four hundred new works, in association with the Arts Council; and though broadly based – its Programme Director, John Manduell, aims to produce a balanced programme of music – it provides an irreplaceable showcase for contemporary composers.

The first piece written for the Academy to perform at Cheltenham was Martin Dalby's 'Concerto Martin Pescatore'. The composer explains how the work came to be written: 'I played second viola [while studying in Italy between 1963 and 1965] in a group called "L'Orchestra dell'Accademia di Napoli" – a group similar in constitution . . . to the basis of the Academy of St Martin in the Fields – strings 4-3-2-2-1 . . . We did a number of terrible tours around the Continent where I was thought by my Italian colleagues to be somewhat eccentric. One of these eccentricities was my ability to consume vast amounts of food. They therefore thought it apt to call me Martin Pescatore [the Italian for "kingfisher"] and continually asked me to write a Concerto Martin Pescatore for them. I

never did. In the end the work was written specially for the
Academy of St Martin in the Fields with all this history at the back
of my mind. . . . The music is built of tiny motifs, many of them
derived from other music. . . . Shapes are taken from Ravel's song
"Le Martin Pecheur" from "Histoires Naturelles", and the "Kingfisher's Call" as portrayed in Messiaen's "Catalogue d'Oiseaux".
. . . There are also continuous throbbing noises which give the taste
to the work's texture which are my musical versions of the strange
sounds that kingfisher chicks make when feeding. I borrowed a tape
of various kingfisher sounds from the BBC's effects library.'

Though dedicated to Piera Guarino, the director of L'Orchestra
dell'Accademia di Napoli, the piece was written with the Academy
very much in mind. 'Knowing the virtuosity of each member, there
are solo parts for all, or at least 3-3-2-2-1, which is the minimum
performing strength. . . . Knowing too the skill of certain members
in chamber music, the work is conceived as an overgrown chamber
work. This is the reason for the unconventional system of barring
and notation. It was designed to be played without conductor, the
leader giving the main cues and the other principals at times leading
their own sections, sometimes independently of the main body,
sometimes leading the whole ensemble for a few bars. Being laid
out in this way and for these reasons, it becomes somewhat imprac-
tical when there is a conductor. . . . [The performance at] Cheltenham was nervous, at least I was. I hadn't been able to attend the
preliminary rehearsals and Brendel had pinched most of the final
one. . . . I remember [Neville] being perturbed about conducting
my style of free notation. I don't blame him. He added bar lines to
some passages which I disapproved of (and still do), believing that
they confuse rather than clarify. In the end, or possibly in the
circumstances, he was right: the final performance was extremely
exciting and very beautiful.'

The Times, in a review of an Academy concert in 1973, expressed
the view that 'Nothing speaks louder of this group's distinction
than the willingness of our elder musical statesmen to recast their
earlier works for it,' referring specifically to a work the Academy
had premièred at the Cheltenham Festival the previous year – 'Two
Contrasts for String Orchestra', adapted by Sir Arthur Bliss from
movements of his Second String Quartet. Whatever the group's

Left, *Katy Woolf;* right, *Sir Lennox Berkeley*

distinction, the performance was a near-disaster; a change of heart by Sir Arthur resulted in last-minute alterations to the final bars of the piece – observed punctiliously by half the players but totally forgotten by the remainder. The 'Contrasts' ended in confusion, to Sir Arthur's justifiable displeasure and, given that he was President of the Festival Committee, the Academy's embarrassed apprehension. Nevertheless, in the following year they were invited to participate in the Festival's celebration of Sir Lennox Berkeley's seventieth birthday with a performance of his 'Antiphon for String Orchestra'. The piece was commissioned for them, and Sir Lennox recalls, 'I had in mind the brilliant playing and particularly the attack and precision. . . . It was obvious, even if one had not known it, that the conductor was himself a violinist! "Antiphon" is not very long, and [Neville] would have liked me to add another movement that would be in a somewhat lighter vein to show off the virtuosity of his players, but I didn't feel that it would have made the right ending for this particular piece. I did consider the idea, though.'

New music can pose problems not only in performance but also in practical terms; the manuscripts of modern composers are often extremely unwieldy, and the required seating plans can pose severe problems. Katy, on her first solo appearance as the Academy's Concerts Manager, was faced with one such problem. 'It was a concert in Cheltenham, the first I'd done completely on my own – and I was terribly keen, everything was going to be wonderful. There was this contemporary piece in the middle of the first half which involved a complicated change from the normal seating arrangement, so I'd carefully stuck pieces of tape everywhere to show me where to put the chairs and stands; I practised the change three times, but there was no way I could do it in less than five minutes, which is an awfully long time ... So during the concert I made my début rearranging chairs: everything went smoothly, I started to relax – and then, just before Neville went on for the last piece, he said casually, "We should have got a bouquet for Iona – do you think you could achieve something?", as though it was all my fault for forgetting it. I knew we never got her a bouquet normally, he was just making it up to torment me on my first concert. The last piece was only due to last fifteen minutes, so I rushed across to this canteen where I'd happened to notice some flowers decorating the room and charged over to the washing-up lady, shouting "Who's responsible for these flowers? I want some". She pointed out a formidable-looking lady, and I went up and explained that I needed a bouquet – within the next eight minutes. She was *marvellous* – she leapt at a pillar and started tearing flowers off it, with cries of "These are rather nice" as she ripped them down. We got some tinfoil and some clingfilm from the washing-up lady – it made really quite a presentable bouquet – and I rushed backstage just as Neville was coming off – his face was a study as he took the flowers, he never believed I was going to do it, and I thought "That's one for me."'

The piece which had occasioned Katy's chair-shifting efforts was Nicholas Maw's 'Life Studies', a set of eight studies composed between 1971 and 1978 specifically for the Academy, and performed by them at the Cheltenham Festival in various stages of completion – five were premièred in 1974, two more in 1978. This has been the Academy's most sustained collaboration with a contemporary composer, and the completed work interestingly reflects both their abilities and their needs. One of the orchestra's principal requirements for the piece was that they should be able to tour with it. This determined the size of the forces for which it was to be

Nicholas Maw and Neville Marriner

written and, indirectly, their disposition. Nicholas Maw remembers, 'Neville warned me not to put in a part for bass trumpet or saxophone or something obscure . . . so I agreed to write a piece for the absolute basic band. He raised one eyebrow and said "Do you know what that is?" and described it to me – ten violins, two violas, two cellos, and one double bass. . . . I started thinking about it – ten violins etc. – and thought "Why not split it into two septets of five violins, one viola and one cello each, with the bass in the middle, party to both sides?" . . . . With two septets, one on each side . . . [I] wrote things which were very strongly contrasted – one group doing one thing, the other doing another, things thrown between the two.' To emphasise the antiphonal effect, and to make it possible for the piece to be performed without conductor – as it would have to be on tour – the players were to be seated in a semi-circle, with the double bass equidistant from the two septets.

From the requirement that the piece be suitable for touring also came the final conception of the work's form. The Academy patently needed a piece that could be adapted to changing circumstances – the other works on a programme, for example, or the particular players available. Maw recalls: 'What was needed was obviously something made up of a lot of small parts. Then I had the

206

idea that, as every single member of the orchestra is such a brilliant player, I would write a showpiece for them, something that showed them off to what I hoped was the best advantage. It was at that point that I conceived the idea of doing a set of studies . . . [but] for fifteen players as opposed to one.' The work was to be a set of studies which could be performed in varying combinations – Maw had in mind the *Études* of Chopin: 'Although people tend nowadays to do the whole lot as a [single] piece, that's not how they're written.' He sees the study, or set of studies, as a legitimate form of composition, provided that the resulting works, as well as being exercises in technique, are musically interesting: 'Chopin's *Études* are music as well. That is what I hope the "Life Studies" are.'

The name given to the work reflects the inspiration behind its composition. Maw is unwilling to give a blow-by-blow account of the thoughts behind the piece, preferring his audience to listen to the music without the distraction of musical detective work. However, he has explained: 'They're called "Life Studies" – a title pinched from Robert Lowell – because every one of the pieces is based in some sense on personal experience, either memories of the past or a private evocation of a particular bit of landscape or memory of a certain type of person . . . For instance, the one with the double bass is based on memories of going to a jazz club in New York and hearing Ray Brown play. . . . The second is based on two fragments of Chopin . . . I can remember as a small boy falling off to sleep hearing my father practising Chopin downstairs – and these phrases became so deeply embedded in my memory . . . I can remember falling off to sleep with them blurring and going round in my mind, and I hope that this is to some extent conveyed in the piece.'

'Life Studies' was extremely well received, and in 1979 Argo decided to pursue further their policy of recording English string music: with Academy recordings of Elgar, Vaughan Williams, Butterworth, Britten and Tippett already in the catalogue, they undertook to record Maw's work (now completed by the addition of an eighth study, not previously performed at Cheltenham) with support from the Arts Council, which had helped to finance the original commission. Nicholas Maw attended the sessions and regarded the recording, which was produced by James Mallinson, as 'In a sense, a second creative stage in the composition. . . . When

Nicholas Maw,
Neville Marriner,
Stephen Shingles
and James
Mallinson

the composer turns up at the rehearsals, it is generally the first time he has heard the piece being played.... Sometimes with orchestral pieces you get some real surprises. It's healthy that you should ... it shows that you're moving on, not just getting into a rut. If you don't get surprises, it means that you're only doing things that you know will work, and things you've done before.' Although a considerable amount of work had been done on the piece at Cheltenham, the Academy had not yet given a complete performance (Study No. 2 had been radically revised, and, because of a shortage of rehearsal time, had not been performed with the other seven in 1978); in the recording studios it was possible to analyse the work in minute detail and adjustments were seen to be necessary. Maw observes, 'If something that I had written didn't actually work, or if the balance was wrong, then we changed it. What is on that disc does not always correspond exactly to what is shown on the page.... I am always pragmatic about this – I take the opposite line from someone like Stravinsky, who always insisted that what was down in the score was down in the score and that was it.'

Maw's approach to collaboration with the performer is tactful: 'It is extremely unwise for any composer to turn up too early to any rehearsals. He should stay out of the way, let the players come to grips with the piece in their own fashion, make a lot of mistakes, swear at him in private – and *then* he should turn up towards the end, when he can possibly be the most help. He's got to know *how* to be of help; you must not interfere all the time, and if you're going to interfere at all, you must interfere at the right time.' He prizes a compliment he received from Harley Usill – 'He said I'd been the most use he'd ever seen a composer be in the recording studio' – but he does not believe the composer has a *right* to be present. Neville has commented: 'We like if possible to have the composer there at recording sessions. If he's got a particular sound in his head and we're not getting it, then it's valuable to have him there to sort out the practical difficulties. . . . Generally speaking, the first performance on record with the composer present is considered to be the definitive version, and you should go out of your way, if he's available, to play it by the rule book – to make sure he's there.'

Neville greatly admires 'Life Studies', and the piece, with or without conductor, has become part of the Academy's touring repertoire. The reviews of the record were outstanding, speaking of 'antiphonal ingenuity', 'dramatic virtuosity', and 'a formidably impressive score'. But perhaps the most gratifying comment, for Nicholas Maw, Argo and the Academy alike, came in *Records & Recordings*, which spoke of the disc as 'a blow struck for English music'.

15

Nice To Have You Join Us

Seen in a San Francisco newspaper:

> My car radio has provided me with my only exposure to classical
> music. Many's the time I've driven to work with the Juilliard String
> Quartet and returned home with Leonard Bernstein and the New
> York Philharmonic. Transported by music, I have found the auto-
> mobile to be an ideal acoustic shell. The only thing that bothers me
> about radio music is the bizarre selection of orchestras and conduc-
> tors. For instance, the announcer will frequently insist that I am about
> to hear a performance by 'Neville Marriner conducting the Academy
> of St Martin *in the fields*' (italics my own). Why must he conduct in the
> fields? What kind of sadist is this Neville Marriner? Dragging those
> kids and their heavy instruments outside in that God-awful English
> weather and expecting them to play their hearts out. I must confess
> that the boys and girls of St Martin's do a bang-up job, but the sound
> of that chill wind roaring off the heath in the background sends
> shivers up and down my steering-column.

When the Academy went to the United States in 1980, the question
most often asked was, 'Why haven't you been before?' – a reasonable query, given that it had taken the orchestra twenty-one years to
make its first appearance in America in full strength. The most
obvious consequence of this long delay was that, although the name
'Academy of St Martin in the Fields' was extremely well-known
through gramophone records, the general conception in the States
of the personalities, organisation and *modus operandi* behind the
name was a trifle hazy – as the querulous listener with the goose-
pimpled steering-column attests. One critic (Andrew L. Pincus,
writing in the *Berkshire Eagle*) even expressed doubts as to the
orchestra's existence: 'Until last Friday, it had seemed to me that the
Academy of St Martin in the Fields was a product of that British
imagination that gave us Monty Python and all those other lunatic

radio, television and film comedians. You know, the St Martin blokes didn't really exist. Some chap with a computer just sat in a recording studio, grinding out all those LPs of concerti grossi, sinfonias and bright, bouncy Haydn symphonies that fill the FM airways day and night.'

The exposure the Academy's records have been given on American radio stations is extraordinary: Neville estimates that every major classical music channel in North America gives them an average of half an hour every day, and he has known the odd 24-hour stretch of uninterrupted Academy. Their name has certainly been aired frequently enough to prompt the cartoon printed by the record magazine *Stereo Review* in March 1979 – a gibe the orchestra cheerfully accepts from a magazine which has presented it with two awards, one for its recording of Handel's Opus 6 concertos in 1969, and for Vivaldi's 'L'Estro Armonico' in 1978. The Academy have also fared remarkably well in popularity polls conducted by local radio stations among their listeners. However, the listeners were in effect voting for a characteristic sound and style rather than for the performers themselves, about whom little was known in the States. The reticence of the Academy's record-sleeve notes as far as personal details are concerned was remarked upon by

211

Iona Brown directing the Academy in rehearsal in the USA, 1980 (left, Colin Sauer)

a reviewer in the American *Musical Quarterly*: 'We may even be grateful that we are spared the personality build-up: there is not a word about the lives and hobbies of the performers.... If other readers ... are as tired as I am of record-jackets that combine the worst features of hard-selling confession-writing and gossip-mongering, they will join me in hailing this record for its modesty and seemliness, as well as for its other qualities.'

Another problem for the Academy in establishing a clear identity was that the conductorless chamber orchestra which has proliferated in Europe over the past three decades is still unfamiliar in the United States. Chamber orchestral repertoire is increasingly popular, not least for economic reasons: the comparatively high fees commanded by American musicians make projects for smaller groups ever more attractive to orchestral managements and promoters. However, chamber works are performed more often than not by shrunken symphony orchestras depleted for the occasion, rather than by small orchestras working together regularly on this repertoire – and such chamber orchestras as do exist in America are generally conducted. A chamber ensemble led from the front desk was thus a novelty – and reviewers regularly thought it helpful to explain to their readers the role of the Academy's director, describing Iona variously as 'concertmistress', 'leader', 'first chair violinist conducting while playing', 'soloist-conductor', and 'occasional traffic cop', and likening the Academy in performance to 'sixteen people with individual steering wheels, gas pedals and brakes, trying to drive a single car over a difficult course'.

The variety of forms in which the Academy began to record in the 1970s, and the increasing diversity of their repertoire, added to the general perplexity – and the name, a stumbling-block everywhere outside England, appeared to generate particular confusion in the States. The American cellist Lynn Harrell, with whom the Academy have worked regularly since 1975, remembers his initial acquaintance with the orchestra: 'My first thought was "What a crummy name for a great group." It conjured up thoughts of a latter-day Friar Tuck in the pastures with the daisies talking to Juliet about alchemy.' For the *Akron Beacon Journal* it conjured up quite different thoughts of 'a church-run prep school in the British hinterlands'.

Nor was the Academy's image as a conductorless ensemble made any clearer by their association with Neville – who has been known in America since the early 1970s as a symphonic conductor. It was on the strength of the reputation he had built during the 1960s as the director of the Academy that Neville was invited to found a similar ensemble in California – but this time to conduct it as well. The Los Angeles Chamber Orchestra was set up at the instigation of a group of music-lovers in Beverly Hills, headed by Richard Colburn (who, as Neville has pointed out, 'kept the orchestra afloat almost single-handed'). It was as Dick's guest that Neville developed a taste for the American way of life, at least in its more glamorous aspects – which included having both Phil Spector and Norma Shearer as neighbours. The Marriners were given the run of the Colburn guest house, glass-fronted, with marble floors, mirrored walls, chandeliers and, as Neville describes it, 'a swimming-pool as big as a rugger pitch, fringed with jacaranda trees and orange blossom'. He once remarked, dazed by his return to a fog-bound England, 'After a time, you really believe you live like that . . . in perpetual sunshine to the endless chink of ice in tall glasses.'

213

In Los Angeles, Neville acquired a working knowledge of the American music profession, and it was there rather than in England that his conducting career took root. As he explains, 'At home they'd seen me as a fiddle player and then as the director of a chamber orchestra – so to come back a third time as a symphonic conductor would have been one change too many.' But in America he was not generally known as a violinist; audiences had no preconceptions, and musicians none of the resentments that English orchestral players might have felt towards one of their own number 'risen from the ranks'. On the contrary, where it was known that he had played for thirteen years as a second fiddle in a symphony orchestra, this was counted as a positive advantage. Stephen Wright, a director of the concert agency Harold Holt and Neville's general manager, has called his reputation among orchestral musicians 'really extraordinary; his musicianship and his knowledge of how to get results from players are quite remarkable in the symphonic field' – the outcome of years of experience, observing from the inside the efforts of other conductors to 'get results'.

From 1972, Neville's conducting career was vigorously promoted by Stephen Wright (then with the American agency Shaw Concerts). At first the invitations were almost all to conduct baroque and early classical works – Handel, Mozart, and Haydn – and, as Neville remarks, 'I got a lot of sawn-off symphony orchestras, attracted by the prestige attached to my work with the Academy in this kind of music.' However, he became increasingly convinced that the lessons he had learned conducting chamber orchestras could be translated effectively in symphonic terms – that a chamber orchestral background was, in fact, in many ways an ideal preparation: after all, as Bruno Walter once observed, 'In order to be a good conductor, one must above all know how to perform chamber music.' Gradually, as his repertoire broadened, he began to conduct full symphonic works – often as a quid pro quo: 'At first I would get half a concert for the larger symphonies, then I was given alternate concerts to do them in – and finally I began to be accepted as a symphonic conductor, with no reservations.'

From appearances with orchestras at their various summer festivals – the Chicago Symphony at Ravinia, the Boston Symphony at Tanglewood, the Cleveland Orchestra at Blossom, and the

214

*Neville Marriner,
Music Director of
the Minnesota
Orchestra*

Detroit Symphony at the Meadowbrook Festival (of which he was subsequently made Director) – he graduated to regular guest appearances in both summer and winter seasons with some of North America's leading orchestras, in Cleveland, New York, Boston, Chicago, Los Angeles, San Francisco, Washington, Buffalo, Detroit, Vancouver and Montreal. By 1979 his American career as a symphonic conductor was secure, guaranteed by his first permanent link with a US symphony orchestra, his appointment as Music Director of the Minnesota Orchestra, based in Minneapolis.

The Minnesota appointment, and his ambitious plans for the orchestra ('I'd like to make it an orchestra with an instantly recognisable style – like the Cleveland Orchestra under George Szell') were described in an article by Christopher Porterfield in *Time*, and by 1980 Neville had established a considerable American reputation. He was on the books of a large and influential agency, Columbia Artists Management Inc. – 'I think they have a corner in conductors: they've got a hundred and four, the same number as Haydn's symphonies' – and in Minneapolis his appointment was flamboyantly publicised by Richard Cisek, the orchestra's General Manager.

Flamboyant publicity

Throughout this period the Academy's records with Neville continued to pour out, and the orchestra continued to be inextricably associated with him in the public mind. As one critic (Clifford A. Ridley) remarked, 'The names of conductor Marriner and London's Academy of St Martin in the Fields have been linked on so many recordings over so many years that the very idea of one without the other seems like an unresolved cadence, like Gladys Knight without her Pips.' But since the Academy's American image (as the *Stereo Review* awards demonstrate) was still principally that of a baroque ensemble, while Neville was known to be extending his conducting repertoire to include the largest Romantic works, the sense of mystification was, if anything, deepened. Nevertheless, as Neville has said, this state of affairs had its advantages: 'There was a kind of reverse prestige about the Academy always being in the States on record, and never there in the flesh; people were *more* intrigued by this organisation, which they had always heard in optimum conditions, that is to say, on gramophone records – and the longer they stayed away, the more interest there was bound to be when the time came for them to go.'

Between 1975 and 1980 the Academy's relations with the USA became increasingly cordial. Throughout Neville's time as Artistic

216

Director of the South Bank Festival, the list of soloists contained a preponderance of American artists – among them Lynn Harrell, Garrick Ohlsson, Jessye Norman, Jaime Laredo, Murray Perahia and the Cleveland Quartet (with whom the Academy shared an interesting concert featuring both quartet and orchestral versions of Beethoven's 'Grosse Fuge'). In 1976, the year of the US Bicentennial celebrations, the Festival had a specifically American theme; and to commemorate the Bicentenary the Academy issued a record of music by American composers – Barber, Copland, Ives, Cowell and Creston. Invitations to tour were beginning to come in from American promoters, and the Academy were enthusiastic – but the question of finance presented difficulties. Promoters required a period of at least six weeks to make a tour financially viable, but the players' other commitments always prevented them from leaving England for that length of time.

The problem was to remain insurmountable for several years. Eventually a Chamber Ensemble tour was planned for 1980 – but this was brought forward a year when in 1979 the Ensemble was invited at very short notice to replace another European octet. The two-week tour took the group from one side of North America to the other (they played, among other places, in Washington, Los Angeles, Stanford, Dallas, Minneapolis and Montreal) and, as Malcolm Latchem recalls, 'The most notable aspect of the trip – apart from excellent crits – was the fantastic hospitality we were shown, which included a visit to Niagara Falls, and the students at Colorado Springs driving us many miles to show us the marvellous country round about.'

The precedent had been set – and the following year, in the week of the Presidential Election, the Academy (the sixteen band under Iona's direction) finally went to North America. Their three-week tour, made possible by sponsorship from the British company Andry Montgomery Ltd, took them up the north-east coast of America, into Canada, with appearances in Toronto, Kingston and London, Ontario, and across into Michigan and Ohio, ending with concerts in Boston, Washington and Carnegie Hall. The programmes were carefully chosen to display the full range of the Academy's chamber orchestral repertoire, from Handel, Vivaldi and Mozart through Mendelssohn, Schubert, Grieg and

217

Left, *Raymund Koster;* right, *Roger Smith*

Tchaikovsky to Bartok and Stravinsky. 'The Four Seasons' with Iona as soloist was, as usual, ecstatically received – but the twentieth-century repertoire came as something of a surprise in places where the Academy's image as 'little baroquists' lingered on.

The concerts were sold out nearly everywhere – even in Buffalo, on the night of the televised Carter/Reagan debate. Critics hailed the Academy as variously a 'crackerjack bunch of musicians' (*Akron Beacon Journal*), a 'seamless musical unit' (*Cleveland Plain Dealer*) and 'international superstars of the chamber circuit' (*Buffalo Evening News*). On occasion they singled out individuals for particular praise – Raymund Koster, for example, the Academy's regular double bass player since the departure of John Gray for Australia in 1977, and Roger Smith, playing first cello in the absence of Denis Vigay. But in general they concentrated on the unanimity and spirit of the orchestra's playing. The remark most appreciated by the orchestra came from Greg Ladewski in Ann Arbor, Michigan – 'The audience responded warmly and with obvious affection; reacting, perhaps, as much to that remarkable community of friends on the stage as to the fine performance.'

218

Unanimity and spirit – Colin Sauer, Roger Garland and Malcolm Latchem

Malcolm Russell

219

The highlight of the tour for Sylvia was the finding of the perfect coach driver: 'Everyone said we were crazy to be travelling by bus – it was, after all, to be a 2500-mile journey altogether – but the bus gave us self-sufficiency. We carried our own music stands and double bass stool, and the girls could hang their evening dresses at the back to save them getting crumpled. We had a company manager, from Columbia Artists, and a lorry-driver-cum-odd-job-man for when anything went wrong; in the lorry, we had the harpsichord we had brought from home, with Malcolm Russell to look after it – it was ideal.' (Malcolm Russell's role was significant enough to rate both a note in every programme and, in one newspaper, his own review.)

Obviously the bus driver was a key figure, and Sylvia had written to the bus company in advance: 'I said the driver had to be exceptionally nice, as he was going to be very much a part of the team effort – and the moment we met Earl Grubbs in Pittsburgh, we knew it was going to be all right. He was extremely nervous at the prospect of taking an orchestra round – most of his work is with old people and children – but he soon grew accustomed to the idea, and even started coming to the concerts: the Holberg Suite was what he liked best . . . He couldn't have been more helpful and friendly – he showed us the pictures of his three daughters and Earl Junior – and when we go to America again we'll move heaven and earth to have him with us.'

The Academy's 1980 tour underlined the extent to which their concert career (though not their career in the recording studio) had diverged from Neville's, for while the sixteen band was touring with Iona, Neville was making a concert tour of the East Coast with the Minnesota Orchestra. Their paths crossed repeatedly, finally meeting in New York, where the two orchestras gave concerts in Carnegie Hall within forty-eight hours of one another. Neville was a little preoccupied in New York. It was his first appearance with the Minnesota Orchestra at Carnegie Hall, and the night before the concert had been spent combating the fire which had broken out in the sitting-room of his eighteenth-floor hotel suite. He and Molly did, however, celebrate the Academy's twenty-first birthday on 13 November 1980, and enlivened the festivities with wine brought round from their (slightly charred) hotel.

Top left, *Chuck Lambertz,
the company manager;* top
right, *Neil Cowit, the
lorry-driver-
cum-odd-job-man;* below left,
Earl Grubbs, the driver;
below right, *Andy McGee,
the artist*

221

In future, the American careers of Neville and the Academy are likely to converge more closely. Neville will remain first and foremost a symphonic conductor: he once said, 'Now that Bob Dart is no longer here, I tend to feel my path lies forward to the nineteenth century rather than backward to the seventeenth' – and hence forward to the full symphony orchestra rather than back to the chamber ensemble. But he looks forward very much to working with the Academy in America, the suggestion being that in the next two or three years, rather than simply repeating the pattern of the first tour, the orchestra should travel more widely and appear in all its different forms. Neville speculates: 'We could give several concerts with the Chorus and the larger orchestra, and I could perhaps take the larger orchestra to some of the summer festivals. Then both Chorus and sixteen band could go on to give concerts on their own – Laszlo could conduct the choir in performances of *a capella* music, and the sixteen band under its director might perhaps do a tour of the West Coast. As for the Chamber Ensemble, a repeat visit is already planned.'

The Academy's 'recordings-before-appearances' approach, perfected in Europe, has been applied most conspicuously to America. It is interesting that it should have been so effective in a country which (to the outsider, at least) appears to consider the 'personal touch' an all-important ingredient of success. Lynn Harrell has his own explanation. He has known the Academy for six years – though their relationship, as he recalls, did not get off to the most comfortable of starts: 'I was very nervous before the first concerto rehearsal, I remember. I had never rehearsed at the church before, and the journey seemed endless. My hands were icy cold – a mixture of anticipation and fear of disappointment, I suppose – the possibilities of musical and artistic achievement with such a group were so high. I arrived five minutes late. I had never met Neville before, and he was waiting in front of the orchestra, since he had begun the rehearsal. As I started to unlatch my cello case, he launched into the opening *tutti* of the concerto. I could sense, even not knowing him, a kind of dare, a challenge to get there in time to come in with poise, as though I'd had the half hour warm-up I should have had. I sheepishly shuffled towards my seat. Without missing a beat, Neville looked down and smiled, with a look that said "Nice to

Lynn Harrell

have you join us." '

Lynn sees the Academy's skill at ensemble playing as the crucial factor in their success, both as a solo group and with a soloist. 'I didn't think that in the professional orchestral music scene there could exist a group of such virtuosos dedicated to true chamber music playing. . . . Their virtuosity is of such a high individual level that they can devote a much greater proportion of concentration not just to following the soloist, but really playing *with him*.' He is also impressed by the sense of enjoyment they generate in their playing, and the discipline which underlies it: 'Neville is the least bossy of conductors, but he has an iron will . . . he seems to be the easy-going relaxed orchestra man, but when he says "I don't know – what do you think? – could it perhaps be a little louder?", you know you'd better play twice as loud.'

Above all, Lynn relishes the Academy's *Britishness* – their dislike of the oversentimental and embarrassment at the overblown, and their fondness for understatement: 'Their understatement of a compliment is extreme – they'll say "Jolly good" ... one of Neville's "Oh, well done"'s is like a twenty-minute standing ovation.' The Academy have 'what is to me typically English deadpan demeanour – the hauteur of the *maitre d'* of the best restaurant in the world might be similar. It can be, for an American, thoroughly unnerving.'

Lynn's picture of the Academy in 1980 provides an intriguing contrast with that of Hans Tecker and Jan Rubinstein, who in the late 1960s promoted the orchestra in Holland as being the last word in relaxed geniality. It is impossible to decide whether the comparison reflects on the formality of the Dutch or the informality of the Americans – or it could simply be that the Academy have changed in the last decade. Either way, the American response has been overwhelmingly positive: to quote the orchestra's most effusive review of the 1980 tour – 'When they created this one, as they say, they broke the mould.'

16

They Must Have Sold Them All

It seems to us as musicians that St Martin's is the ideal place for this exciting project. Its position, its architecture (contemporary with the music we shall explore), its vitality, its willingness to accept new ideas and cast its cloak over new groups of people; there could be no other church where the Academy could find so suitable a home. We shall often play elsewhere and take the name of St Martin into places where it is seldom heard, but this is our home, from which we start and to which we return.

John Churchill, in the *St Martin's Review*, October 1958

The Academy have never lost sight of their links with St Martin's. After John Churchill emigrated to Canada in 1967, the ties weakened for a few years as the orchestra's career became increasingly centred on the recording studio, but in 1973 the relationship was restored to its previous vigour with the aid of the Reverend Austen Williams and the new Master of Music, the organist Robert Vincent.

In September of that year, the first ever Academy Festival was held at St Martin's. Described by Sylvia as 'a large home-grown effort', the Festival looked back to the orchestra's early concerts in the church: one of the pieces performed – Corelli's Concerto Grosso Opus 6, No. 7 – had been included both in the 1959/60 series of concerts at St Martin's ('A Survey of the Baroque Concerto'), and on the first 'Recital' record – whose cover bore a photograph of the church. The programmes were almost entirely baroque – 'The Four Seasons', the Bach Double Violin Concerto, the Brandenburg Concertos – straying beyond the eighteenth century only for the Chamber Ensemble's programme of Mendelssohn, Brahms and Martinu, and for the Rossini String Sonata in C (a piece included

Left, *Kenneth Heath's drawing of St Martin-in-the-Fields;* right, *Kenneth Heath*

largely for sentimental reasons and for the solo work of Ken Heath and John Gray). The majority of soloists were drawn, as usual, from within the orchestra – Alan Loveday for the 'Seasons', Iona Brown and Carmel Kaine for the Bach Double. The remainder were old friends – George Malcolm, Frans Brüggen (with whom the orchestra had worked during the 1969 series of concerts in the Queen Elizabeth Hall), and Maurice André (a regular companion on Academy tours of Germany, and a great favourite with the players).

The bond with St Martin's was further strengthened by the appointment in 1975 of the Reverend Christopher Walker as one of the church's curates. An early and enthusiastic member of the Academy Chorus, he was also an invaluable ally in arranging concerts at the church – as part of the 1976 celebrations for the 250th anniversary of the present building, for example, and to launch the Organ Fund Appeal in 1977. The following year saw a dual-purpose concert in the church, arranged simultaneously to mark the 300th anniversary of Vivaldi's birth, and to raise money for riding facilities for the disabled.

1978 was also the year in which church and orchestra joined to commemorate the death of Ken Heath, one of the Academy's earliest members and their principal cellist for almost nineteen years. Denis Vigay, who had the unenviable task of replacing him, has said of Ken, 'He had the spirit of the Academy in him – he was a big factor in keeping people together.' He was ferociously dedicated to keeping the orchestra's standards consistently high, and made great demands on himself to do it. Trevor Connah remembers an occasion during the *tour gastronomique* when Ken was the only one to experiment with *bouillabaisse:* seriously unwell in consequence, he nevertheless insisted on playing in subsequent performances – 'He was only ill in the interval, never the concert.'

Ken was an integral part of the Academy's public image. Audiences came to look for him in the front row, immensely dignified and immaculately dressed, with his little goatee and the mien of an elder statesman: as John Gray puts it, 'He gave an air of respectability to the orchestra.' He was a talented and enthusiastic amateur artist, taking every opportunity on tour to sketch or paint the places the Academy visited. Several of the players possess sheets of hotel writing-paper or the backs of envelopes covered by Ken with sketches made in the odd spare moment from the windows of buses or trains, for paintings to be completed later. He was also a man of great kindness, and had a keen (if sometimes cryptic) sense of humour. The artist's response to his own performance is not always

The back of one of Kenneth Heath's envelopes

227

as spiritual as his audience might suppose, and John remembers with affection the set of sayings which Ken used to mutter at appropriate moments to the players around him. 'At the end of every concert he would always, without fail, say, "Thank your mother for the rabbit – and tell her the laundry's fourpence" or four francs, or four marks, depending where we were.' John also remembers him wreaking havoc at a formal reception in Tokyo by explaining to a bemused waiter the difference between 'an ambassador's gin-and-tonic' and 'a bedroom gin-and-tonic', and insisting that only the latter were suitable for consumption by the English – with the result that the waiter, properly concerned to observe the finer points of protocol, ladled out gin in ruinous quantities for the rest of the evening.

Ken, who died in March 1977, was (and still is) very much missed by the Academy. For Steve, who had been in the Army with him and was a constant companion on tour, certain pieces the orchestra plays are still closely associated with him. The commemorative concert at St Martin's was both a personal remembrance from Ken's friends and a means of launching the Kenneth Heath Memorial Fund, a trust fund which provides awards enabling established professional musicians to take sabbatical leave. Ken had epitomised the busy professional – during his years with the Academy he had also been principal cellist with the LSO, and later with the BBC Symphony Orchestra – and had felt strongly enough about the contribution such musicians make to national life to write, in 1971, a letter to *The Times*. In it he expressed the opinion that English musicians were given far less official support, moral or financial, than their counterparts in other countries, and he suggested that better publicity for their achievements would both improve record earnings and encourage overworked performers by making known their contribution to the national income.

This theme was picked up by George Malcolm in his tribute to Ken: 'The standards of English professional musicianship, frequently underestimated in their native country, are very high ones and are esteemed as such throughout the rest of the musical world. It is men like Ken Heath, with his undemonstrative but undeviating perfectionism, who create and maintain those standards.' These sentiments formed the basis of the Appeal that appeared in the programme, signed by John Amis, Dame Janet Baker, Raymond Leppard, Hugh Maguire, George Malcolm, Neville Marriner, Yehudi Menuhin and Sir Peter Pears, all of whom had known Ken as continuo player, principal cellist, and friend: 'Players like Ken Heath are vital to the musical life of this country. Most have been orchestral players. They go on to form chamber orchestras and ensembles. Some become conductors. To do this, a lot of time has to be devoted to practice, study, rehearsal and building up repertoire. It all means pressure and risk, particularly for those with young families. When successful, these artists not only give great pleasure, they also earn the country valuable export income from recordings, television and live music. But once on the treadmill, it is almost impossible for them to take time off. Sabbaticals could help in two ways. Primarily, by supporting and encouraging new ventures; secondly, by providing an opportunity for recharging after long arduous periods of work. Knowing Ken, we are sure that this is something he would have wished, and we would like to perpetuate his memory in this way.'

The Academy's relationship with St Martin's was by now thoroughly cemented again – although their physical proximity has never been quite as close as some seem to believe: John Davy and the other vergers still regularly have to turn away eager visitors expecting to find the players tuning up in the crypt. However, to be able to use the church even occasionally for concerts is a great asset: as the orchestra has grown, it has become increasingly difficult to accommodate all the players on the altar steps – but St Martin's is the one place where the Academy will submit without a murmur to being squashed.

In 1979 Neville was made a Commander of the British Empire in the Queen's Birthday Honours List, for his services to music as 'the founder and director of the Academy of St Martin in the Fields'. When he went to Buckingham Palace to receive the honour, to his delight he discovered the Reverend Austen Williams, who was to be made a Companion of the Victorian Order at the same Investiture. The Reverend Prebendary Williams (as he then became) has been the orchestra's most stalwart supporter from the beginning, and has always felt that there was something special in the relationship between St Martin's and the Academy: it was a more than happy

Academy regulars (left to right – Raymund Koster, Susan Lynn, Colin Sauer, Roger Garland, David Woodcock, Iona Brown, Malcolm Latchem, Anthony Jenkins, Marilyn Taylor, Peter Poole, Stephen Shingles, Douglas Wieland, Denis Vigay, Andrew McGee, Roger Smith)

coincidence that the representatives of church and orchestra should receive their honours together.

It was quite natural and highly appropriate that in 1980, when the Academy came of age as a professional ensemble, they should celebrate their twenty-first anniversary at St Martin's. For a week at the end of July the orchestra displayed, as *The Daily Telegraph* remarked, 'the versatility and flexibility that have been from the start two of its most durable assets', in a festival which opened with Neville conducting the expanded Academy in Handel's 'Fireworks Music'. For the rest of the week the stage was held by the sixteen band – Academy regulars Iona Brown, Malcolm Latchem, Colin Sauer, Andrew McGee, Roger Garland, Marilyn Taylor, Susan Lynn, Douglas Wieland, David Woodcock and Elizabeth Perry, violins; Stephen Shingles and Anthony Jenkins, violas; Denis Vigay and Roger Smith, cellos; Raymund Koster, double bass; and Alistair Ross and John Birch alternating at the harpsichord. Under Iona's direction they played programmes which were largely baroque (including 'The Four Seasons' by candlelight); Iona also led the Chamber Ensemble in the Mendelssohn and Schubert Octets – and the celebrations ended with orchestra and Academy Chorus under Laszlo Heltay performing the B Minor Mass. The Festival coincided neatly with the hottest week of the year, and orchestra and audience sweltered together by candlelight. However, as *The Financial Times* wrote after the first concert, 'It was clear that anyone who might not previously have been numbered among the loyal Academy audience had joined the enthusiastic partisans.' As a bonus for the festival week, on the day following the opening concert, the orchestra's first digital record – a recital of Dvorak, Wagner, Grieg, Tchaikovsky and Fauré, produced by John Fraser for EMI – appeared at the top of the list of best-selling classical records compiled by *Melody Maker* and published in *The Sunday Times*.

Neville's CBE marked not only his personal dedication to the Academy, but also the orchestra's status as a part of the English musical establishment and an institution in its own right – a status hinted at as far back as 1975, by Stephen Walsh writing in *The Times*: 'Rumour has it that the Academy of St Martin in the Fields is nowadays one of the three most famous things about England (the others, in no particular order, are Laura Ashley and Earl Grey).' It is the most-often recorded chamber orchestra in the world, with almost two hundred and fifty records to its name – 'The history of the Academy of St Martin in the Fields', as *HiFi News & Record Review* once commented, 'has been the history of the LP in this country' – and its remarkable career has been dotted with awards

Sessions for the Academy's first digital recording – Neville Marriner and John Fraser

The surviving Gold Disc (left to right – Kenneth Wilkinson, Iona Brown, John Kehoe, Neville Marriner, Stan Goodall, Harley Usill, Chris Hazell)

betokening huge record sales. The most recent was in 1978, when the orchestra received a Gold Disc for sales of more than a million records (a fast-receding landmark) on the Argo and Decca labels alone. This Disc is carefully preserved – unlike its predecessors, one of which, presented in Japan, was accidentally bounced down the steps of a JAL DC-10 and broken; the other, played on a gramophone in a spirit of experiment, turned out to be gold-painted Mantovani.

Yet the Academy are uncomfortably aware that their success has brought with it certain hazards. Neville explains, 'Once you are well-known, people never want you to change – and they become quite offended if you do. Promoters invariably ask you to play the same pieces – and from their point of view, they're right, the Brandenburgs always sell. But if you're not careful, the shine goes off things' – and an orchestra as much in demand as the Academy faces the risk of becoming complacent and losing the urge to improve. In Neville's view, 'The worst thing that could happen to the orchestra would be for it to become merely professional; it would be a waste of everything we've worked for,' and Mike

232

Bremner reiterates this: 'What matters more than anything else is that they should not become a routine band.... What distinguishes the Academy is that every member feels that he has something to give and has been allowed to give it: if they lose that, it would be a great shame.'

In one sense, Academy work has become more routine: where it once occupied less than three months of a player's year, it now accounts for seven or eight, and some members devote their time exclusively to the orchestra. From being the oasis, it risks becoming 'The Job'. For this reason the players are particularly aware of the need to remain fresh, and insist that there is still a great deal to be achieved. As Malcolm Latchem remarks, 'If an orchestra isn't on its way up, it's probably on its way down,' and the Academy are intent on setting themselves new objectives.

Their first priority is fresh repertoire, both on record and in concert. One obvious way for the Academy to regenerate their repertoire would be to play more contemporary music: in America the players were often asked why they did not perform more British music, which has prompted them to review a variety of twentieth-century English works for inclusion in their future programmes. However, the commercial drawbacks of contemporary music are well-known: the pieces require more rehearsal time, there are copyright fees (sometimes high), and they appeal, as yet, to a minority audience. For these reasons, recording companies are reluctant to record them and promoters, when offered programmes including contemporary works, balk more often than not. (Sylvia laments, 'They won't even take "Verklärte Nacht": it's such a *marvellous* piece, the Academy play it beautifully – and strictly speaking, it's not even twentieth-century; but they take one look, think "Schoenberg – twelve-tone", and visions of empty concert halls float before their eyes.')

At the other extreme, there is always a ready market for baroque music – but here the objection might be levelled that for the Academy, this is very much 'more of the same'. As far as recordings are concerned, Chris Hazell refutes this suggestion with some force: 'It's *never* the same.... There's so much more that one can achieve within the same framework.... A record's never perfect – and while it's not perfect, there are always things to aim for.' There is actually a surprising amount of baroque and early classical repertoire which the Academy have neither performed in concert nor recorded – Geoffrey Crankshaw points, for example, to Boccherini and the English school of Arne, Stanley and others. In addition, the development of digital recording techniques may have particular advantages for the Academy in their baroque recordings, in emphasising the clarity and precision which have always been their hallmarks.

It is more fashionable at present to use contemporary instruments (or modern copies) to play baroque music, and one or two Academy members have felt that the repertoire should perhaps be left to 'authentic' groups. There are a large number of people, however, who simply prefer Vivaldi, Bach and Handel played on modern instruments, regardless of musicological argument, and there is no reason why the two schools should not continue to co-exist peacefully, given that the end they are pursuing is essentially the same: as Sir Colin Davis puts it, 'The question of whether or not to use authentic instruments is superficial to the *real* problem – which is how you make music. The problem of expression in, for example, a Mozart aria remains – it won't be put off or avoided by playing with an old instrument.'

Neville continues to explore symphonic repertoire with the augmented orchestra, and in the 1980s the Academy are likely to be recording as a small symphony orchestra on all three record labels with which they are associated. For Philips they are to record the complete symphonies of Beethoven and Schubert; for Argo they have recently completed recordings of Mendelssohn's 'Scottish' and 'Italian' Symphonies; and EMI are also interested in their larger repertoire, possibly in digital recordings. Neville wants particularly to concentrate with the Academy on the music of 'the composers who wrote for the beginnings of the modern symphony orchestra, with flutes, oboes, bassoons, horns, trumpets and timpani – starting really at Mozart's time, but going some way beyond Beethoven.' After that, the Academy may proceed with some caution, in the knowledge that once the orchestra is expanded significantly beyond its most usual symphonic strength of between thirty-five and sixty players, the risk of blurring its distinctive character is increased. In Chris Hazell's view, 'The principal point of using any particular

artist is playing to their strength. . . . There wouldn't be much sense in taking the first three desks out of a symphony orchestra to play Vivaldi or Handel . . . so why bring outsiders in and blow up the Academy bigger than it is essentially?'

The augmented Academy completing their cycle of the Mozart Symphonies for Philips

All concerned are sensitive to the danger of spreading the Academy too thinly. On the other hand, the wider the variety of repertoire tackled, the more interesting the work becomes for the members. So the Academy's aim for the future will be to explore new repertoire – symphonic, chamber and choral – without losing their essential identity, preserving in whatever they do the characteristics which Peter Gammond has described as typical of their performances: 'A taste that is creative and life-giving, a sense of and concern for style in whatever is being played, and a technical polish and precision which releases rather than inhibits the inner spirit, the true expressive impulse.'

To maintain these standards, the orchestra recognises that it will have to keep a balance in its composition between maturity and freshness, and, to complement the early members' years of experience and understanding of the Academy approach, there is a constant search for new blood. Neville emphasises, 'We are always looking for young people to come into the Academy and grow up with the style – a new generation of players,' and Hugh Maguire adds, 'The sort of person I would like to see coming in ... are the young chamber music players, the people who play in string quartets. They're the ones who are mad keen – as we used to be. We used to go to Cornwall Gardens and rehearse all night for nothing.'

This type of player is not always easy to find. Recruits have to be prepared to submit to the discipline of playing in a particular style, evolved by others over a long period – but at the same time they are expected, as John Gray has pointed out, 'to step out of line just enough to add a stamp of originality and excellence ... within the overall framework'. In this respect the Academy have been compared both to King's College Choir, by Robert Tear, and to the Duke Ellington Orchestra, by Peter Gammond: each member has an individual contribution to make, but he makes it within the framework of a common style. The Academy style is not in itself hard to pick up, given that much of it is marked by Neville into the music, but it is not to everyone's taste, nor can it readily assimilate all kinds of playing. Denis Vigay explains: 'Anyone coming in to the Academy has got to be adaptable ... and we've had one or two players in the past who just couldn't blend: their tone was too prominent and there was an edge to the sound, or they weren't aware of the dynamic levels at which one had to play, or maybe their virtuosity carried them away rhythmically.'

The right people are also the hardest to secure. Neville observes, 'If we pick out the best young musicians in the country, they are precisely the ones who are going to be enticed away – to be the leader of this orchestra, or the first violin in that quartet: it's only *easy* to make an orchestra of players whom nobody else is after.' However, it is on the successful choice of players that the durability of the orchestra will depend. Malcolm Latchem reflects: 'There's a table in Salisbury Cathedral which is supposed to be over a thousand years old; not one piece of it is original – over the years it has gradually been replaced, bit by bit – but as a whole, it's been in existence for a thousand years. In the same way, Academy members can come and go – but if we select them carefully, the style will remain the same'.

*Malcolm Latchem
and Roger
Garland (with
Andrew McGee
in the
background)*

In the 1980s there are several wholly new avenues open to the Academy. There is the possibility of wider experience in opera. The orchestra has already made two opera recordings for Philips – Purcell's *Dido and Aeneas* and Mozart's *Die Entführung aus dem Serail*, both under the baton of Sir Colin Davis – and in 1979 the Academy spent a sunny and successful month at the Festival in Aix-en-Provence, preparing and performing Mozart's *Marriage of Figaro*. Neville is soon to conduct them in performances of Rossini's *La Cenerentola*, and at least one Rossini opera – *The Barber of Seville* – is soon to be recorded for Philips. There is the possibility of an annual Academy Festival at St Martin's, about which Steve Shingles is particularly enthusiastic: 'What better than for people from all parts of the world, when visiting London, to be able to hear the Academy *at* St Martin-in-the-Fields?' There is the possibility that selected Academy editions might be published; that the players will embark on a concert series with Alfred Brendel, performing Mozart piano concertos in the capital cities of Europe; that the orchestra might be involved in the rapidly expanding world of video recording. Above all, there is the certainty of more frequent concert tours in Europe and America for the sixteen band and, increasingly, for the Chamber Ensemble: as Malcolm has remarked, 'The Ensemble is a

*The Academy
rehearsing 'The
Four Seasons' in
Provence*

growing interest – the Far East, Australia, New Zealand, the States
again – people wanting to write us new works – it's all growing.'

*   *   *

Outwardly, the Academy of St Martin in the Fields has changed
dramatically over twenty-one years. Raymond Keenlyside
reminisces: 'The Academy that I can see in my mind's eye is a few
ardent musically-minded characters sitting in Cornwall Gardens –
and subsequently, full of the joys of spring, doing those first very
successful records.' The orchestra no longer fits into Neville and
Molly's drawing-room in Cornwall Gardens and, with as many as
two dozen recordings to be made a year and at least three months'
touring to be accommodated, the joys of spring occasionally wear a
little thin. But the ardour remains. Geoffrey Crankshaw has
remarked: 'Right up to the present day they have played as though
each concert was a new thing – and this is remarkable for people
who have played together for so long. To my mind, this is their
most important characteristic of all – the sheer enthusiasm, which
seems to be inexhaustible.... I've seen the Academy at recording
sessions: they go off into corners and discuss and practice – they
never stop.... They have a sense of total participation.'

238

To very few of the members is the Academy just a job. Simon Preston makes this clear: 'You don't just go along and play the notes and say "What time do we finish?" – there's no way with the Academy of staying uninvolved. I don't think there's any other orchestra like it.' The players have accepted responsibility to the Academy; in moving away from the safety in numbers to be found in a symphony orchestra each has taken the decision, in Dame Janet Baker's words, 'to stand up and be counted'. Tristan Fry puts it more graphically: 'A lot of bands will wait for somebody else to have a go first.... The Academy does tend to go in and give it one – each fiddle player is there concentrating, and when they see the baton go down, they're there.'

In return they get a kind of satisfaction they can perhaps find nowhere else. John Gray has summed up his feelings on seventeen years with the orchestra: 'I got everything out of playing with the Academy – it was the one thing I looked forward to above everything else. It was the greatest musical thing in my life, and always has been.' Playing for pleasure – even at a time when the music

1964, Kingsway Hall (clockwise – Alex Lindsay, Neville Marriner, Norman Nelson, Trevor Connah, Raymond Keenlyside, Michael de Saulles, Malcolm Latchem, Roger Lord, Michael Dobson, Denis Vigay, Roger Birnstingl, Kenneth Heath, Simon Streatfeild, Stephen Shingles)

239

profession is as tightly bound as any other by the need to be financially viable – is still at a premium, and the Academy will exist for just as long as this attitude survives.

There is little danger, at any rate, of the players taking the Academy or their success for granted. After twenty-one years of critical acclaim and popular success, people are still getting the name wrong: one European music-lover, writing to the Royal Festival Hall for details of concerts in London, enquired earnestly after 'the orchestra St Mariners in the Field'. And after two hundred and fifty records – mono, stereo, quadrophonic and digital – it is still possible to try to buy an Academy record and fail. Neville complains, 'We may have made hundreds of recordings; but when I go into a shop, all I can find are everybody else's. The only way I can cheer myself up is to think, "My God! They must have sold them all."'

1980, St John's, Smith Square – Neville Marriner conducting the Academy and Chorus of St Martin in the Fields

Discography

As at 13 November 1980

Albicastro   Concerto a 4, Op. 7 No. 6/
Marriner *L'Oiseau-Lyre*

Albinoni   Concerto a 5, Op. 5 No. 5/
Marriner *L'Oiseau-Lyre*
Trumpet Concerto in C/ Wilbraham/
Marriner *Argo*
Adagio in G minor/ Marriner *EMI*

Albrechtsberger   Concerto a 5 in E/
Wilbraham/ Marriner *Argo*

Arne   Harpsichord Concerto No. 5 in
G minor/ Malcolm/ Marriner *Decca*
Overture No. I/ Marriner *Decca*
Songs – 'Bacchus and Ariadne' and
'Fair Caelia love pretended'/ Tear/
Marriner *Argo*

Avison/Scarlatti   Concertos   Op.   9
Nos. 1–12/ Marriner *Philips*
Concerto Op. 9 No. 11/ Marriner
L'Oiseau-Lyre

Bach, C. P. E.   Harpsichord Concerto
in   C   minor/   Malcolm/   Marriner
Decca
Symphony No. 2/ Marriner *Decca*
Magnificat/ Palmer, Watts, Tear,
Roberts/ King's College/ Ledger
Argo

Bach, J. C.   Harpsichord Concerto in
A/ Malcolm/ Marriner *Decca*
Symphonies Op. 3 Nos. 1–6/ Mar-
riner *Philips*

Bach, J. S.
Concertos
Violin Concerto in A minor, BWV
1041/ Szeryng/ Marriner *Philips*
Violin Concerto in E, BWV 1042/
Szeryng/ Marriner *Philips*
Concerto for two violins, BWV
1043/ Szeryng, Hasson/ Marriner
Philips
Brandenburg Concertos Nos. 1–6,
BWV 1046–51/ Loveday, Brown,
Black, Munrow, Turner, Tuckwell,
Malcolm, Monteux/ Marriner *Philips*
Oboe Concerto in F, tr. BWV 1053/
Black/ Marriner *Argo*
Concerto for oboe d'amore and
strings, tr. BWV 1055/ Black/ Mar-
riner *Argo*
Flute Concerto in G minor, tr. BWV
1056/ Bennett/ Marriner *Argo*
Concerto for violin and oboe, tr.
BWV 1060/ Kaine, Miller/ Marriner
Argo
Triple Concerto for violin, oboe,
flute and strings, tr. BWV 1063/
Kaine, Black, Bennett/ Marriner *Argo*
Concerto for three violins, tr. BWV
1064/ Kaine, Studt, Thomas/ Mar-
riner *Argo*

Misc. orchestral
'Jesu, Joy of Man's Desiring' from
Cantata 147, arr. Connah/ Marriner
EMI

241

Bach, J. S. *misc. orchestral – contd.*
Sinfonia from *Christmas Oratorio*/ Marriner *EMI*
Suites 1–4, BWV 1066–9/ Marriner *Argo*
Suites 1–4, BWV 1066–9/ Marriner *Philips*
'Air in G', from Suite 3, BWV 1068/ Marriner *EMI*
'The Art of Fugue'/ Marriner *Philips*
'The Musical Offering'/ Marriner *Philips*

Vocal/Choral
Christmas Oratorio/ Ameling, Baker, Tear, Fischer-Dieskau/ King's College/ Ledger *HMV*
Aria – 'Bereite dich, Zion' (*Christmas Oratorio*)/ Baker/ Marriner *EMI*
Magnificat/ Palmer, Watts, Tear, Roberts/ King's College/ Ledger *Argo*
Aria – 'Et exultavit' (Magnificat)/ Baker/ Marriner *EMI*
Mass in B Minor/ Marshall, Baker, Tear, Ramey/ Academy Chorus/ Marriner *Philips*
Cantata 56, 'Ich will den Kreuzstab gerne tragen'/ Shirley-Quirk/ St Anthony Singers/ Marriner *L'Oiseau-Lyre*
Cantata 82, 'Ich habe genug'/ Shirley-Quirk/ Marriner *L'Oiseau-Lyre*
Cantata 147, 'Herz und Mund und Tat und Leben'/ Ameling, Baker, Partridge/ King's College/ Willcocks *HMV*
Cantata 159, 'Sehet, wir gehn hinauf gen Jerusalem'/ Baker, Tear, Shirley-Quirk/ St Anthony Singers/ Marriner *L'Oiseau-Lyre*
Cantata 170, 'Vergnügte Ruh', beliebte Seelenlust'/ Baker/ St Anthony Singers/ Marriner *L'Oiseau-Lyre*
Cantata 202, 'Weichet nur, betrübte Schatten'/ Ameling/ Marriner *EMI*
Cantata 209, 'Non sa che sia dolore'/

Ameling/ Marriner *EMI*
Motet – 'Der Geist hilft unsrer Schwachheit auf', BWV 226/ King's College/ Willcocks *HMV*
Motet – 'Fürchte dich nicht', BWV 228/ King's College/ Willcocks *HMV*
Motet – 'Lobet den Herrn alle Heiden', BWV 230/ King's College/ Willcocks *HMV*
Aria – 'Saget, saget mir geschwinde' (*Easter Oratorio*)/ Baker/ Marriner *EMI*
Aria – 'Bist du bei mir' (Notebook of Anna Magdalena Bach)/ Baker/ Marriner *EMI*
Aria – 'Es is vollbracht' (*St John Passion*)/ Baker/ Marriner *EMI*
Aria – 'Hochgelobter Gottesohn' (Cantata 6)/ Baker/ Marriner *EMI*
Aria – 'Ach, bleibe doch' (Cantata 11)/ Baker/ Marriner *EMI*
Aria – 'Wohl euch ihr auserwählen Seelen' (Cantata 34)/ Baker/ Marriner *EMI*
Aria – 'Gelobet sei der Herr' (Cantata 129)/ Baker/ Marriner *EMI*
Aria – 'Komm, du süsse Todesstunde' (Cantata 161)/ Baker/ Marriner *EMI*
Aria – 'Lobe, Zion, deinen Gott' (Cantata 190)/ Baker/ Marriner *EMI*

Barber   Adagio for Strings/ Marriner *Argo*

Bartok   'Music for Strings, Percussion and Celeste'/ Marriner *Argo*
Divertimento/ Marriner *Argo*

Beethoven   Romance No. 1 for violin and orchestra/ Suk/ Marriner *HMV*
Romance No. 2 for violin and orchestra/ Suk/ Marriner *HMV*
Symphony No. 1/ Marriner *Philips*
Symphony No. 2/ Marriner *Philips*
Symphony No. 4/ Marriner *Philips*
'Grosse Fuge'/ Marriner *Philips*
12 Minuets, WoO 7/ Marriner *Philips*
12 German Dances, WoO 8/ Marriner *Philips*

12 Country Dances, WoO 14/ Marriner *Philips*

12 Contredanses/ Marriner *EMI*

C Major Mass/ Palmer, Watts, Keyte/ St John's College/ Guest *Argo*

Bellini Oboe Concerto in E flat/ Lord/ Marriner *L'Oiseau-Lyre*

Bizet Symphony in C/ Marriner *Argo*

Bloch Concerto Grosso/ Marriner *EMI*

Blow Anthem – 'Blessed is the man'/ Brett, Langridge/ King's College/ Willcocks *Argo*
Anthem – 'Cry aloud and spare not'/ Brett, Langridge/ King's College/ Willcocks *Argo*
Anthem – 'God spake sometime in visions'/ Brett, Langridge/ King's College/ Willcocks *Argo*
Anthem – 'I was glad when they said unto me'/ Brett, Langridge/ King's College/ Willcocks *Argo*
Anthem – 'O sing unto the Lord'/ Brett, Langridge/ King's College/ Willcocks *Argo*

Boccherini String Quintet Op. 13 No. 5 (excerpt)/ Marriner *HMV (digital)*
String Quintet Op. 13 No. 5 (excerpt)/ Marriner *Philips*
Guitar Quintets Nos. 4–6/ P. Romero/ ASM Chamber Ensemble *Philips*

Boieldieu Harp Concerto in C/ Robles/ Brown *Argo*

Bononcini Sinfonia No. 10 in D/ Smithers, Laird/ Marriner *Philips*
Aria – 'Deh più a me non v'ascondete'/ Baker/ Marriner *Philips*

Boyce Symphonies Nos. 1–8/ Marriner *Argo*
Song – 'Momus to Mars'/ Tear/ Marriner *Argo*

Bree, van Allegro for 4 string quartets/ Marriner *Philips*

Britten 'Simple Symphony'/ Marriner *EMI*
Variations on a theme of Frank Bridge/ Marriner *Argo*
Nocturne, Op. 60/ Tear/ Marriner *Argo*
St Nicholas Cantata/ Tear/ King's College/ Willcocks *HMV*

Butterworth 'A Shropshire Lad'/ Marriner *Argo*
'The Banks of Green Willow'/ Marriner *Argo*
'Two English Idylls'/ Marriner *Argo*

Caccini Aria – 'Amarilli mia bella'/ Baker/ Marriner *Philips*

Caldara Aria – 'Come raggio di sol'/ Baker/ Marriner *Philips*
Aria – 'Sebben crudele mi fai languir'/ Baker/ Marriner *Philips*
Aria – 'Selve amiche'/ Baker/ Marriner *Philips*

Cesti Aria – 'Intorno all'idol mio'/ Baker/ Marriner *Philips*

Charpentier Magnificat/ Lott, Harrhy, Brett, Partridge, Roberts/ King's College/ Ledger *EMI*
Te Deum/ Lott, Harrhy, Brett, Partridge, Roberts/ King's College/ Ledger *EMI*

Cherubini Etude No. 2 in F for horn and strings/ Tuckwell/ Marriner *L'Oiseau-Lyre*
Horn Concerto in F/ Tuckwell/ Marriner *EMI*

Clarke Trumpet Voluntary/ Wilbraham/ Marriner *Philips*

Copland 'Quiet City'/ Marriner *Argo*

Corelli Concerti Grossi Op. 6 Nos. 1–12/ Marriner *Argo*
Concerto Grosso Op. 6 No. 1/ Marriner *L'Oiseau-Lyre*
Concerto Gross Op. 6 No. 7/ Marriner *L'Oiseau-Lyre*

Cowell Hymn and Fuguing Tune

Cowell – *contd.*
No. 10 for oboe and strings/Nicklin/
Marriner *Argo*

Creston 'A Rumor'/ Marriner *Argo*

Delius Air and Dance/ Marriner *Argo*
'A Song Before Sunrise'/ Marriner
Argo
Intermezzo and Serenade from 'Hassan'/ Marriner *Argo*
Intermezzo from 'Fennimore and
Gerda'/ Marriner *Argo*
'La Calinda' from 'Koanga'/ Marriner *Argo*
'On Hearing the First Cuckoo in
Spring'/ Marriner *Argo*
'Summer Night on the River'/ Marriner *Argo*
'The Walk to the Paradise Garden'/
Marriner *Argo*
'Two Aquarelles'/ Marriner *EMI*

Dittersdorf Harp Concerto in A
(transp. Pilley)/ Robles/ Brown *Argo*
Sinfonia Concertante for double
bass, viola and orchestra/ Slatford,
Shingles/ Marriner *EMI*

Donizetti String Quartet in D, arr. for
string orchestra/ Marriner *Argo*

Durante Aria – 'Danza fanciulla gentile'/ Baker/ Marriner *Philips*

Dvorak Serenade for Strings, Op. 22/
Marriner *Argo*
Nocturne in B minor, Op. 40/ Marriner *HMV (digital)*

Elgar Serenade for Strings, Op. 20/
Marriner *Argo*
Introduction and Allegro, Op. 47/
Marriner *Argo*
Elegy for Strings, Op. 58/ Marriner
Argo
'Sospiri', Op. 70/ Marriner *Argo*
Suite from 'The Spanish Lady'/ Marriner *Argo*

Fasch Trumpet Concerto in D/ Wilbraham/ Marriner *Argo*

Fauré Pavane, Op. 50/ Marriner
HMV (digital)

'Cantique de Jean Racine', Op. 11/
Bond, Luxon/ St John's College/
Guest *Argo*
Requiem, Op. 48/ Bond, Luxon/ St
John's College/ Guest *Argo*

Forster Horn Concerto in E flat/
Tuckwell/ Marriner *EMI*

Francheschini Sonata in D for two
trumpets, strings and continuo/ Wilbraham, Laird/ Marriner *EMI*

Gabrieli, G. Canzon a 8/ Philip Jones
Brass Ensemble/ Marriner *Argo*
Canzon per Sonar Noni Toni/ Marriner *L'Oiseau-Lyre*
Canzon Prima a 4, 'La Spiritata'/
Philip Jones Brass Ensemble/ Marriner *Argo*
Canzon Prima a 5/ Philip Jones Brass
Ensemble/ Marriner *Argo*
Canzon Primi Toni No. 1 a 8/ Philip
Jones Brass Ensemble/ Marriner *Argo*

Geminiani Concerto Grosso Op. 3
No. 3/ Marriner *L'Oiseau-Lyre*

Giordani Song – 'Caro mio ben'/
Baker/ Marriner *Philips*

Giuliani Guitar Concerto, Op. 30/ P.
Romero/ Marriner *Philips*
Guitar Concerto, Op. 36/ P.
Romero/ Marriner *Philips*
Introduction, Theme with Variations, and Polonaise, Op. 65/ P.
Romero/ Marriner *Philips*
Guitar Concerto, Op. 70/ P.
Romero/ Marriner *Philips*

Gluck 'Dance of the Blessed Spirits'
from *Orfeo et Eurydice*/ Marriner *EMI*
'Don Juan' – complete ballet/ Marriner *Decca*

Grétry Concerto in C for flute, two
horns and strings/ Monteux/ Marriner *L'Oiseau-Lyre*
Air – 'Eprise d'un feu téméraire' from
Anacréon chez Polycrate/ Eda-Pierre/
Marriner *Philips*
Air – 'Plus d'ennemis dans mon
empire' from *Céphale et Procris*/

Eda-Pierre/ Marriner *Philips*
Air – 'Comme un éclair' from *La fausse magie*/ Eda-Pierre/ Marriner *Philips*
Air – 'Je ne le dis qu'à vous' from *La fausse magie*/ Eda-Pierre/ Marriner *Philips*
Air – 'Je crains de lui parler' from *Richard Coeur de Lion*/ Eda-Pierre/ Marriner *Philips*

Grieg   Two Elegiac Melodies, Op. 34/ Marriner *Argo*
Two Elegiac Melodies, Op. 34/ Marriner *HMV (digital)*
Holberg Suite, Op. 40/ Marriner *Argo*

Grossi   Sonata a 5 No. 11 in C for trumpet, bassoon, strings and continuo/ Smithers/ Marriner *Philips*

Handel
Concertos
Concerti Grossi Op. 3 Nos. 1–6/ Marriner *Argo*
Keyboard Concertos Op. 4 Nos. 1–6/ Malcolm/ Marriner *Argo*
Harp Concerto in B flat, (Op. 4 No. 6)/ Robles/ Brown *Argo*
Concerti Grossi Op. 6 Nos. 1–12/ Marriner *Decca*
Concerto Grosso Op. 6 No. 1/ Marriner *L'Oiseau-Lyre*
Concerto Grosso Op. 6 No. 4/ Marriner *L'Oiseau-Lyre*
Concerto Grosso Op. 6 No. 6/ Marriner *L'Oiseau-Lyre*
Keyboard Concertos Op. 7 Nos. 1–6/ Malcolm/ Marriner *Argo*
Concerti a Due Cori Nos. 1–3/ Marriner *Philips*
Concerto a Due Cori No. 1/ Marriner *EMI*
Concerto a Due Cori No. 3/ Marriner *EMI*
Oboe Concerto No. 1 in B flat/Lord/ Marriner *Argo*
Oboe Concerto No. 2 in B flat/Lord/ Marriner *Argo*
Variant in F of Oboe Concerto No. 2/ Lord/ Marriner *Argo*
Oboe Concerto No. 3 in G minor/ Lord/ Marriner *Argo*
Concerto in B flat for treble recorder/ Munrow/ Marriner *EMI*
Concerto in F for treble recorder/ Petri/ Brown *Philips*
Keyboard Concerto in F, No. 13 (Second Set)/ Malcolm/ Marriner *Argo*
Keyboard Concerto in A, No. 14 (Second Set)/ Malcolm/ Marriner *Argo*
Keyboard Concerto in D minor, No. 15/ Malcolm/ Marriner *Argo*
Keyboard Concerto in F, No. 16/ Malcolm/ Marriner *Argo*
Sonata from 'Il trionfo del tempo e del disinganno'/ Malcolm/ Marriner *Argo*

Misc. orchestral
Alexander's Feast/ Marriner *Philips*
'Arrival of the Queen of Sheba' from *Solomon*/ Marriner *Argo*
'Arrival of the Queen of Sheba' from *Solomon*/ Marriner *Philips*
Dream Music from *Ariodante/Alcina*/ Marriner *Argo*
'Fireworks Music' (complete)/ Marriner *Argo*
'Fireworks Music' (complete)/ Marriner *Philips*
Hunting Scene from *Il Pastor Fido II*/ Marriner *Argo*
Largo from *Xerxes*/ Marriner *EMI*
Overture and ballet music from *Alcina*/ Marriner *Argo*
Overture and ballet music from *Ariodante*/ Marriner *Argo*
Overture and Hornpipe in D/ Marriner *Philips*
Overture to *Agrippina*/ Marriner *EMI*
Overture to *Arianna*/ Marriner *EMI*
Overture to *Berenice*/ Marriner *Argo*
Overture to *Berenice*/ Marriner *EMI*
'Pastoral' Symphony from *Messiah*/ Marriner *HMV*

245

Handel *misc. orchestral – contd.*

'Water Music' (complete)/ Marriner
Philips
'Water Music' (Suite in D, Suite in F,
Suite in G)/ Marriner *Argo*

Vocal / Choral

Acis and Galatea/ Gomez, Tear, Lan-
gridge, Luxon/ Marriner *Argo*
Hercules/ Harper, Watts, Bowman,
Tear/ King's College/ Ledger *EMI*
Jephtha/ Marshall, Hodgson, Rolfe-
Johnson, Esswood, Keyte/ Southend
Boys Choir/ Academy Chorus/ Mar-
riner *Argo*
Messiah – complete/ Bowman, Tear,
Luxon/ King's College/ Willcocks
HMV
Messiah – complete/ Ameling,
Reynolds, Langridge, Howell/
Academy Chorus/ Marriner *Argo*
Messiah – Choruses ('And the glory
of the Lord', 'And He shall purify',
'For unto us a child is born', 'Glory to
God', 'His yoke is easy', 'Behold the
Lamb of God', 'Surely, He hath
borne our griefs', 'And with His
stripes', 'All we like sheep', 'He
trusted in God', 'Lift up your heads',
'Let all the angels of the Lord', 'The
Lord gave the Word', 'Let us break
their bonds', 'Hallelujah', 'Since by
man came death', 'Worthy is the
Lamb', 'Amen'/ King's College/
Willcocks *HMV*
Messiah – Christmas Music (Overture, Nos. 2–9, 12–14, 17–21)/ Jen-
nings, Tear, Carol Case/ King's Col-
lege/ Willcocks *HMV*
Messiah – highlights ('Comfort ye',
'Ev'ry valley', 'And the glory of the
Lord', 'Behold, a virgin', 'O thou
that tellest', 'For unto us a child is
born', 'And suddenly there was with
the angel', 'Glory to God', 'Rejoice
greatly', 'Behold the Lamb of God',
'He was despised', 'All we like
sheep', 'Hallelujah', 'I know that my
Redeemer liveth', 'The trumpet shall

sound', 'Worthy is the Lamb',
'Amen'/ Ameling, Reynolds, Lan-
gridge, Howell/ Academy Chorus/
Marriner *Argo*
Messiah – highlights ('And the glory
of the Lord', 'And He shall purify',
'For unto us a child is born', 'And
suddenly there was with the angel',
'Glory to God', 'His yoke is easy',
'Behold the Lamb of God', 'Surely
He hath borne our griefs', 'And with
His stripes', 'All we like sheep', 'All
they that see Him', 'He trusted in
God', 'Lift up your heads', 'Unto
which of the angels', 'Let all the
angels of God worship Him', 'The
Lord gave the Word', 'How beautiful
are the feet', 'Why do the nations',
'Let us break their bonds asunder',
'Hallelujah', 'Since by man came
death', 'Then shall be brought to
pass', 'O death where is thy sting?',
'But thanks be to God', 'Worthy is
the Lamb', 'Amen'/ Ameling,
Reynolds, Langridge, Howell/
Academy Chorus/ Marriner *Argo*
Chandos Anthem – 'As pants the
hart'/Cantelo, Partridge/King's Col-
lege/ Willcocks *Argo*
Chandos Anthem – 'In the Lord will I
put my trust'/ Friend, Langridge/
King's College/ Willcocks *Argo*
Chandos Anthem – 'I will magnify
thee'/Friend, Langridge/King's Col-
lege/ Willcocks *Argo*
Chandos Anthem – 'Let God arise'/
Vaughan, Young, Robinson/ King's
College/ Willcocks *Argo*
Chandos Anthem – 'O praise the
Lord with one consent'/ Vaughan,
Young, Robinson/ King's College/
Willcocks *Argo*
Chandos Anthem – 'The Lord is my
light'/ Cantelo, Partridge/ King's
College/ Willcocks *Argo*
Ode for St Cecilia's Day/ Cantelo,
Partridge/ King's College/ Willcocks
Argo
Aria – 'O ruddier than the cherry'

from *Acis and Galatea*/ Robinson/ Ledger *Argo*

Aria – 'Cangio d'aspetto' from *Admeto*/ Greevy/ Leppard *Argo*

Aria – 'Verdi prati' from *Alcina*/ Greevy/ Leppard *Argo*

Aria – 'Pensa a chi geme' from *Alcina*/ Robinson/ Ledger *Argo*

Aria – 'Convey me' from *Alexander Balus*/ Greevy/ Leppard *Argo*

Aria – 'Revenge, Timotheus cries' from *Alexander's Feast*/ Robinson/ Ledger *Argo*

Aria – 'Care selve' from *Atalanta*/ Greevy/ Leppard *Argo*

Aria – 'Si, tra i ceppi' from *Berenice*/ Robinson/ Ledger *Argo*

Aria – 'La rondinella' from *Clori Tirsi Fileno*/ Greevy/ Leppard *Argo*

Aria – 'Se un bell'ardire' from *Ezio*/ Robinson/ Ledger *Argo*

Aria – 'The god of battle' from *Hercules*/ Robinson/ Ledger *Argo*

Aria – 'Arm, arm ye brave' from *Judas Maccabaeus*/ Robinson/ Ledger *Argo*

Aria – 'La Speranza e giunta' from *Otho*/ Greevy/ Leppard *Argo*

Aria – 'Vieni o figlio' from *Otho*/ Greevy/ Leppard *Argo*

Aria – 'Voglio dire' from *Partenope*/ Greevy/ Leppard *Argo*

Aria – 'Lascia ch'io pianga' from *Rinaldo*/ Greevy/ Leppard *Argo*

Aria – 'Dove Sei' from *Rodelinda*/ Greevy/ Leppard *Argo*

Aria – 'Honour and arms' from *Samson*/ Robinson/ Ledger *Argo*

Aria – 'Leave me, loathsome light' from *Semele*/ Robinson/ Ledger *Argo*

Aria – 'Peace crowned with roses' from *Susanna*/ Robinson/ Ledger *Argo*

Aria – 'Wide spread his name' from *Theodora*/ Robinson/ Ledger *Argo*

Aria – 'Look down, harmonious Saint'/ Tear/ Marriner *Argo*

Aria – 'Meine Seele hört im Sehen'/ Tear/ Marriner *Argo*

Aria – 'Susse Stille'/ Tear/ Marriner *Argo*

Haydn, F. J.

Concertos

Cello Concerto in C/ Rostropovich *EMI*

Cello Concerto in D/ Rostropovich *EMI*

Trumpet Concerto in E flat/ Stringer/ Marriner *Argo*

Trumpet Concerto in E flat/ Wilbraham/ Marriner *EMI*

Excerpt from Trumpet Concerto in E flat/ Wilbraham/ Marriner *Philips*

Horn Concerto No. 1 in D/ Tuckwell/ Marriner *Argo*

Horn Concerto No. 2 in D/ Tuckwell/ Marriner *Argo*

Harpsichord Concerto in D/ Malcolm/ Marriner *Decca*

Organ Concerto in C/ Preston/ Marriner *Argo*

Misc. orchestral

Symphony No. 22, 'The Philosopher'/ Marriner *Philips*

Symphony No. 31, 'Horn Signal'/ Marriner *Philips*

Symphony No. 43, 'Mercury'/ Marriner *Philips*

Symphony No. 44, 'Mourning'/ Marriner *Philips*

Symphony No. 45, 'Farewell'/ Marriner *Philips*

Symphony No. 48, 'Maria Theresia'/ Marriner *Philips*

Symphony No. 49, 'La Passione'/ Marriner *Philips*

Symphony No. 52/ Marriner *Philips*

Symphony No. 53, 'L'Imperiale'/ Marriner *Philips*

Symphony No. 55, 'The Schoolmaster'/ Marriner *Philips*

Symphony No. 59, 'Fire'/ Marriner *Philips*

Symphony No. 73, 'The Hunt'/ Marriner *Philips*

Symphony No. 82, 'The Bear'/ Marriner *Philips*

247

Haydn, F. J. *misc. orchestral – contd.*
Symphony No. 83, 'The Chicken'/ Marriner *Philips*
Symphony No. 85, 'La Reine'/ Marriner *Philips*
Symphony No. 92, 'Oxford'/ Marriner *Philips*
Symphony No. 94, 'Surprise'/ Marriner *Philips*
Symphony No. 96, 'Miracle'/ Marriner *Philips*
Symphony No. 100, 'Military'/ Marriner *Philips*
Symphony No. 101, 'The Clock'/ Marriner *Philips*
Symphony No. 103, 'Drumroll'/ Marriner *Philips*
Symphony No. 104, 'London'/ Marriner *Philips*
Overture *Acide e Galatea*/ Marriner *Argo*
Overture in D/ Marriner *Decca*
Pieces for Mechanical Clock/ Scott/ Guest *Argo*
Six German Dances/ Marriner *Argo*
String Quartet No. 17, Op. 3 No. 5 (excerpt)/ Marriner *Philips*
'The Seven Last Words'/ Marriner *EMI*

Vocal/choral
The Creation/ Harper, Tear, Shirley-Quirk/ King's College/ Willcocks *HMV*
Mass No. 5 in B flat, 'Missa Brevis – St Johannis de Deo – Kleine Orgelmesse'/ Smith, Watts, Tear, Luxon/ St John's College/ Guest *Argo*
Mass No. 6 in C, 'Missa Cellensis – Mariazeller'/ Smith, Watts, Tear, Luxon/ St John's College/ Guest *Argo*
Mass No. 7 in C, 'Paukenmesse'/ Cantelo, Watts, Tear, McDaniel/ St John's College/ Guest *Argo*
Mass No. 8 in B flat, 'Heiligmesse'/ Cantelo, Minty, Partridge, Keyte/ St John's College/ Guest *Argo*
Mass No. 10 in B flat, 'Theresienmesse'/ Spoorenberg, Greevy,

Mitchison, Krause/ St John's College/ Guest *Argo*
Mass No. 11 in B flat, 'Schöpfungsmesse'/ Cantelo, Watts, Tear, Robinson/ St John's College/ Guest *Argo*
Mass No. 12 in B flat, 'Harmoniemesse'/ Spoorenberg, Watts, Young, Rouleau/ St John's College/ Guest *Argo*

Haydn, M.
Duo Concertante for viola and organ/ Shingles, Preston/ Marriner *Argo*
Horn Concerto in D/ Tuckwell/ Marriner *Argo*
Divertimento for viola, cello and double bass/ Shingles, Heath, Slatford/ Marriner *EMI*
Six Minuets/ Marriner *Argo*
'Ave Regina'/ Cantelo, Watts, Tear, McDaniel/ St John's College/ Guest *Argo*

Hertel Concerto a 5/ Wilbraham/ Marriner *Argo*

Hindemith Fünf Stücke, Op. 44 No. 4/ Marriner *Argo*

Holst 'St Paul's Suite'/ Marriner *EMI*

Hook Song – 'The Lass of Richmond Hill'/ Tear/ Marriner *Argo*

Hummel Trumpet Concerto in E/ Wilbraham/ Marriner *Argo*

Iacchini Trattenimento per camera in D for trumpet, strings and continuo/ Smithers/ Marriner *Philips*

Ives Symphony No. 3/ Marriner *Argo*

Jacob Five Pieces for harmonica/ Reilly/ Marriner *Argo*

Kёyper Romance and Rondo for double bass and orchestra/ Slatford/ Marriner *EMI*

Leclair Flute Concerto Op. 7 No. 3/ Monteux/ Marriner *L'Oiseau-Lyre*

Locatelli Concerto Grosso Op. 1 No. 9/ Marriner *L'Oiseau-Lyre*

Introduzione Teatrale Op. 4 No. 4/ Marriner *Philips*

Loeillet Flute Concerto in D/ Monteux/ Marriner *L'Oiseau-Lyre*

Lotti Aria – 'Pur dicesti, o bocca bella'/ Baker/ Marriner *Philips*

Mahler 'Lieder eines fahrenden Gesellen'/ Tear/ Marriner *Argo*

Manfredini Concerto in G minor, Op. 3 No. 10/ Marriner *L'Oiseau-Lyre*

Martin 'Petite Symphonie Concertante' for harp, harpsichord, piano and double string orchestra/ Ellis, Preston, Ledger/ Marriner *EMI*

Martini Aria – 'Plaisir d'amour'/ Baker/ Marriner *Philips*

Maw 'Life Studies'/ Marriner *Argo*

Mendelssohn Piano Concerto in A major/ Ogdon/ Marriner *Argo*
Piano Concerto No. 1, Op. 25/ Perahia/ Marriner *CBS*
Piano Concerto No. 2, Op. 40/ Perahia/ Marriner *CBS*
Concerto in E for two pianos/ Ogdon, Lucas/ Marriner *Argo*
String Symphony No. 9/ Marriner *Argo*
String Symphony No. 10/ Marriner *Argo*
String Symphony No. 12/ Marriner *Argo*
Octet, Op. 20/ ASM Octet/ Maguire *Argo*
Octet, Op. 20/ ASM Chamber Ensemble/ Brown *Philips*
Scherzo from Octet, Op. 20/ Marriner *EMI*
Quintet in B flat, Op. 87/ ASM Chamber Ensemble *Philips*
Scherzo from 'A Midsummer Night's Dream'/ Marriner *Philips*

Monteverdi Mass in four parts (1640)/ Turner, Birts, Keene/ St John's College/ Guest *Argo*

Mass in four parts (1651)/ Turner, Birts, Keene/ St John's College/ Guest *Argo*
'Laudate pueri'/ Turner, Birts, Keene/St John's College/Guest *Argo*
'Ut queant laxis'/ Turner, Birts, Keene/St John's College/Guest *Argo*

Moody Little Suite for Harmonica/ Reilly/ Marriner *Argo*

Mozart, L. Trumpet Concerto in D/ Wilbraham/ Marriner *Argo*
Horn Concerto in D/ Tuckwell/ Marriner *EMI*
'Haydn Toy Symphony'/ Marriner *EMI*

Mozart, W. A.
Concertos
Concertone for two violins, K. 190/ Brown, Kaine/ Marriner *Argo*
Bassoon Concerto, K. 191/ Chapman/ Marriner *Philips*
Violin Concerto, K. 216/ Loveday/ Marriner *Argo*
Violin Concerto, K. 216/ Brown *Argo*
Violin Concerto, K. 218/ Brown *Argo*
Adagio in E for violin and orchestra, K. 261/ Suk/ Marriner *HMV*
Sinfonia Concertante, K. 297b/ Civil, Brymer, Chapman, Monteux, Black/ Marriner *Philips*
Concerto for flute, harp and orchestra, K. 299/ Monteux, Ellis/ Marriner *Philips*
Flute Concerto, K. 313/ Monteux/ Marriner *Philips*
Oboe Concerto, K. 314/ Black/ Marriner *Philips*
Andante for flute and orchestra, K. 315/ Monteux/ Marriner *Philips*
Sinfonia Concertante for violin and viola, K. 364/ Loveday, Shingles/ Marriner *Argo*
Rondo for horn and orchestra, K. 371/ Civil/ Marriner *Philips*
Rondo for horn and orchestra, K. 371/ Tuckwell/ Marriner *EMI*

Mozart, W. A. *Concertos – contd.*
Rondo in F for violin and orchestra, K. 373/ Suk/ Marriner *HMV*
Horn Concerto, K. 412/ Civil/ Marriner *Philips*
Horn Concerto, K. 412/ Tuckwell/ Marriner *EMI*
Horn Concerto, K. 417/ Civil/ Marriner *Philips*
Horn Concerto, K. 417/ Tuckwell/ Marriner *EMI*
Horn Concerto, K. 447/ Civil/ Marriner *Philips*
Horn Concerto, K. 447/ Tuckwell/ Marriner *EMI*
Fragment of Horn Concerto in E, K. 494a/ Tuckwell/ Marriner *EMI*
Horn Concerto, K. 495/ Civil/ Marriner *Philips*
Horn Concerto, K. 495/ Tuckwell/ Marriner *EMI*
Clarinet Concerto, K. 622/ Brymer/ Marriner *Philips*

Piano concertos
Piano Concerto, K. 271/ Brendel/ Marriner *Philips*
Concerto for two pianos, K. 365/ Brendel, Cooper/ Marriner *Philips*
Concert Rondo, K. 382/ Brendel/ Marriner *Philips*
Concert Rondo, K. 386/ Brendel/ Marriner *Philips*
Piano Concerto, K. 414/ Brendel/ Marriner *Philips*
Piano Concerto, K. 415/ Brendel/ Marriner *Philips*
Piano Concerto, K. 449/ Brendel/ Marriner *Philips*
Piano Concerto, K. 453/ Brendel/ Marriner *Philips*
Piano Concerto, K. 456/ Brendel/ Marriner *Philips*
Piano Concerto, K. 466/ Brendel/ Marriner *Philips*
Piano Concerto, K. 482/ Brendel/ Marriner *Philips*
Piano Concerto, K. 488/ Brendel/ Marriner *Philips*

Piano Concerto, K. 491/ Brendel/ Marriner *Philips*
Piano Concerto, K. 503/ Brendel/ Marriner *Philips*
Piano Concerto, K. 595/ Brendel/ Marriner *Philips*

Misc. orchestral
Symphony No. 1, K. 16/ Marriner *Philips*
Symphony No. 4, K. 19/ Marriner *Philips*
Symphony No. 5, K. 22/ Marriner *Philips*
Symphony No. 6, K. 43/ Marriner *Philips*
Symphony No. 7a, K.E. 45a/ Marriner *Philips*
Symphony No. 8, K. 48/ Marriner *Philips*
Symphony No. 9, K. 73/ Marriner *Philips*
Symphony No. 10, K. 74/ Marriner *Philips*
Symphony No. 11, K. 84/ Marriner *Philips*
Symphony No. 12, K. 110/ Marriner *Philips*
Symphony No. 13, K. 112/ Marriner *Philips*
Symphony No. 13, K. 112/ Marriner *Argo*
Symphony No. 14, K. 114/ Marriner *Philips*
Symphony No. 14, K. 114/ Marriner *Argo*
Symphony No. 15, K. 124/ Marriner *Philips*
Symphony No. 15, K. 124/ Marriner *Argo*
Symphony No. 16, K. 128/ Marriner *Philips*
Symphony No. 16, K. 128/ Marriner *Argo*
Symphony No. 17, K. 129/ Marriner *Philips*
Symphony No. 18, K. 130/ Marriner *Philips*

Symphony No. 19, K. 132/Marriner *Philips*

Symphony No. 20, K. 133/Marriner *Philips*

Symphony No. 21, K. 134/Marriner *Philips*

Symphony No. 22, K. 162/Marriner *Philips*

Symphony No. 23, K. 181/Marriner *Philips*

Symphony No. 23, K. 181/Marriner *Argo*

Symphony No. 24, K. 182/Marriner *Philips*

Symphony No. 24, K. 182/Marriner *Argo*

Symphony No. 25, K. 183/Marriner *Philips*

Symphony No. 25, K. 183/Marriner *Argo*

Symphony No. 26, K. 184/Marriner *Philips*

Symphony No. 26, K. 184/Marriner *Argo*

Symphony No. 27, K. 199/Marriner *Philips*

Symphony No. 27, K. 199/Marriner *Argo*

Symphony No. 28, K. 200/Marriner *Philips*

Symphony No. 29, K. 201/Marriner *Philips*

Symphony No. 29, K. 201/Marriner *Argo*

Symphony No. 30, K. 202/Marriner *Philips*

Symphony No. 31, K. 297, 'Paris'/ Marriner *Philips*

Andante for Symphony No. 31, K. 297, 'Paris'/ Marriner *Philips*

Symphony No. 32, K. 318/Marriner *Philips*

Symphony No. 32, K. 318/Marriner *Argo*

Symphony No. 33, K. 319/Marriner *Philips*

Symphony No. 34, K. 338/Marriner *Philips*

Symphony No. 35, K. 385, 'Haffner'/ Marriner *Philips*

Symphony No. 36, K. 425, 'Linz'/ Marriner *Philips*

Symphony No. 37, K. 444 (introduction)/ Marriner *Philips*

Symphony No. 38, K. 504, 'Prague'/ Marriner *Philips*

Symphony No. 39, K. 543/Marriner *Philips*

Symphony No. 40, K. 550/Marriner *Philips*

Symphony No. 41, K. 551, 'Jupiter'/ Marriner *Philips*

Symphony No. 42, K. 75/ Marriner *Philips*

Symphony No. 43, K. 76/ Marriner *Philips*

Symphony No. 44, K. 81/ Marriner *Philips*

Symphony No. 45, K. 95/ Marriner *Philips*

Symphony No. 46, K. 96/ Marriner *Philips*

Symphony No. 47, K. 97/ Marriner *Philips*

Symphony No. 55, K.E. 45b/ Marriner *Philips*

Symphony in C (Overture *Il Re Pastore*, K.208, and Finale, K. 102)/ Marriner *Philips*

Symphony in D, K. 45 (Excerpts from *La finta semplice*)/ Marriner *Philips*

Symphony in D (Overture and Andante grazioso from *Ascanio in Alba*, K. 111, and Finale, K. 120)/ Marriner *Philips*

Symphony in D, K. E. 141a (Overture *Il sogno di Scipione*, K. 126, and Finale, K. 163)/ Marriner *Philips*

Symphony in D (Overture *La finta giardiniera*, K. 196, and Finale, K. 121)/ Marriner *Philips*

Symphony in G, 'Neue Lambacher'/ Marriner *Philips*

'Die Schlittenfahrt' (German Dance No. 3, K. 605)/ Marriner *EMI*

Divertimento, K. 136/Marriner *Argo*

Mozart, W. A. *misc. orchestral – contd.*
Divertimento, K. 137/Marriner *Argo*
Divertimento, K. 138/Marriner *Argo*
Divertimento, K. 334/Marriner *Argo*
Excerpt from Divertimento K. 334/ Marriner *Philips*
Divertimento for flute, oboe, two horns, bassoon and strings/Marriner *Philips*
Divertimento for two flutes, bassoon, two trumpets, drums and strings/ Marriner *Philips*
Divertimento for two oboes, bassoon, two horns and strings/ Marriner *Philips*
Divertimento for two oboes (two flutes), bassoon, two horns and strings/ Marriner *Philips*
Divertimento for two oboes, two horns and strings/ Marriner *Philips*
Divertimento for strings/ Marriner *Philips*
'Les Petits Riens', K. Anh. 10/ Marriner *EMI*
March, K. 335 No. 1/ Marriner *EMI*
March, K. 408 No. 2/ Marriner *Philips*
Minuet in C, K. 409/ Marriner *Philips*
Overture to *La finta semplice*, K. 51/ Marriner *EMI*
Overture to *Lucio Silla*, K. 135/ Marriner *EMI*
Overture to *Il Re Pastore*, K. 208/ Marriner *EMI*
Overture to *Idomeneo*, K. 336/ Marriner *Philips*
Overture to *Der Schauspieldirektor*, K. 486/ Marriner *EMI*
Serenata Notturna, K. 239/ Marriner *Argo*
Serenade No. 8, K. 286 (Notturno for four orchestras)/ Marriner *Argo*
Serenade No. 13, K. 525, 'Eine Kleine Nachtmusik'/ Marriner *Argo*
Serenade No. 13, K. 525, 'Eine Kleine Nachtmusik'/ Marriner *EMI*
Three Contredanses (for flute and bassoon; flute, oboe and bassoon; two horns and strings)/ Marriner *Philips*

Two Contredanses (for flute, two horns and strings; oboe, clarinet and bassoon)/ Marriner *Philips*

Vocal / Choral
'Exsultate Jubilate', K. 165/ Spoorenberg/ Marriner *Argo*
Litaniae Lauretanae B.M.V., K. 195/ Cotrubas, Watts, Tear, Shirley-Quirk/ Schola Cantorum of Oxford/ Marriner *Argo*
Coronation Mass, K. 317/ Cotrubas, Watts, Tear, Shirley-Quirk/ Schola Cantorum of Oxford/ Marriner *Argo*
C Minor Mass, K. 427/ Marshall, Palmer, Rolfe-Johnson, Howell/ Academy Chorus/ Marriner *Philips*
'Et incarnatus est' from C Minor Mass, K. 427/ Spoorenberg/ Marriner *Argo*
Requiem, K. 626/ Cotrubas, Watts, Tear, Shirley-Quirk/ Academy Chorus/ Marriner *Argo*
Die Entführung aus dem Serail (including five alternative arias and duets – 'Welch ängstliches Beben', K. 389; 'Schon lacht der holde Frühling', K. 580; 'Männer suchen stets zu maschen', K. 433; 'Müsst ich auch durch tausend Drachen', K. 435; 'Ich möchte wohl der Kaiser sein', K. 539)/ Eda-Pierre, Burrowes, Burrows, Tear, Lloyd, Jurgens/ John Alldis Choir/ Davis *Philips*
Aria – 'L'Amero' from *Il Re Pastore*, K. 208/ Spoorenberg/ Marriner *Argo*
Aria – 'Se il Padre' from *Idomeneo*, K. 366/ Spoorenberg/ Marriner *Argo*
Aria – 'Padre germani addio' from *Idomeneo*, K. 366/ Spoorenberg/ Marriner *Argo*
Recitative and Aria – 'Non più, tutto ascoltai . . . non temper, amato bene', K. 490/ Norman/ Marriner *Philips*
Recitative and Aria – 'Ch'io mi scordi di te?', K. 505/ Norman/ Marriner *Philips*

Nielsen Little Suite/ Marriner *Argo*

Pachelbel   Canon a 3 on a ground in D/ Marriner *EMI*

Paisiello   Aria – 'Nel cor più non mi sento'/ Baker/ Marriner *Philips*

Pergolesi   Magnificat/ Vaughan, Baker, Partridge, Keyte/ King's College/ Willcocks *Argo*
Aria – 'Ogni pena più spietata'/ Baker/ Marriner *Philips*

Philidor   Récitatif et air – 'O Ciel, se pourrait-il? ... Quel espoir est pour moi' from *La belle esclave*/ Eda-Pierre/ Marriner *Philips*
Air – 'De la coquette volage' from *Les femmes vengées*/ Eda-Pierre/ Marriner *Philips*
Air – 'Tout dormait' from *Mélide ou le navigateur*/ Eda-Pierre/ Marriner *Philips*
Récitatif et air – 'Respirons un moment ... O toi qui né peut m'entendre' from *Tom Jones*/ Eda-Pierre/ Marriner *Philips*

Piccinni   Aria – 'O notte o dea del mistero'/ Baker/ Marriner *Philips*

Poulenc   Concert   Champêtre   for harpsichord and orchestra/ Malcolm/ Brown *Argo*
Concerto in G minor for organ, timpani and strings/ Malcolm/ Brown *Argo*

Prokoviev   'Visions Fugitives', Op. 22 (arr. Barshai)/ Marriner *Argo*
Symphony No. 1, Op. 25, 'Classical'/ Marriner *Argo*

Purcell   Sinfonia from 'The Yorkshire Feast Song'/ Smithers/ Marriner *Philips*
Trumpet Overture from 'The Indian Queen'/ Smithers/ Marriner *Philips*
Chacony in G minor/ Marriner *EMI*
Rondo from *Abdelazer*/ Marriner *Philips*
Dido and Aeneas/ Veasey, Donath, Bainbridge, Patterson, Shirley-

Quirk/ John Alldis Choir/ Davis *Philips*
'Funeral Music for Queen Mary'/ King's College/ Ledger *EMI*
Anthem – 'Blessed are they that fear the Lord'/ King's College/ Ledger *EMI*
Anthem – 'Hear my prayer, O Lord'/ King's College/ Ledger *EMI*
Anthem – 'Jehova, quam multi sint hostes mei'/ St John's College/ Guest *Argo*
Anthem – 'Lord, how long wilt thou be angry'/ St John's College/ Guest *Argo*
Anthem – 'My beloved spake'/ King's College/ Ledger *EMI*
Anthem – 'My beloved spake'/ St John's College/ Guest *Argo*
Anthem – 'O sing unto the Lord a new song'/ St John's College/ Guest *Argo*
Anthem – 'Rejoice in the Lord alway'/ King's College/ Ledger *EMI*
Anthem – 'Remember not, Lord, our offences'/ King's College/ Ledger *EMI*
Anthem – 'They that go down to the sea in ships'/ St John's College/ Guest *Argo*
Anthem – 'Who hath believed our report'/ St John's College/ Guest *Argo*

Quantz   Flute Concerto in D 'pour Potsdam'/ Monteux/ Marriner *L'Oiseau-Lyre*

Rameau   'La Poule'/ Marriner *Philips*

Respighi   'The Birds'/ Marriner *EMI*
'Three Botticelli Pictures'/ Marriner *EMI*

Ricciotti   Concertino No. 4 in F minor/ Marriner *Philips*

Rodrigo   Concierto   Andaluz/ Los Romeros/ Marriner *Philips*
Concierto de Aranjuez/ P. Romero/ Marriner *Philips*

Rodrigo – *contd.*
Concierto Madrigal/ Angel and Pepe Romero/ Marriner *Philips*
Fantasia para un Gentilhombre/ P. Romero/ Marriner *Philips*

Rossini Overture to *Armida*/ Marriner *Philips*
Overture to *Bianca e Faliero*/ Marriner *Philips*
Overture to *Demetrio e Polibio*/ Marriner *Philips*
Overture to *Edipo a Colone*/ Marriner *Philips*
Overture to *Edoardo a Cristina*/ Marriner *Philips*
Overture to *Ermione*/ Ambrosian Singers/ Marriner *Philips*
Overture to *Guillaume Tell*/ Marriner *Philips*
Overture to *Il barbiere di Siviglia*/ Marriner *Philips*
Overture to *Il Signor Bruschino*/ Marriner *Philips*
Overture to *Il Turco in Italia*/ Marriner *Philips*
Overture to *Il viaggio a Reims*/ Marriner *Philips*
Overture to *La cambiale di matrimonio*/ Marriner *Philips*
Overture to *La Cenerentola*/ Marriner *Philips*
Overture to *La gazza ladra*/ Marriner *Philips*
Overture to *L'inganno felice*/ Marriner *Philips*
Overture to *L'Italiana in Algieri*/ Marriner *Philips*
Overture to *La scala di seta*/ Marriner *Philips*
Overture to *La Siège de Corinthe*/ Marriner *Philips*
Overture to *Maometto II*/ Marriner *Philips*
Overture to *Otello*/ Marriner *Philips*
Overture to *Ricciardo e Zoraide*/ Ambrosian Singers/ Marriner *Philips*
Overture to *Semiramide*/ Marriner *Philips*
Overture to *Tancredi*/ Marriner *Philips*
Overture to *Torvaldo e Dorliska*/ Marriner *Philips*
Sinfonia 'al Conventello'/ Marriner *Philips*
String Sonatas Op. 4 Nos. 1–6/ Marriner *Argo*
Excerpt from String Sonata Op. 4 No. 3/ Marriner *Philips*
Duetto for cello and double bass/ Heath, Slatford/ Marriner *EMI*

Sammartini Concerto in F for descant recorder/ Munrow/ Marriner *EMI*
Concerto in F for descant recorder/ Petri/ Brown *Philips*

Sarri Aria – 'Sen corre l'agnelletta'/ Baker/ Marriner *Philips*

Scarlatti, A. Aria – 'Già il sole dal Gange'/ Baker/ Marriner *Philips*
Aria – 'Sento nel core'/ Baker/ Marriner *Philips*
Aria – 'Spesso vibra per suo gioco'/ Baker/ Marriner *Philips*

Schmelzer Sonata a 5 in C/ Smithers/ Marriner *Philips*

Schoenberg 'Verklärte Nacht', Op. 4/ Marriner *Argo*

Schubert Rondo in A for violin and orchestra, D. 438/ Suk/ Marriner *HMV*
Entr'acte in B flat from *Rosamunde*/ Marriner *EMI*
Excerpt from *Rosamunde*/ Marriner *Philips*
Octet in E, Op. posth. 166/ ASM Chamber Ensemble/ Brown *Philips*
Mass in A flat, D. 678/ Eathorne, Greevy, Evans, Keyte/ St John's College/ Guest *Argo*
Mass in E flat, D. 950/ Palmer, Watts, Bowen, Evans, Keyte/ St John's College/ Guest *Argo*

Shostakovich Concerto for piano, trumpet and strings/ Ogdon, Wilbraham/ Marriner *Argo*

Sibelius 'Kuelema'/ Marriner *Argo*
'Rakestava'/ Marriner *Argo*

Stradella Aria – 'Ragion sempre addita'/ Baker/ Marriner *Philips*

Strauss, R. 'Metamorphosen'/ Marriner *Argo*

Stravinsky 'Apollo'/ Marriner *Argo*
Capriccio/ Ogdon/ Marriner *Argo*
'Pulcinella'/ Marriner *Argo*

Tausky Concertino for Harmonica/ Reilly/ Marriner *Argo*

Tchaikovsky String Quartet No. 1, Op. 11 (excerpt)/ Marriner *Philips*
String Quartet No. 1, Op. 11 (excerpt)/ Marriner *HMV (digital)*
Serenade for Strings, Op. 48/ Marriner *Argo*
'Souvenir de Florence', Op. 70/ Marriner *Argo*

Telemann Concerto in F, 'Musique de Table', Set 2/ Marriner *L'Oiseau-Lyre*
Viola Concerto in G/ Streatfeild/ Marriner *L'Oiseau-Lyre*
Viola Concerto in G/ Shingles/ Marriner *Argo*
Concerto in C for treble recorder/ Petri/ Brown *Philips*
Suite in A minor for treble recorder, strings and continuo/ Munrow/ Marriner *EMI*
Concerto a 4 'di Melante' in D for trumpet, strings and continuo/ Smithers/ Marriner *Philips*
Trumpet Concerto in D/ Wilbraham/ Marriner *Argo*
Trumpet Concerto in D/ Wilbraham/ Marriner *EMI*
Horn Concerto in D/ Tuckwell/ Marriner *EMI*
'Don Quichotte' Suite/ Marriner *Argo*
Overture 'des Nations Anciens et Modernes'/ Marriner *Argo*
Overture in C for three oboes, bassoon and strings/ Marriner *Argo*

Overture in C 'Hamburger Ebb und Fluth'/ Marriner *Argo*
Overture in D for two oboes, two horns and strings/ Marriner *Argo*

Tippett Concerto for Double String Orchestra/ Marriner *Argo*
'Fantasia Concertante on a Theme of Corelli'/ Marriner *Argo*
'Little Music for String Orchestra'/ Marriner *Argo*

Torelli Concerto Musicale, Op. 6 No. 10/ Marriner *L'Oiseau-Lyre*
Sonata a 5 No. 7 in D for trumpet, strings and continuo/Smithers/Marriner *Philips*
Sonata a 5 No. 7 in D for trumpet, strings and continuo/ Wilbraham/ Marriner *EMI*

Vaughan Williams Concerto grosso for string orchestra/ Marriner *Argo*
'The Lark Ascending'/ Brown/ Marriner *Argo*
Oboe Concerto in A minor/ Nicklin/ Marriner *Argo*
Romance for Harmonica/ Reilly/ Marriner *Argo*
'Fantasia on a Theme by Thomas Tallis'/ Marriner *Argo*
'Fantasia on Greensleeves'/ Marriner *Argo*
Five variants of 'Dives and Lazarus'/ Marriner *Argo*
Prelude: 'Rhosymedre'/ Marriner *EMI*

Vejvanovsky 'Balletti pro Tabula'/ Philip Jones Brass Ensemble/ Marriner *Argo*
'Harmonia Romana'/ Philip Jones Brass Ensemble/ Marriner *Argo*
Intrada in C for two trumpets, strings and continuo/ Smithers, Laird/ Marriner *Philips*
'La Posta'/ Philip Jones Brass Ensemble/ Marriner *Argo*
Sonata Natalis/ Philip Jones Brass Ensemble/ Marriner *Argo*

Vejvanovsky – *contd.*
Sonata Tribus/ Philip Jones Brass Ensemble/ Marriner *Argo*

Vivaldi Concertos Op. 3 Nos. 1–12, 'L'Estro Armonico'/ Loveday, Brown, Kaine, Gillard, Thomas/ Marriner *Argo*
Concerto Op. 3 No. 10/ Marriner, Nelson, Howard, Jarvis/ Marriner *L'Oiseau-Lyre*
Concertos Op. 4 Nos. 1–12, 'La Stravaganza'/ Loveday, Kaine/ Marriner *Argo*
Concertos Op. 8 Nos. 1–4, 'The Four Seasons'/ Loveday/ Marriner *Argo*
Concertos Op. 9 Nos. 1–12, 'La Cetra'/ Brown, Latchem/ Brown *Argo*
Cello Concerto in C minor, RV 401/ Heath/ Marriner *L'Oiseau-Lyre*
Flute Concerto in C minor, RV 441/ Bennett/ Marriner *Argo*
Piccolo Concerto in C, RV 443/ Bennett/ Marriner *Argo*
Concerto in C for sopranino recorder (or piccolo), RV 443/ Petri/ Brown *Philips*
Oboe Concerto in F, RV 456/ Black/ Marriner *Argo*
Bassoon Concerto in A minor, RV 498/ Gatt/ Marriner *Argo*
Concerto in D minor for two oboes, RV 535/ Black, Nicklin/ Marriner *Argo*
Concerto in C for two trumpets, RV 537/ Jones, Wilbraham/ Marriner *Argo*
Concerto in F for two horns, RV 539/ Brown, Davis/ Marriner *Argo*
Concerto Grosso in D, RV 562a/ Marriner *Philips*
Concerto in F for two oboes, bassoon, two horns and violin, RV 569/ Black, Nicklin, Gatt, Brown, Davis, Brown/ Marriner *Argo*
Concerto in F for two oboes, bassoon, two horns and violin, RV 574/ Black, Nicklin, Gatt, Brown, Davis,

Brown/ Marriner *Argo*
Gloria/ Vaughan, Baker, Partridge, Keyte/ King's College/ Willcocks *Argo*
Magnificat/ Palmer, Watts, Tear, Roberts/ King's College/ Ledger *Argo*

Viviani Sonata No. 1 for trumpet and continuo/ Wilbraham/ Marriner *EMI*
Sonata No. 2 for trumpet and continuo/ Wilbraham/ Marriner *EMI*

Wagner Adagio for clarinet and strings/ Brymer/ Marriner *Argo*
'Siegfried Idyll'/ Marriner *Argo*
'Siegfried Idyll'/ Marriner *HMV* (digital)

Walton 'Façade' – an Entertainment/ Fielding, Flanders/ Marriner *EMI*
Sonata for string orchestra/ Marriner *Argo*
Two pieces for strings from music for *Henry V*/ Marriner *EMI*

Warlock 'Capriol' Suite/ Marriner *Argo*
Serenade/ Marriner *Argo*

Weber Concertino in E minor for horn, Op. 43/ Tuckwell/ Marriner · *EMI*

Webern Fünf Sätze, Op. 5/ Marriner *Argo*

Williamson 'The Happy Prince'/ Stevens, Cantelo, Lehane, Kells, Rex, Allister, Humphrey, Price/ Guildhall Chamber Choir/ Dods *Argo*

FUTURE RELEASES (1981/2)

Bach, J. S. Brandenburg Concertos Nos. 1–6, BWV 1046–51/ Pini, Szeryng, Holliger, Petri, Selin, Bernard, Malcolm, Rampal/ Marriner *Philips*

Beethoven Violin Concerto, Op. 61/ Brown/ Marriner *Argo*

Septet, Op. 20/ ASM Chamber Ensemble *Philips*

Handel   Concerti Grossi Op. 6 Nos. 1–12/ Brown *Philips*
Trio Sonatas/ ASM Chamber Ensemble *Philips*

Haydn, F. J.   *The Creation*/ Mathis, Baldin, Fischer-Dieskau/ Academy Chorus/ Marriner *Philips*
The Seasons/ Mathis, Jerusalem, Fischer-Dieskau/ Academy Chorus/ Marriner *Philips*

Mendelssohn   Symphony   No.   3, 'Scottish'/ Marriner *Argo*
Symphony No. 4, 'Italian'/ Marriner *Argo*

Stich-Punto   Horn Concertos/ Tuckwell/ Marriner *EMI*

Torroba   Concierto Iberico for four guitars/ Los Romeros/ Marriner *Philips*
Dialogos for guitar and orchestra/ P. Romero/ Marriner *Philips*

Vivaldi   Concertos Op. 8 Nos. 1–4, 'The Four Seasons'/ Brown *Philips*
Recorder Concertos Op. 10 Nos. 1–6/ Petri/ Brown *Philips*

BOX SETS
(see full discography for soloists and conductor)

Handel
Concerti Grossi Ops. 3 & 6 *Decca*
Complete Concertos for Keyboard and Orchestra   *Decca*
Concertos Op. 4 Nos. 1–6
Concertos Op. 7 Nos. 1–6
Concertos 13 & 14 (Second Set)
Concertos 15 & 16
Sonata from 'Il trionfo del tempo e del disinganno'

Haydn, F. J.
Name Symphonies   *Philips*
Symphony No. 22, 'The Philosopher'

Symphony No. 43, 'Mercury'
Symphony No. 44, 'Mourning'
Symphony No. 48, 'Maria Theresia'
Symphony No. 49, 'La Passione'
Symphony No. 55, 'The Schoolmaster'
Symphony No. 59, 'Fire'
Symphony No. 85, 'La Reine'
Symphony No, 94, 'Surprise'
Symphony No. 96, 'Miracle'
Symphony No. 100, 'Military'
Symphony No. 103, 'Drum Roll'

Eight Name Symphonies   *Philips*
Symphony No. 31, 'Horn Signal'
Symphony No. 45, 'Farewell'
Symphony No. 73, 'The Hunt'
Symphony No. 82, 'The Bear'
Symphony No. 83, 'The Chicken'
Symphony No. 92, 'Oxford'
Symphony No. 101, 'The Clock'
Symphony No. 104, 'London'

Six Last Masses   *Argo*
Mass No. 7, 'Paukenmesse'
Mass No. 8, 'Heiligmesse'
Mass No. 10, 'Theresienmesse'
Mass No. 11, 'Schöpfungsmesse'
Mass No. 12, 'Harmoniemesse'
with
Mass No. 9, 'Nelson Mass' – King's College/ London Symphony Orchestra/ Willcocks

Mozart, W. A.
Complete Wind Concertos   *Philips*
Bassoon Concerto, K. 191
Sinfonia Concertante, K. 297b
Concerto for Flute and Harp, K. 299
Flute Concerto, K. 313
Oboe Concerto, K. 314
Andante for flute and orchestra, K. 315
Rondo for horn and orchestra, K. 371
Horn Concerto, K. 412
Horn Concerto, K. 417
Horn Concerto, K. 447
Horn Concerto, K. 495
Clarinet Concerto, K. 622

Thirteen Piano Concertos   *Philips*
Piano Concerto, K. 271

Mozart, W. A. – *contd.*
Concert Rondo, K. 382
Concert Rondo, K. 386
Piano Concerto, K. 414
Piano Concerto, K. 415
Piano Concerto, K. 449
Piano Concerto, K. 453
Piano Concerto, K. 456
Piano Concerto, K. 459
Piano Concerto, K. 466
Piano Concerto, K. 482
Piano Concerto, K. 488
Piano Concerto, K. 491
Piano Concerto, K. 503
Piano Concerto, K. 595

'*Mozart Live*'—   *Philips*
Overture to *Idomeneo*, K. 336
Recitative and Aria – 'Non più, tutto
ascoltai . . . non temper, amato bene',
(K. 490)
Piano Concerto, K. 503
Recitative and Aria – 'Ch'io mi scordi
di te?', (K. 505)
Symphony No. 40, K. 550

The Early Symphonies   *Philips*
Symphony No. 1, K. 16
Symphony No. 4, K. 19
Symphony No. 5, K. 22
Symphony No. 6, K. 43
Symphony No. 7a, K.E. 45a
Symphony No. 8, K. 48
Symphony No. 9, K. 73
Symphony No. 10, K. 74
Symphony No. 11, K. 84
Symphony No. 12, K. 110
Symphony No. 13, K. 112
Symphony No. 14, K. 114
Symphony No. 15, K. 124
Symphony No. 16, K. 128
Symphony No. 17, K. 129
Symphony No. 18, K. 130
Symphony No. 19, K. 132
Symphony No. 20, K. 133
Symphony No. 42, K. 75
Symphony No. 43, K. 76
Symphony No. 44, K. 81
Symphony No. 45, K. 95
Symphony No. 46, K. 96

Symphony No. 47, K. 97
Symphony No. 55, K.E. 45b
Symphony in G, 'Neue Lambacher'
Symphony in D, K.E. 141a (Over-
ture *Il sogno di Scipione*, K. 126, and
Finale, K. 163)
Symphony in C (Overture *Il Re Pas-
tore*, K. 208, and Finale, K. 102)
Symphony in D (Overture and
Andante grazioso from *Ascanio in
Alba*, K. 111, and Finale, K. 120)
Symphony in D (Overture *La finta
giardiniera*, K. 196, and Finale, K. 121)
Symphony in D, K. 45 (Excerpts
from *La finta semplice*)

The Late Symphonies   *Philips*
Symphony No. 21, K. 134
Symphony No. 22, K. 162
Symphony No. 23, K. 181
Symphony No. 24, K. 182
Symphony No. 25, K. 183
Symphony No. 26, K. 184
Symphony No. 27, K. 199
Symphony No. 28, K. 200
Symphony No. 29, K. 201
Symphony No. 30, K. 202
Symphony No. 31, K. 297, 'Paris'
Symphony No. 32, K. 318
Symphony No. 33, K. 319
Symphony No. 34, K. 338
Symphony No. 35, K. 385, 'Haffner'
Symphony No. 36, K. 425, 'Linz'
Symphony No. 37, K. 444 (introduc-
tion)
Symphony No. 38, K. 504, 'Prague'
Symphony No. 39, K. 543
Symphony No. 40, K. 550
Symphony No. 41, K. 551, 'Jupiter'
Minuet in C, K. 409
Andante for Symphony No. 31,
K. 297, 'Paris'

Rossini
String Sonatas 1–6 *Argo*
(with Donizetti – String Quartet in D)

The Complete Overtures   *Philips*
Overture to *Armida*

Overture to *Bianca e Faliero*
Overture to *Demetrio e Polibio*
Overture to *Edipo a Colone*
Overture to *Edoardo a Cristina*
Overture to *Ermione*
Overture to *Guillaume Tell*
Overture to *Il barbiere di Siviglia*
Overture to *Il Signor Bruschino*
Overture to *Il Turco in Italia*
Overture to *Il viaggio a Reims*
Overture to *La cambiale di matrimonio*
Overture to *La Cenerentola*
Overture to *La gazza ladra*
Overture to *La scala di seta*
Overture to *La Siège de Corinthe*
Overture to *L'inganno felice*
Overture to *L'Italiana in Algieri*
Overture to *Maometto II*
Overture to *Otello*
Overture to *Ricciardo e Zoraide*
Overture to *Semiramide*
Overture to *Tancredi*
Overture to *Torvaldo e Dorliska*
Sinfonia 'al Conventello'

Vivaldi
  'Antonio Vivaldi'   *Argo*
  'L'Estro Armonico', Op. 3 Nos.
  1–12
  'La Stravaganza', Op. 4 Nos. 1–12
  'The Four Seasons', Op. 8 Nos. 1–4
  'La Cetra', Op. 9 Nos. 1–12
  Cello Concerto, RV 401
  Flute Concerto, RV 441
  Piccolo Concerto, RV 443
  Oboe Concerto, RV 456
  Bassoon Concerto, RV 498
  Concerto for two oboes, RV 535
  Concerto for two horns, RV 539
  Concerto for two oboes, bassoon, two horns and violin, RV 569
  Concerto for two oboes, bassoon, two horns and violin, RV 574

ANTHOLOGIES
(see full discography for soloists and conductor)

Academy Con Amore   *Philips*
  J. C. Bach   Symphony Op. 3 No. 3

Bach   Brandenburg Concerto No. 2
Haydn   String Quartet No. 17, Op.
3 No. 5 (excerpt)
Mozart   Bassoon Concerto, K. 191

Academy Encores   *Argo*
  Bach   Air in G from Suite 3
  Handel   Air and Hornpipe from 'Water Music'/ Overture to *Berenice*
  Haydn   Trumpet Concerto in E flat
  Mozart   'Eine Kleine Nachtmusik'/ Minuet from Divertimento, K. 334

Academy in Concert I   *EMI*
  Albinoni   Adagio in G minor
  Bach   Air in G from Suite 3/ Sinfonia from *Christmas Oratorio*
  Beethoven   Twelve Contredanses
  Handel   Minuet from Overture to *Berenice*/ 'Pastoral' Symphony from *Messiah*
  Mendelssohn   Scherzo from Octet, Op. 20
  Mozart   March in D, K. 335 No. 1/ 'Die Schlittenfahrt', German Dance No. 3, K. 605
  Pachelbel   Canon

Academy in Concert II   *EMI*
  Bach   'Jesu, Joy of Man's Desiring' from Cantata 147
  Gluck   'Dance of the Blessed Spirits' from *Orfeo et Eurydice*
  Handel   Largo from *Xerxes*
  L. Mozart   'Haydn' Toy Symphony
  Mozart   'Eine Kleine Nachtmusik'
  Schubert   Entr'acte from *Rosamunde*

Airs d'Opéras Comiques   *Philips*
  Grétry   Air – 'Eprise d'un feu téméraire' from *Anacréon chez Polycrate*
  Air – 'Plus d'ennemis dans mon empire' from *Céphale et Procris*
  Air – 'Je ne le dis qu'à vous' from *La fausse magie*
  Air – 'Je crains de lui parler' from *Richard Coeur de Lion*
  Philidor   Récitatif et air – 'O Ciel, se pourrait-il? ... Quel espoir est pour moi' from *La belle esclave*

259

Airs d'Opéras Comiques – contd.
Air – 'De la coquette volage' from *Les femmes vengées*
Air – 'Tout dormait' from *Mélide ou le navigateur*
Récitatif et air – 'Respirons un moment ... O toi qui ne peut m'entendre' from *Tom Jones*

American Music   Argo
Barber   Adagio for Strings
Copland   'Quiet City'
Cowell   Hymn and Fuguing Tune No. 10
Creston   'A Rumor'
Ives   Symphony No. 3

Arie Amorose   Philips
Bononcini   Aria – 'Deh più a me non v'ascondete'
Caccini   Aria – 'Amarilli mia bella'
Caldara   Aria – 'Come raggio di sol'
Aria – 'Sebben crudele mi fai languir'
Aria – 'Selve amiche'
Cesti   Aria – 'Intorno all'idol mio'
Durante   Aria – 'Danza fanciulla gentile'
Giordani   Aria – 'Caro mio ben'
Lotti   Aria – 'Pur dicesti, o bocca bella'
Martini   Aria – 'Plaisir d'amour'
Paisiello   Aria – 'Nel cor più non mi sento'
Pergolesi   Aria – 'Ogni pena più spietata'
Piccinni   Aria – 'O notte o dea del mistero'
Sarri   Aria – 'Sen corre l'agnelletta'
A. Scarlatti   Aria – 'Già il sole dal Gange'
Aria – 'Sento nel core'
Aria – 'Spesso vibra per suo gioco'
Stradella   Aria – 'Ragion sempre addita'

Baroque Festival   Argo
'Arne   Harpsichord Concerto No. 5 in G minor

Bach Flute Concerto (tr. BWV 1056)
Violin and Oboe Concerto (tr. BWV 1060)
Fasch   Trumpet Concerto in D
Handel   Concerto Grosso Op. 3 No. 1
Harpsichord Concerto No. 15 in D minor
Oboe Concerto No. 3 in G minor
Telemann   Trumpet Concerto in D
Viola Concerto in G
Vivaldi   Concerto for one violin, Op. 4 No. 1
Concerto for two violins, Op. 3 No. 8
Concerto for four violins, Op. 3 No. 10
Concerto for two trumpets, RV 537

Baroque Trumpet Anthology   Philips
Bononcini   Sinfonia No. 10
Grossi   Sonata a 5 No. 11
Iacchini   Trattenimento per camera in D
Purcell   Sinfonia from 'The Yorkshire Feast Song'
Trumpet Overture from 'The Indian Queen'
Schmelzer   Sonata a 5 in C
Telemann   Concerto a 4 'di Melante'
Torelli   Sonata a 5 No. 7
Vejvanovsky   Intrada in C

Baroque Trumpet Concerti   Argo
Albinoni   Trumpet Concerto in C
Fasch   Trumpet Concerto in D
Hertel   Concerto a 5
Telemann   Trumpet Concerto in D

Concert à la Carte   Philips
Boccherini   Quintet Op. 13 No. 5 (excerpt)
Clarke   Trumpet Voluntary
Handel   'Arrival of the Queen of Sheba'
Haydn   String Quartet No. 17, Op. 3 No. 5 (excerpt)

Discography

Trumpet Concerto in E flat (excerpt)
Mendelssohn Scherzo from 'A Midsummer Night's Dream'
Mozart Divertimento K. 334 (excerpt)
Purcell Rondo from *Abdelazer*
Rossini String Sonata Op. 4 No. 3 (excerpt)
Schubert *Rosamunde* (excerpt)
Tchaikovsky String Quartet Op. 11 No. 1 (excerpt)

Eighteenth-Century Flute Concertos L'Oiseau-Lyre
Grétry Flute Concerto in C
Leclair Flute Concerto in C, Op. 7 No. 3
Loeillet Flute Concerto in D
Quantz Flute Concerto in D, 'pour Potsdam'

English String Music EMI
Britten 'Simple Symphony'
Delius 'Two Aquarelles'
Holst 'St Paul's Suite'
Purcell Chacony in G minor
Vaughan Williams Prelude: 'Rhosymedre'
Walton Two pieces for strings from music for *Henry V*

Festival of English Music Argo
Britten Variations on a theme of Frank Bridge
Butterworth 'A Shropshire Lad'
'The Banks of Green Willow'
'Two English Idylls'
Elgar Serenade for Strings, Op. 20
Introduction and Allegro, Op. 47
Elegy for Strings, Op. 58
'Sospiri', Op. 70
Suite from 'The Spanish Lady'
Tippett Concerto for Double String Orchestra
Fantasia Concertante on a Theme of Corelli
'Little Music for String Orchestra'
Vaughan Williams Fantasia on a

Theme by Thomas Tallis
Fantasia on 'Greensleeves'
Five Variants of 'Dives and Lazarus'
'The Lark Ascending'

Harp Concertos of the Eighteenth Century Argo
Boieldieu Harp Concerto in C
Dittersdorf Harp Concerto in A
Handel Harp Concerto in B flat, Op. 4 No. 6

Horn Concertos EMI
Cherubini Horn Concerto in F
Forster Horn Concerto in E flat
L. Mozart Horn Concerto in D
Telemann Horn Concerto in D
Weber Concertino in E minor, Op. 43

Italian Concertos L'Oiseau-Lyre
Bellini Oboe Concerto in E flat
Cherubini Etude No. 2 for horn and strings
Corelli Concerto Grosso Op. 6 No. 1
Geminiani Concerto Grosso Op. 3 No. 3
Vivaldi Cello Concerto RV 401

Italian Concertos L'Oiseau-Lyre
Bellini Oboe Concerto in E flat
Cherubini Etude No. 2 for horn and strings
Corelli Concerto Grosso Op. 6 No. 1
Concerto Grosso Op. 6 No. 7
Geminiani Concerto Grosso Op. 3 No. 3
Locatelli Concerto Grosso Op. 1 No. 9
Manfredini Concerto in G minor, Op. 3 No. 10
Torelli Concerto Musicale, Op. 6 No. 10
Vivaldi Cello Concerto RV 401
Concerto Op. 3 No. 10

Living Baroque Philips
Bach Ricercare a 6 from 'The Musical Offering'
Clarke Trumpet Voluntary

Italian Concertos – contd.
Handel 'Arrival of the Queen of Sheba'
Purcell Rondo from *Abdelazer* Trumpet Overture From 'The Indian Queen'
Rameau 'La Poule'
Ricciotti Concertino No. 4 in F minor
Torelli Sonata a 5, No. 7 in D
Vivaldi Concerto Grosso in D, RV 562a

Music for Double Bass   EMI
Dittersdorf Sinfonia Concertante for double bass, viola and orchestra
M. Haydn Divertimento for viola, cello and double bass
Këyper Romance and Rondo for double bass and orchestra
Rossini Duetto for cello and double bass

Music for Flute and Orchestra   Argo
Bach Flute Concerto in G minor, (tr. BWV 1056)
Vivaldi Flute Concerto in C minor, RV 441
Piccolo Concerto in C, RV 443

Orchestral Works (digital)   HMV
Boccherini String Quintet Op. 13 No. 5 (excerpt)
Dvorak Nocturne in B minor, Op. 40
Fauré Pavane, Op. 50
Grieg Two Elegiac Melodies, Op. 34
Tchaikovsky String Quartet No. 1, Op. 11 (excerpt)
Wagner 'Siegfrid Idyll'

Recital by the Academy of St Martin in the Fields   L'Oiseau-Lyre
Albicastro Concerto a 4, Op. 7 No. 6
Corelli Concerto Grosso, Op. 6 No. 7
Handel Concerto Grosso, Op. 6 No. 6

Locatelli Concerto Grosso, Op. 1 No. 9
Torelli Concerto Musicale, Op. 6 No. 10

Recital for Strings   L'Oiseau-Lyre
Gabrieli, G. Canzon per Sonar Noni Toni
Handel Concerto Grosso Op. 6 No. 4
Telemann Viola Concerto in G
Vivaldi Concerto Op. 3 No. 10

Recital – Robert Tear   Argo
Arne Song – 'Bacchus and Ariadne' Song – 'Fair Caelia love pretended'
Boyce Song – 'Momus to Mars'
Handel Aria – 'Look down, harmonious Saint'
Aria – 'Meine Seele hört im Sehen'
Aria – 'Süsse Stille'
Hook Song – 'The Lass of Richmond Hill'

Recorder Concertos   EMI
Handel Concerto in B flat for treble recorder
Sammartini Concerto in F for descant recorder
Telemann Suite in A minor for treble recorder

Recorder Concertos   Philips
Handel Concerto in F for treble recorder
Sammartini Concerto in F for descant recorder
Telemann Concerto in C for treble recorder
Vivaldi Concerto in C for sopranino recorder (or piccolo), RV 443

Rise of the Symphony   Philips
J. C. Bach Symphonies Op. 3 Nos. 1–6
Beethoven Symphonies Nos. 1 and 2
Haydn Symphonies Nos. 52 and 53
Mozart Symphonies Nos. 35 and 40

Discography

Romances: Rondos: Adagios   *EMI*
  Beethoven   Romance No. 1 for violin and orchestra
  Romance No. 2 for violin and orchestra
  Mozart   Adagio in E for violin and orchestra, K. 261
  Rondo in C for violin and orchestra, K. 373
  Schubert   Rondo in A for violin and orchestra, D. 438

Scandinavian Music   *Argo*
  Grieg   Two Elegiac Melodies, Op. 34
  Nielsen   Little Suite
  Sibelius   Kuelema
  Rakestava

Second Recital by the Academy of St Martin in the Fields   *L'Oiseau-Lyre*
  Albinoni   Concerto a 5, Op. 5 No. 5
  Avison   Concerto Op. 9 No. 11
  Handel   Concerto Grosso Op. 6 No. 1
  Manfredini   Concerto in G minor, Op. 3 No. 10
  Telemann   Concerto in F (Musique de Table, Set 2)

Strings and Brass   *Argo*
  Gabrieli, G.   Canzon a 8
  Canzon Prima a 4 'La Spiritata'
  Canzon Prima a 5
  Canzon Primi Toni No. 1 a 8
  Vejvanovsky   'Balletti pro Tabula'
  'Harmonia Romana'
  'La Posta'
  Sonata Natalis
  Sonata Tribus

Tribute to Holland   *Philips*
  van Bree   Allegro for four string quartets
  Locatelli   Introduzione Teatrale, Op. 4 No. 5
  Ricciotti   Concertino No. 4 in F minor
  Vivaldi   Concerto Grosso in D, RV 562a

Trumpet Concertos   *EMI*
  Francheschini   Sonata in D for two trumpets, strings and continuo
  Haydn   Trumpet Concerto in E flat
  Telemann   Trumpet Concerto in D
  Torelli   Sonata a 5, No. 7 in D
  Viviani   Sonatas Nos. 1 and 2 for trumpet and continuo

Trumpet Concertos   *Argo*
  Albrechtsberger   Trumpet Concerto in E
  Hummel   Trumpet Concerto in E
  L. Mozart   Trumpet Concerto in D

Trumpet Concertos   *Argo*
  Albinoni   Trumpet Concerto in C
  Albrechtsberger   Trumpet Concerto in E
  Fasch   Trumpet Concerto in D
  Hertel   Concerto a 5
  Hummel   Trumpet Concerto in E
  L. Mozart   Trumpet Concerto in D
  Telemann   Trumpet Concerto in D

Works for Harmonica and Orchestra *Argo*
  Jacob   Five Pieces
  Moody   Little Suite
  Tausky   Concertino
  Vaughan Williams   Romance

Works for Orchestra   *Philips*
  Bach   Brandenburg Concerto No. 3
  Mozart   Horn Concerto in E flat, K. 417
  Mozart   Symphony No. 10, K. 74
  Purcell   Trumpet Overture from 'The Indian Queen'
  Rossini   Overture to *La scala di seta*
  Telemann   Concerto a 4 'di Melante'

World of the Academy I   *Argo*
  Handel   'Arrival of the Queen of Sheba'
  Haydn   Six German Dances
  Mendelssohn   Scherzo from Octet, Op. 20
  Mozart   Divertimento K. 136
  Rossini   String Sonata Op. 4 No. 1

263

List of Illustrations

We should like to thank everyone who has helped to supply the illustrations for this book; we are particularly grateful to Mike Evans for the cover photography.

List of Illustrations and Acknowledgements

266

List of Illustrations and Acknowledgements

267

List of Illustrations and Acknowledgements

Every effort has been made to attribute illustrations correctly. We apologise for any omissions or inadequacies; they are unintentional, and will be remedied in future editions.

269

Index

N.B. The surnames of players who have appeared regularly with the Academy are printed in capitals. Page numbers in italics refer to illustrations.